The Psychology of Prejudice and Discrimination

**Recent titles in
Race and Ethnicity in Psychology**

Sources of Stress and Relief for African American Women
Catherine Fisher Collins

Playing with Anger: Teaching Coping Skills to African American Boys through
Athletics and Culture
Howard C. Stevenson Jr., editor

The Psychology of Prejudice and Discrimination

VOLUME 1
RACISM IN AMERICA

Edited by
Jean Lau Chin

Foreword by
Joseph E. Trimble

PRAEGER PERSPECTIVES

Race and Ethnicity in Psychology
Jean Lau Chin, John D. Robinson, and Victor De La Cancela
Series Editors

Westport, Connecticut
London

Library of Congress Cataloging-in-Publication Data

The psychology of prejudice and discrimination / edited by Jean Lau Chin ; foreword by Joseph E. Trimble.
    p. cm.—(Race and ethnicity in psychology, ISSN 1543-2203)
    Includes bibliographical references and index.
    ISBN 0-275-98234-3 (set : alk. paper)—ISBN 0-275-98235-1 (v. 1 : alk. paper)—ISBN 0-275-98236-X (v. 2 : alk. paper)—ISBN 0-275-98237-8 (v. 3 : alk. paper)—ISBN 0-275-98238-6 (v. 4 : alk. paper) 1. Prejudices—United States. I. Chin, Jean Lau. II. Series.
BF575.P9P79 2004
303.3'85'0973—dc22   2004042289

British Library Cataloguing in Publication Data is available.

Library of Congress Catalog Card Number: 2004042289
ISBN: 0-275-98234-3 (set)
        0-275-98235-1 (Vol. 1)
        0-275-98236-X (Vol. 2)
        0-275-98237-8 (Vol. 3)
        0-275-98238-6 (Vol. 4)
ISSN: 1543-2203

First published in 2004

Praeger Publishers, 88 Post Road West, Westport, CT 06881
An imprint of Greenwood Publishing Group, Inc.
www.praeger.com

Printed in the United States of America

The paper used in this book complies with the Permanent Paper Standard issued by the National Information Standards Organization (Z39.48-1984).

10 9 8 7 6 5 4 3 2

Copyright Acknowledgment

Contents

Foreword

Civilized men have gained notable mastery over energy, matter, and inanimate nature generally and are rapidly learning to control physical suffering and premature death. But, by contrast, we appear to be living in the Stone Age so far as our handling of human relations is concerned.

(Gordon W. Allport, 1954, p. ix)

Although written over fifty years ago, the haunting words of the eminent social psychologist Gordon W. Allport may ring true today. His intent then was to clarify the various elements of the enormously complex topic of prejudice. Since the writing of his now well-cited and highly regarded text on prejudice, social and behavioral scientists have made great strides in furthering our knowledge of the field. Since 1950, for example, thousands of books, journal articles, and book chapters have been devoted to studying prejudice and discrimination. Professor Allport would be somewhat pleased with the numbers because that was partly his expectation when he said, "So great is the ferment of investigation and theory in this area that in one sense our account will soon be dated. New experiments will supersede old, and formulations of various theories will be improved" (1954, p. xiii). But has there been that much improvement that we have moved away from a Stone Age understanding of human relations to a higher level of sophistication? The question begs for an answer, but that can wait until later.

Let me back up for a moment to explore another line of thought and inquiry that bears directly on the significance and importance of this wonderful set of books on the psychology of prejudice and discrimination. For as long as I can remember, I have been deeply interested in the origins of, motives in, and attitudes about genocide and ethnocide; as a young child I did not use those horrific terms, as I did not know them then. But I did know about their implied destructive implications from stories passed along by sensitive teachers, ancestors, and elders. The deep social psychological meaning of the constructs later became an intense interest of mine as a graduate student in the turbulent 1960s, an era filled with challenges and protestations of anything regarding civil rights, discrimination, racism, sexism, and prejudice. During that era I threw my mind and spirit into the study of Allport's writings on prejudice—not merely to study them, but to explore every nuance of his scholarly works to expand the depth of my understanding and expecting to come away with fewer questions and more answers. I was not disappointed in my exploration. I was baffled, though, because I recognized more so just how complicated it was to prevent and eradicate prejudice and discrimination.

As I write these thoughts, I am reminded of a sign that was once posted over the porch roof of an old restaurant and tavern in a rural South Dakota community adjacent to an American Indian reservation. The sign was hand-painted in white letters on a long slat of weathered wood; it was written in the Lakota language, and the English translation read, "No dogs or Indians allowed." The store was and is still owned by non-Indians. The offensive, derogatory sign is no longer there—likely torn down years ago by angry protestors from the nearby reservation. While the sign is gone, the attitude and intent of the message still linger in and around the rustic building, except that it is more insidious, pernicious, and guileful now. The prevailing prejudicial and loathsome attitude is a reflection of many of the residents of the small town. Many of the town's residents tolerate Native Americans because they dependent on them economically, but their bigoted and closed-minded convictions are unwilling to accept Native Americans as equals and provide them with freedom of movement and expression.

The wretched, mean-spirited, pernicious attitudes present in that rural South Dakota town symbolize the prevailing changes in attitudes and behavior across North America—the blatant signs are gone, but in many places and for many individuals the prejudicial attitudes persist, sometimes in sly and subtle forms. On other occasions they are overt and repulsive. Chapters in these volumes summarize and explore the social and psychological motives and reasoning behind the persistence of prejudicial attitudes and discriminatory practices. They go beyond the conclusions drawn by Professor Allport and other early writers on the topic and take us into domains represented by those who have experienced prejudice and discrimination firsthand, as did their ancestors. Indeed, a voice not included in early studies on prejudice and discrimination is intensified and deepened as more and more ethnic groups and women are represented in the social and behavioral sciences than in years gone by.

Stories and anecdotes, too, recounted by the rising groups of diverse scholars and researchers, lend a new authenticity to the literature. Some of the accounts provide a different perspective on historical events involving racial hatred that provide more thorough descriptions of the details and perspectives. Revisionist historical approaches have a place in the study of prejudice and discrimination because for so long the authentic voices of the victims were muffled and muted. For example, as a consequence of European contact, many Native American communities continue to experience individual and community trauma, a "wound to the soul of Native American people that is felt in agonizing proportions to this day" (Duran & Duran, 1995, p. 27). The cumulative trauma has been fueled by centuries of incurable diseases, massacres, forced relocation, unemployment, economic despair, poverty, forced removal of children to boarding schools, abuse, racism, loss of traditional lands, unscrupulous land mongering, betrayal, broken treaties—the list goes on. Brave Heart and DeBruyn (1998) and Duran and Duran (1995) maintain that postcolonial "historical and intergenerational trauma" has left a long trail of unresolved grief and a "soul wound" in Native American communities that contribute to high levels of social and individual problems such as alcoholism, suicide, homicide, domestic violence, child abuse, and negative career ideation. The presence of Native American scholars contributed a voice that was suppressed for decades because some feared the consequences if these scholars told their stories. The stories and accounts of past racial events and their corresponding trauma also were not told because there were few visible ethnic scholars available.

Decades ago the topics of prejudice and discrimination largely emphasized race and, more specifically, the racial experiences of black Americans. Over the years the topic has expanded to include the experiences of other ethnic groups, women, the elderly, those with disabilities, those with nonheterosexual orientations, and those with mixed ethnic heritages. The volumes edited by Jean Lau Chin expand the concepts of diversity and multiculturalism to add a broader, more inclusive dimension to the understanding of prejudice and discrimination. The addition of new voices to the field elevates public awareness to the sweeping effects of prejudice and discrimination and how they are deeply saturated throughout societies.

The amount of scholarly attention devoted to the study of prejudice and discrimination closely parallels the growth of ethnic diversity interests in psychology. Until about thirty years ago, psychology's mission appeared to be restricted to a limited population as references to blacks, Asian Americans, Native American and Alaska natives, Hispanics, Pacific Islanders, and Puerto Ricans were almost absent from the psychological literature; in fact, the words *culture* and *ethnic* were rarely used in psychological textbooks. The long absence of culture in the web of psychological inquiry did not go unnoticed. About three decades ago, ethnic minority and international psychologists began questioning what the American Psychological Association meant by its use of *human* and to whom the vast body of psychological knowledge applied. America's ethnic psychologists and those from other countries, as well as a small handful of North American psychologists, argued that American psychology did not include what constituted the world's population. They claimed that findings were biased, limited to studies involving college and university students and laboratory animals, and therefore not generalizable to all humans. Comprehensive literature reviews reinforced their accusations and observations.

Accusations of imperialism, cultural encapsulation, ethnocentrism, parochialism, and, in some circles of dissent, of "scientifically racist" studies, run the gamut of criticisms hurled at the field of psychology during that period. Robert Guthrie (1976), for example, writing in his strongly worded critique of psychology, *Even the Rat Was White*, argues that culture and context were not taken seriously in the history of psychological research. Given these conditions and the myopia of the profession, it is no small wonder that prejudice and discrimination were not given more widespread attention. The topic was not perceived as salient and important enough for extensive consideration. The four volumes in this set are a testament to the amount of change and emphasis that are focused on ethnicity, culture, and the topics of prejudice and discrimination.

The changing demographics in the United States call into question the relevance of a psychology that historically has not included ethnic and racial groups and that fostered a research agenda that was ethnocentric and bound by time and place. This can no longer be tolerated, as the rapid growth of ethnic minority groups in the United States amplifies the need for more attentiveness on the part of the social and behavioral sciences. Consider the population projections offered by the U.S. Bureau of the Census. By 2050, the U.S. population will reach over 400 million, about 47 percent larger than in 2000 (U.S. Bureau of the Census, 2001). The primary ethnic minority groups—specifically, Hispanics, blacks, Asian Americans, and Native American and Alaska Natives—will constitute almost 50 percent of the population in 2050. About 57 percent of the population under the age of eighteen, and 34 percent over the age of 65, will be ethnic minorities.

America never was and likely will not be a melting pot of different nationalities and ethnic groups for another century or two. As the mixture and size of ethnic groups increase, we are faced with the disturbing possibility that an increase in prejudice and discrimination will occur accordingly. Given this possibility, the topics covered in these volumes become even more worthy of serious consideration, especially the ones that emphasize prevention. Given the demographic changes and the topical changes that have occurred in the social and behavioral sciences, the extensive contents of these four volumes are a welcome addition to the field. Editor Jean Lau Chin and her long list of chapter authors are to be congratulated for their monumental effort. The volumes are packed with useful and wonderfully written material. Some is based on empirical findings, some on firsthand experiences. The blend of various writing styles and voice adds to the breadth of coverage of the topic. The many points of view provided by the contributors will help shape the direction of research and scholarly expression on a topic that has been around since the origins of humankind. We can hope that the contributions of these four volumes will move the field of human relations from a perceived Stone Age level of understanding to one where we believe we are moving closer to eliminating prejudice, discrimination, and the vile hatred they engender.

Joseph E. Trimble
Professor of Psychology
Western Washington University
Bellingham, WA
March 21, 2004

REFERENCES

Allport, G. W. (1954). *The nature of prejudice*. Garden City, NY: Doubleday.

Brave Heart, M. Y. H., & DeBruyn, L. (1998). The American Indian holocaust: Healing unresolved grief. *American Indian and Alaska Native Mental Health Research, 8*(2), 56–78.

Duran, E., & Duran, B. (1995). *Native American postcolonial psychology*. Albany, NY: State University of New York Press.

Guthrie, R. (1976). *Even the rat was white: A historical view of psychology*. New York: Harper & Row.

U.S. Bureau of the Census. (2001). *Census of the population: General population characteristics, 2000*. Washington, DC: Government Printing Office.

Introduction

Prejudice and discrimination are not new. The legacy of the Pilgrims and early pioneers suggested a homogenous, mainstream America. Our early emphasis on patriotism in the United States resulted in a false idealization of the melting pot myth. Prejudice and discrimination in American society were overt and permeated all levels of society, that is, legislation, government, education, and neighborhoods. In the 1960s, attempts to eradicate prejudice, discrimination, and racism were explicit—with an appeal to honor and value the diversity within different racial and ethnic groups. This soon extended to other dimensions of diversity, including gender, disability, and spirituality. However, long after the war to end slavery, the civil rights movement of the 1960s, desegregation in the schools, and the abolition of anti-Asian legislation—indeed, in the midst of growing public debate today regarding gay marriage—we still see the pernicious effects of prejudice and discrimination in U.S. society.

Prejudice and discrimination toward differences in race, ethnicity, gender, spirituality, and disability have had negative psychological consequences, and they continue in primarily covert forms. Bias and disparities still exist and result in inequity of services, opportunities, and practices in American society. Combating prejudice and discrimination in today's environment warrants some different strategies. We live in an environment of heightened anxiety due to war and terrorism. Thanks to technological advances in communication, travel, and the

Internet, news and information from all parts of the world are almost instantaneously brought to us. We live in a global economy with a narrowing of borders between countries and groups. Generations of immigrants have resulted in the U.S. population becoming so diverse that there may soon be no single majority group within most major cities. Technological advances have eliminated the biological advantage of males in strength and the biological "limitations" of women of childbearing age in the work environment. Yet, the more things change, the more they stay the same. Irrational and unjust perceptions of other people remain—more subtle, perhaps, but they remain.

This four-volume set, *The Psychology of Prejudice and Discrimination*, takes a fresh look at that issue that is embedded in today's global environment. Images, attitudes and perceptions that sustain prejudice and discrimination are more covert, but no less pernicious. What people say, believe, and do all reflect underlying bias. **We do not claim here to address every existing form of prejudice or discrimination, nor do we cite every possible group targeted today. What we offer are insights into a range from the most to least recognized, or openly discussed, forms of this injustice.** Each chapter offers new perspectives on standing issues, with practical information about how to cope with prejudice and discrimination. The "toolbox" at the end of each chapter suggests steps to be taken at different levels to combat prejudice and discrimination and to achieve change. At the individual level, self-reflection needs to occur by both the victims and perpetrators of discrimination. Practitioners, educators, and all who deliver services potentially impart a bias perpetuating prejudice and discrimination. At the systems level, communities and policymakers must join together and have the will to combat discrimination.

How does one remain "whole" or validate one's identity despite persistent assaults to self-esteem from prejudice and discrimination? How does one raise children or teach amid societal institutions that perpetuate bias? Culturally competent principles and practices are needed to provide a framework for managing diversity and valuing differences.

Volume 1, *Racism in America*, looks at stereotypes, racial bias, and race relations. How do we avoid internalizing racism or accepting negative messages about a group's ability and intrinsic worth? How do we address institutionalized racism that results in differential access to goods, service, and opportunities of society? Volume 2, *Ethnicity and Multiracial Identity*, looks at discrimination toward differences due to immigration, language, culture, and mixed race. Volume 3,

Bias Based on Gender and Sexual Orientation, looks at gender bias, women's issues, homophobia, and oppression of gay/lesbian lifestyles. Volume 4, *Disability, Religion, Physique, and Other Traits*, strives to examine less-spotlighted bias against other forms of difference, and begins the difficult dialogue that must take place if we are to eradicate prejudice and discrimination.

Written for today's people and environment, these volumes are rich with anecdotes, stories, examples, and research. These stories illustrate the emotional impact of prejudice and discrimination throughout history and as it still strikes people's lives today. While the chapters spotlight psychology, they interweave history, politics, legislation, social change, education, and more. These interdisciplinary views reflect the broad contexts of prejudice and discrimination that ultimately affect identity, life adjustment, and well-being for every one of us.

Please take with you the strategies for change offered in the toolbox at the end of each chapter. Change needs to occur at all levels: individual, practitioner/educator, and community. The intent of the toolboxes is to move us from the emotional to the scholarly to action and empowerment. They are intended to encourage and compel readers to begin individual change that will spur community and social action. With each person who reads these volumes, gains understanding, and finds the motivation or method to help make his or her small part of the world a more just and open-minded place, we have moved closer to making our goal a reality.

Jean Lau Chin

CHAPTER 1

The Causes of Racial Prejudice: A Behavior-Analytic Perspective

Afua Arhin
Bruce A. Thyer

> Not as many theories have been offered on the subject of racial bias as one would think. . . .
>
> (Katz, 2003, p. 898)

According to the theory of the *tabula rasa,* all persons are born with a mind that serves as a blank slate, upon which experience imprints knowledge. Furthermore, all persons are born innately good, independent, and equal (Locke, 1975). Assuming that this principle holds true, it is very interesting to find that racial prejudice is found in very young children (Aboud, 1988), with white children in particular expressing prejudice against blacks and other minority groups (Corenblum & Annis, 1993). Katz notes that "by the age of six years, over half of the white children in [Katz's] longitudinal study showed significant degrees of pro-white, anti-black bias" (2003, p. 897). Racial prejudice is a phenomenon found between, and even within, so-called racial categories, and it pervades human history and contemporary life. For example, in 1935, a survey of Princeton undergraduate men asked them to rank various racial groups in terms of the undergraduates' preferences for associating with them. Blacks were rated very low, indicating that these well-educated college undergraduates tended to avoid contact with them. This survey was conducted almost seventy years ago (Katz &

Braly, 1935). In the recent *National Longitudinal Survey of College Freshmen*, 3,924 students were surveyed on their racial attitudes, aspirations, and motivations. It was found that black, Latino, Asian, and white youth saw themselves and each other as tending to discriminate against members of other groups. White, Latino, and Asian students were more likely to stereotype blacks as poor, violence-prone, welfare-dependent, and lazy. Stereotypes of Latino people also followed a similar pattern. Asians were stereotyped as hardworking, intelligent, preferring to be self-sufficient, and tending to stick to tasks (Charles & Massey, 2003). It is striking how little change is evident among the views of college students.

Even more compelling is the recent novel study by Bertrand and Mullainathan (2003), who sent out fictitious resumes, each with either a "black-sounding" name or a "white-sounding" name, to companies in Boston and Chicago that were advertising employment opportunities. "White" names received 50 percent more callbacks for job interviews. This disparity even occurred among companies that advertised themselves as "equal opportunity employers." It is clear from this finding that we are far away from achieving a color-blind society in which people are judged by the content of their character rather than by the color of their skin. Blacks and others continue to frequently encounter overt and subtle acts of racism in everyday contemporary American life (Swim, Hyers, Cohen, Fitzgerald, & Bylsma, 2003).

Discrimination on the basis of skin color is expressed not only by white individuals, but also by darker-complected individuals such as blacks and Puerto Ricans, in that these racial groups express preferences for individuals with lighter skin tones (Hall, 2002; Hunter, 2002). Furthermore, it has been shown that these preferences significantly affect how individuals, regardless of race, interact and treat each other (Hill, 2002). How is it that racial discrimination is such a pervasive issue, even among highly educated individuals? Why do discriminatory attitudes exist and favor a lighter complexion among both whites and people of color? In this chapter we will develop some provisional answers to these questions, drawing upon literature related to the field of behavior analysis (see also Briggs & Paulson, 1996).

A BEHAVIOR-ANALYTIC PERSPECTIVE ON RACIAL PREJUDICE

Regardless of whether racial prejudice is a privately held attitude, the expression of discriminatory verbal statements; or expressed as overt, publicly observable action, it can be seen as a form of human behavior. As such, racial prejudice can be explained in terms of selected principles of learning theory and may, potentially, be preventable or amenable to change using interventions derived from learning theory.

Prejudice can be defined as "an opinion about an individual, group, or phenomenon that is developed without proof or systematic evidence. The prejudgment may be favorable but is more often unfavorable and may become institutionalized in the form of a country's laws or customs" (Barker, 2003, p. 372). *Racism*, the form of discrimination discussed in this chapter, is "stereotyping and generalizing about people, usually negatively, because of their *race*; commonly a basis of *discrimination* against members of racial groups" (Barker, 2003, p. 397). The actions referred to in the above definitions—opinions, laws, customs, stereotyping, and generalizing—are all examples of behavior, which was defined by B. F. Skinner as everything that a human does, regardless of its potential for public observation (1974). Skinner's definition, of course, contrasts starkly with Watson's (1913) much earlier position that the proper study of behavior, and indeed the subject matter of psychology itself, is limited only to investigating publicly observable acts. Therefore, the contemporary field of behavior analysis (the thriving discipline established by Skinner), defines *behavior* as "any action or response by an individual, including observable activity, measurable physiological changes, cognitive images, fantasies, and emotions" (Barker, 2003, p. 42). To the extent that empirically based principles of learning theory may play a role in the establishment of negative attitudes, opportunities exist to understand, intervene, and potentially prevent racial prejudice. We certainly recognize that a wide array of theories—psychological, sociological, sociobiological, and so on—exist and attempt to account for the phenomenon of racism, and we make no pretense at providing a comprehensive overview of such positions. Our much more modest goal is to present to the reader a preliminary account of how, when viewed through the conceptual lens of learning theory, racial prejudice could be established and maintained in children and adults.

Applied behavior analysis is a discipline that overlaps considerably with the domains of other fields concerned with human comportment, such as psychology, sociology, nursing, social work, political science, public administration, and anthropology. While applied behavior analysis can certainly inform certain aspects of these other disciplines, it is slowly emerging as an autonomous discipline with its own journals, professional associations, legal credentialing, and code of ethics. Behavior analysis is based upon the application of principles of empirically based learning theories to the understanding and control of socially significant behavior. Presently there is a focus on explicating the roles of three forms of learning: respondent learning, operant learning, and learning via observation. The following text reviews the fundamental concepts of each type and then illustrates how these learning processes may shape and maintain racial prejudice.

In the conclusion is a discussion of some promising leads derived from these self-same learning theories, which may be relevant to preventing and/or ameliorating racial prejudice.

RESPONDENT LEARNING

To many readers, the term *respondent learning*, or *classical conditioning*, may be synonymous with Pavlov's dogs. The images that come to mind are those of a ringing bell, food, and a salivating dog. This form of learning appears to be possible among virtually all animal species ever tested, including human beings. Explained in brief, certain forms of environmental stimuli can elicit an almost automatic response in humans. A sudden noise elicits a flinch response. A puff of air to the eye elicits a blink. A sharp pain produces a withdrawal reaction. Ingestion of spoiled or toxic food induces nausea and vomiting. The environmental stimuli that elicit these automatic reactions are called *unconditioned stimuli*, and the responses engendered are called *unconditioned responses*. Many, if not most, environmental stimuli do not produce conditioned responses, and such events are called *neutral stimuli*. If, however, a neutral stimulus is paired (either naturally or via a contrived manipulation) with the immediate presentation of an unconditioned stimulus, then after one or more trials the neutral stimulus can come to elicit a reaction similar to that evoked by the unconditioned stimulus, at which point the previously neutral stimulus becomes known as a *conditioned stimulus* and the reaction evoked becomes a *conditioned response*. This model of learning appears to be involved to a considerable degree in the establishment of emotional reactions (both positive and negative) and in the development of avoidance and approach behaviors. Classical conditioning is known to occur among human fetuses and is present immediately after birth and throughout one's lifetime (Bernard & Sontag, 1947; Kisilevsky, Muir, & Low, 1992). Indeed, it seems to be a learning process shared with all living animals, from one-celled organisms to human beings (Hennessey, Rucker, & McDiarmid, 1979).

Respondent learning has obvious adaptive significance for the species. For example, there are profound biological reasons why we begin to avoid oysters after ingesting a single spoiled one. Indeed, such taste aversions are among the easiest to acquire and are difficult to get rid of. The learning theory mechanisms are easy to understand. The taste and smell of sherry were originally a neutral stimulus. But a large quantity of sherry, by itself, is an unconditioned stimulus capable of producing the unconditioned responses of nausea and vomiting. A single experience of pairing the neutral taste and smell of sherry with the convulsive aftereffects caused the taste and smell of sherry to become a conditioned stimulus, capable of causing mild nausea (the conditioned response) all by themselves. This effect has persisted for thirty-five years.

A mild static shock (an unconditioned stimulus) to the fingertip produces pain and an immediate withdrawal response (an unconditioned response). During the winter, when humidity changes, touching a car-door handle often produces an unpleasant shock. After cold weather sets in and individuals have been shocked a few times upon touching the car-door handles, many find themselves pausing a bit before opening their car door, and in some cases having to force themselves to grasp the handle. In this instance, the door handle was initially a neutral stimulus, but after a couple of shocks it became an unconditioned stimulus and evoked the uncontrolled response of withdrawal simply upon being reached for.

Classical learning principles apply not only to simple behaviors, but also to complex behaviors. For example, if selected words are paired with unpleasant stimuli, soon those words themselves can come to evoke conditioned reactions similar to those caused by the unpleasant stimuli (Gale & Jacobson, 1970). Such emotional reactions can include sentiments such as "fear," "aversion," "distaste," and so forth, and in part these emotional reactions are derived from the environmental contexts in which these words occur. Consider the circumstance in which one initially hears words such as *hillbilly, honky, hebe, spic*, and *nigger*. If the circumstances surrounding exposure to these racially laden words are unpleasant and perhaps associated with a strong emotion such as fear or dislike, then the very words themselves may evoke related affective states. Not only affective states but also attitudes seem influenced via classical conditioning processes (Doyo, 1971; Miller, 1966; Staats & Staats, 1957). Such conditioned emotional states associated with initially neutral words seem to be particularly resistant to extinction (Baeyens, Van den Bergh, & Eelen, 1988). If one is raised in a society or culture where certain words are more likely to be uttered in a pejorative context—said with disdain, disgust, suspicion, or fear—then these negative emotions become inextricably intertwined with the very words associated with them.

As noted, respondent learning involves not merely words, but more complex stimuli as well. It is unlikely that any person has encountered a "real-life" Santa Claus or an angel, but if encountered we would likely not be afraid. Similarly, few people in their lives have come across a serial murderer wearing a hockey mask and wielding a chain saw, but imagine finding one in your closet late at night. More realistically, Bar-Tal (1996) found that Israeli children as young as two and a half years old rated a photograph of a male figure more negatively when he was verbally identified as an Arab than when the photo was not labeled. The inculcation of prejudice in very young, perhaps even pre-verbal, children may well involve classical conditioning processes through exposure to frightening images on television; these are unconditioned stimuli that could elicit unconditioned responses of fear and avoidance in the young children.

Emotional reactions can be classically conditioned in the absence of direct "real-life" encounters, but can be acquired vicariously through reading, videotape, or audio presentations, photographs, or listening to scary stories.

Here are some more pertinent examples. Suppose one is frequently exposed to witnessing real or simulated acts of violence on television, in the news, and in videotapes and movies, and that a disproportionate share of the perpetrators are blacks. What not-very-subtle message of such portrayals is conveyed to the audience? No one is immune to such influences. The Reverend Jesse Jackson once recounted how, walking late one night in Washington, DC, he heard footsteps behind him. In looking back he saw that it was a white man, and Jackson felt *relieved* to see that it was not a black man! If someone should have a real-life frightening encounter with a mugger, rapist, or thief, he or she will create negative associations to various stimuli associated with the perpetrator; and the perpetrator's *race* is among the most potentially salient factors available. Through the processes of respondent generalization, other similar-appearing individuals can come to evoke reactions (such as fear and avoidance) initially associated with the original traumatic act.

Classical conditioning is not a part of advanced brain functioning; indeed, conditioned responses are largely not under people's intellectual control, and thus the responses are very difficult to eliminate once established. Despite one's intellectual knowledge that similar-appearing people can be quite different, it is hard to shake off aversive feelings upon encountering a new person similar in appearance or mannerisms to another individual with whom one had a frightening experience. Such responses are not a product of one's intellectual functioning and are difficult to "reason away." As Skinner has noted, "Discrimination is a behavioral process: the contingencies, not the mind, make discriminations" (Skinner, 1974, p. 105).

OPERANT LEARNING

Another major way in which behavioral development occurs is through the interaction between the behavior of a child and the consequences that follow behavior (Bijou, 1995). Operant behavior (behavior that produces effects on one's environment) can be established via several distinct processes. If a behavior is followed by a pleasant consequence and thus becomes more likely in the future, it is labeled *positive reinforcement*. If a behavior is followed by the removal of something unpleasant and thereby increases the likelihood of that behavior recurring, it is called *negative* reinforcement. If a behavior is followed by the presentation of something aversive, and results in a weakening in the future occurrence of that behavior, this process is called *positive punishment*. *Negative punishment* occurs when the consequence of a given behavior results in the removal of something pleasant, and this reduces the likelihood of that behavior recurring. Note that reinforcement occurs if behavior is strengthened, and punishment is operating if behavior is weakened. The adjectives *positive* and *negative* refer to the presentation or removal of stimuli, respectively, not to whether or not a stimulus presented is deemed "good" or "bad." In particular, note that negative reinforcement is quite distinct from punishment in that the former strengthens behavior while the latter weakens it.

Imagine a child who says something like "I hate niggers!" or "I hate honkies." If this statement is met with smiles of approval, pats on the head, or high-fives, then the utterance of such racist opinions will likely be strengthened. If, on the other hand, s/he is scolded, challenged, or slapped, the expression of such views will become less likely. Similarly, if a child listens to music performed by a member of another race or displays a poster in his/her room of a movie star of another race, and meets with ridicule or scorn from parents, peers, or older siblings, the future effects on this type of behavior will be likely quite different than if followed by approval or compliments. This is not uncommon. One of the authors overheard his elementary school-age son say to a friend, "I hate gays!" Neither the boy's mother nor father ever expressed similar views and certainly had not provided any reinforcement for such opinions. It is more likely that such sentiments were picked up via the boy's peers or through exposure to the mass media.

Imagine a white four-year-old who walks into a physician's waiting room, already fearful over anticipating receiving an injection. If the waiting room is full of black adults with whom the child has had little experience, and the child begins to cry and seeks to leave the room, classical conditioning principles related to the environmental association between feeling fearful and subsequent exposure to black people may result in a generalized aversion to blacks. Moreover, if the mother subsequently removes the child from the waiting room, and the child calms down, then his or her escape behavior and complaints of being afraid have been negatively reinforced, and perhaps become more likely in the future. If the mother responds with soothing remarks, petting, and other forms of reassurance, then anxious dependent behavior will have been positively reinforced and again is more likely in the future.

Relatedly, if a child or adolescent verbalizes a racial slur or bullies someone of another race, and his/her peers or parents smilingly approve of or otherwise support these actions, then positive reinforcement may have occurred, with a subsequent increase in the expression of such behaviors in the future. Indeed, the operant learning process called *shaping* may result in a gradual escalation of the magnitude and intensity of racially prejudicial behaviors over time. It certainly seems obvious that audience approval and other positive reinforcers were essential in shaping the content and emotionality of Adolf Hitler's speeches during the 1930s. If fewer people had attended Nazi Party rallies as his anti-Semitic rhetoric escalated, then such behavior would have likely been reduced, as opposed to strengthened over time. In these more contemporary times, it seems obvious that one reason why white supremacist (such as Aryan Nation) or black supremacist (such as Nation of Islam) periodicals flourish is that people buy them! Money is a very potent positive reinforcer!

Another operant learning process is involved with punishment. It is known that one of the side effects of punishment is a tendency to avoid the stimuli associated with punishment. If someone experiences a punitive or otherwise aversive event (a robbery, a paddling at school, bullying, etc.), the most salient features of the perpetrator may become discriminative stimuli for avoidance behavior. A black child punished by a white principal at school may tend to avoid white people in the future, or a white child bullied by a black teenager may similarly avoid blacks.

Apart from contingencies of reinforcement provided in the everyday give and take of human interaction is the community or society establishment of larger-scale sets of consequences, codified as laws. The Nuremberg Laws limiting the civil rights of Jews in Nazi Germany are one egregious example; laws limiting the civil rights of American blacks earlier in our nation's history are another. At one point in America, teaching blacks to read and write was punishable by law, and slave catchers were provided with considerable positive reinforcers in the form of rewards for tracking down escaped slaves. Indeed, all social policies can be viewed through the conceptual lens of learning theory, and analyzed in terms of how contrived conditions of reinforcement and punishment are established and codified into laws (Thyer, 1996).

OBSERVATIONAL LEARNING

Personal contact with contingencies of reinforcement or punishment is not essential in order to learn. One can also acquire new behaviors (including attitudes) by observing the actions of others and witnessing the consequences following these actions. This is called observational learning, modeling, or learning via imitation; and like classical and operant learning processes, learning via imitation also makes sound evolutionary sense. If members of a pack of primates who are the most vocal get picked off by predators more often than those who are quieter, expect the survivors to become a little quieter over the course of their lifetimes, and in turn to pass this tendency on to their offspring, as the louder ones fail to reproduce and the quieter ones have more descendants. If a primate observes a conspecific eating a novel fruit, and this individual later becomes sick, expect the observer of this effect to be less likely to eat that type of fruit.

Learning from the observed consequences experienced by others makes sound evolutionary sense, and like respondent and operant behavioral learning processes, has been documented in a wide array of nonhuman species, including birds (Altshuler & Nunn, 2001), marmosets (Voelkl & Huber, 2000), cows (Veissier, 1993), cats (Karuki & Yanase, 1967), dogs (Adler & Adler, 1977), and chimpanzees

(Hirata & Morimura, 2000), as well as among people. Observational learning is thus highly likely involved in the acquisition, shaping, and maintaining of racial prejudice. Parents, in particular, exert powerful modeling influences over their children. If a child sees his/her parents uttering racist remarks or practicing other racially discriminatory behaviors on a regular or even irregular basis, then one can expect that child to begin displaying similar behaviors. If the child's or adolescent's peers exhibit racist behavior, this behavior can be a powerful influence in establishing a long-term pattern of prejudice. If people see racist behaviors being reinforced, not being followed by punishment, or otherwise tolerated by society at large, expect a society wherein racism flourishes.

The effects of observational learning are particularly powerful when the model is a highly valued or high-prestige individual, or if s/he resembles the observer. Governor George Wallace standing in the doorway to college, literally blocking the admission of black students, was widely applauded by white men in Alabama during the 1960s. If popular musicians loudly sing racist songs to the enthusiastic acclaim of their audience, expect others to model similarly racist actions (Grascia, 2003). If police abuse racial minorities, expect observers, including those watching via television, to be more likely to abuse minorities of color. If many individuals sign on to and read racist web pages, expect such web sites to expand and become ever more florid (Levin, 2002). Music lyrics and videos of "gangsta rap" are very prevalent in today's culture. These explicit lyrics are illustrated by videos depicting sexism, violence, substance abuse, the degradation of women, and inappropriate sexual behavior (Sherman & Dominick, 1986). Many videos are highly reinforcing to watch, and since blacks perform many of them, the imitation of these problematic behaviors by black youth is very likely (Sun & Lull, 1986). Further, these negative images may validate and reinforce racial stereotypes, perpetuating racial prejudice.

Historically, minorities have been very underrepresented on television, and those portrayals that do appear disproportionately represent negative stereotypes. There has been a slight improvement over the years with blacks somewhat more likely to be shown on television, while Latinos, Asians, and Native Americans remain virtually invisible. At present, however, the role of learning via imitation remains a speculative proposition in terms of accounting for racial prejudice. As Katz has recently noted, "no research has been conducted on how children's racial attitudes might be modeled" (2003, p. 899).

POTENTIAL INTERVENTIONS DERIVED
FROM BEHAVIOR ANALYSIS

What can be done to prevent or ameliorate racial prejudice? While genuinely experimental evidence from large-scale studies is lacking, there are a number of intriguing interventions based on social learning that provide some promising leads. An interventive study by Hauserman, Walen, and Behling (1973) employed twenty-five first grade children, including twenty whites and five blacks, as participants in a school-based study of the effects of reinforcement that is delivered contingent upon sitting with a "new friend" each day. The teacher maintained careful records of the children's interracial lunchroom time and free-play time interactions, specifically noting the extent to which the children participated in interpersonal interracial engagements. Following a several-day baseline phase, reinforcers (coupons later exchangeable for snacks) were provided to those children participating in interracial interactions (playing or sitting together, talking, etc.) during lunch. It was found that racial integration strongly increased during lunchtime, when reinforcers were provided, and that this effect generalized to playtimes later that same day when reinforcement was *not* provided. To the extent that social exclusion could indicate racial bias, this simple study demonstrates that elementary operant methods have the potential to encourage black and white children to positively engage with each other to a far greater extent than would normally be the case, and that their likelihood of such engagement generalized to other contexts in which contrived reinforcement was not delivered.

In a controlled nomothetic study, Primac (1980) found that simple verbal praise could enhance the use of positive adjectives by prejudiced white women when free associating to photographs of black persons. This is a powerful demonstration that listener responses exert a strong influence over the spontaneous emission of racially prejudiced remarks made by bigoted individuals (Guerin, 2003). Clearly, the phenomenon of racial prejudice should not be viewed solely as an idiosyncratic or characterological disorder, and it is much more likely to be a function of the social contingencies encountered during everyday life.

A naturalistic experiment was reported by Hamilton, Pinel, and Roskos-Ewoldson (2002), which assessed people's intent to donate money to black interest groups before and after a well-publicized act of racism occurred in the liberal arts college community, which was followed by public counterdemonstrations expressing outrage over the racist event. Behavioral intentions to donate money markedly increased following the racist event and counterprotests. This result may be interpretable in terms of observational learning. As vocal opponents of racism expressed their outrage and racially tolerant views were more widely promoted in the local community, observers would have seen a large array of role models, perhaps some being high-prestige or attractive individuals, displaying anti-racist behavior. This may have promoted similar behaviors among the observers.

A more contrived social psychology experiment by Blanchard, Lilly, and Vaughn (1991) found much the same effect on a small scale. Female college undergraduates were either exposed or not exposed to strong anti-racist opinions during an experimental conversation in small groups. Exposure to these anti-racist sentiments served to enhance the subjects' own endorsement of anti-racist views, which again suggests the powerful effects of modeling influences in ameliorating racial prejudice.

Relatedly, it has been shown that drinking alcohol tends to increase the expression of racial prejudice among college students (Reeves & Nagoshi, 1993), suggesting that one environmental intervention to reduce racist events would be for colleges to work with their local communities to reduce happy hours, the hours during which bars are open, the offering of free drinks to women, and so on.

At present in the United States, racial prejudice expressed as overt discrimination on the basis of race is a crime—for example, in systematically favoring whites over equally qualified blacks in job hiring or in refusing to rent apartments or hotel rooms to minorities of color, and so forth. Criminalizing such behaviors is a step in the right direction, but typically such behaviors are treated by civil penalties, fines levied against corporations, or mandating some form of employee training or restitution for those victimized. A further step in the eradication of racial prejudice would be to strengthen the penalties imposed upon those convicted of overt acts of racial discrimination, so that they receive criminal penalties and not merely fines, or pay some form of restitution up to and including prison sentences. Few interventions could be more potent than a couple of well-publicized CEOs of major corporations being sent to prison for racial discrimination in their companies' job practices.

Respondent learning suggests that exposing young children to members of other races under conditions of happy, pleasant circumstances may engender more favorable appraisals of racially diverse persons than would occur among individuals growing up in a largely racially homogeneous community. Katz's (2003, p. 906) cohort-based longitudinal research shows that "[c]hildren with high racial bias at school entry had much more racially homogenous social environments throughout their early years than did low bias children," and that very early on in life, children prefer to select same-race playmates over those of another race. Early intervention may be required to mitigate such effects. Providing lower dormitory rates for college students who agree to room with a member of another race might be another small step to enhance more liberal racial attitudes and behaviors among older students. To some extent this occurs naturally, but the liberalizing (in a racial sense) effects of education and college life may be promoted in a planned manner. The extent to which such behavioral engineering should be attempted is unknown. For example, would it be wise to disband exclusively black or white fraternities or sororities on campus, or to forcefully integrate historically black colleges and universities? These are not questions about which science may have much to say.

The media over the years have created numerous interventions using modeling to impact racial attitudes and behaviors of children. One example is the *Different and Same* prejudice reduction curriculum for early elementary children, developed by the producers of *Mr. Rogers' Neighborhood* (Lovelace, Scheiner, Dohlberg, Sergui, & Black, 1994). This curriculum consisted of videos of vignettes set in a school environment with animal puppets and racially diverse adult role models, played by live actors to help resolve difficult interracial situations. Overall, the curriculum was effective in positively influencing racial attitudes of children. As demonstrated, the media definitely have a potentially powerful influence on the behavior of young people. But traditional educational programs or diversity workshops appear to be relatively weak methods to inculcate anti-racist behavior (Hill & Augoustinos, 2001).

DISCUSSION

Numerous intervention strategies have been employed to rectify the prevalence of racial bias in children. Such strategies have included the use of multicultural curricula and materials for lessons that highlight the contributions of different racial, ethnic, religious, and other social groups. Other programs focus explicitly on providing counter-stereotypic information about groups (Bishop, 1992).

Despite the variety of racial stereotyping interventions that have been reported in the developmental literature, most interventions have proven ineffective in altering children's negative racial attitudes. This can be argued to be a result of the weaknesses of the theoretical and empirical bases of attitude formation and change on which the interventions are based (Bigler, 1999). It could also be suggested that the environmental (social and physical) conditions responsible for establishing and maintaining racial prejudice are so pervasive in our society that racial prejudice reversal or prevention in children is almost impossible.

Behavioral analysts, however, approach the child's racially related behavior holistically by examining (a) the child as a biological and psychological entity, (b) the environment of development, and (c) the continuous and reciprocal interaction between the behavior of the child and the environment (Bijou, 1995).

From this optimistic behavior-analytic viewpoint, it can be suggested that effective strategies can be employed for change based on learning theory processes. Many behaviors can be strengthened or weakened by the contrived manipulation of the consequences following their occurrence. The types and schedules of reinforcement may influence the strength of racist and nonracist behaviors. In the traditional operant extinction model, reinforcers maintaining a behavior are simply not delivered. In the context of racial prejudice in a child, the extinction condition translates into complete nonreinforcement, either positive or negative, of any racially prejudiced behaviors that the child may exhibit. In a young child, this approach may be more practical to achieve, since his or her environment is more controlled. An alternative to the extinction procedure is the noncontingent reinforcement (NCR) intervention, in which reinforcement is delivered periodically, but not contingent on the specific behavior. For example, a child may be exposed to a stimulus for racial bias, such as watching a racially charged television show as well as two other benign television programs every morning. The mother who provides the same consistent, continuous commentary and attention to the child throughout all three shows, regardless of what shows they are, is exhibiting NCR (rather than emphasizing the racially charged show). NCR control is considered to be the most methodologically appropriate procedure for demonstrating the positive effects of positive reinforcement (Rescorla & Skucy, 1969).

Differential reinforcement of other behaviors (DRO) reverses the contingency by delivering reinforcers for the absence of a specific target behavior during a specified period of time. This suggests that a child who typically exhibits behaviors of racial bias can have this behavior reversed by being reinforced on occasions when such behaviors are not displayed. Positive reinforcement procedures have been found to

Toolbox for Change

For	Images/perceptions	Strategies for change
Individuals		When you hear racist or prejudicial remarks made within your hearing, do not reinforce them by smiling, nodding or verbally agreeing. Instead, gently provide corrective information, or at least inform the speaker that you do not agree with those views, and do not like hearing them.
		Parents should avoid expressing racially discriminatory behavior around their children.
		Try and arrange for children under your responsibility to have the opportunity to positively interact with members of other races.
Community		Leaders can promote community events featuring crossover types of entertainment, likely to appeal to several races.
		Community leaders can be proactive in seeking out deserving members of racial minorities to receive community service awards and other forms of public recognition, or to be placed in appointive offices.
		Law officials can vigorously prosecute hate-crimes and other forms of racial discrimination which violate the law, as opposed to according these a low priority.

continued

Toolbox for Change (continued)

For	Images/perceptions	Strategies for change
Practitioners/ educators	Parents and teachers need to avoid exposing children to media portrayals of racially stereotypical behavior, in terms of books, magazines, television, videos, DVDs, and the theater. Provide access to positive portrayals of members of different races, and to books, music and other creative works created by members of different races.	Teachers can arrange for children in their classes to constructively work and play with each other in bi- or multiracial groupings.

be effective under a number of conditions and may be good techniques for diminishing racial prejudice in the young child. However, this cannot be done well without proper training of parents, preschool educators, and the community at large, in instituting effective contingency management programs.

Another important component of effective strategies is the quality of the environment in which the child is developing. If the child has good peers from whom to learn and to imitate nonracial behaviors, and if s/he is not subjected to a barrage of negative images that promote racism, reinforcement programs may be an effective intervention in the young child.

We freely acknowledge that much of what we have suggested in this chapter is speculative and weakly grounded at best in terms of scientifically credible evidence. However, this behavior-analytic perspective on racial prejudice *is* well supported by a strong theoretical framework, one that has widespread applications to a large array of interpersonal phenomena, and one that has also generated a considerably strong track record of developing effective interventions in related fields. Behavior analysis is also well supported by common sense and practical observations of everyday life. By being grounded solely in terms of environmental events, behavior analysis tends to promote a natural science approach to social issues such as racial prejudice. We believe that the learning theory processes undergirding the behavior-analytic perspective, while not yet offering convincing solutions to the vexing problem of racism, are undoubtedly implicated in the development and maintenance of the problem. We are equally convinced that these will be a part of the solution.

REFERENCES

Aboud, F. E. (1988). *Children and prejudice*. New York: Blackwell.

Adler, L. L., & Adler, H. E. (1977). Ontogeny of observational learning in the dog. *Developmental Psychobiology, 10*, 267–271.

Altshuler, D. L., & Nunn, A. M. (2001). Observational learning in humming-birds. *Auk, 118*, 795–799.

Baeyens, F., Van den Bergh, O., & Eelen, P. (1988). Once in contact, always in contact: Evaluative conditioning is resistant to extinction. *Advances in Behavior Research and Therapy, 10*, 179–199.

Barker, R. L. (Ed.). (2003). *The social work dictionary* (5th ed.). Washington, DC: NASW Press.

Bar-Tal, D. (1996). Development of social categories and stereotyping in early childhood: The case of "the Arab" concept formation, stereo-type, and attitudes by Jewish children in Israel. *International Journal of Intercultural Relations, 20*, 341–370.

Bernard, J., & Sontag, L. W. (1947). Fetal reactivity to tonal stimulation: A preliminary report. *Journal of Genetic Psychology, 70*, 205–210.

Bertrand, M., & Mullainathan, S. (2003). *Are Emily and Greg more employable than Lakisha and Jamal? A field experiment on labor market discrimi-nation*. Cambridge, MA: National Bureau of Economic Research.

Bigler, R. S. (1999). The use of multicultural curricula and materials to counter racism in children. *Journal of Social Issues, 55*, 687–806.

Bijou, S. W. (1995). *Behavior analysis of child development*. Reno, NV: Context Press.

Bishop, R. S. (1992). Multicultural literature for children: Making informed choices. In V. Harris (Ed.), *Teaching multicultural literature in grades K-8* (pp. 37–53). Norwood, CT: Christopher Gordon.

Blanchard, F. A., Lilly, T., & Vaughn, L. A. (1991). Reducing the expression of racial prejudice. *Psychological Science, 2*, 101–105.

Briggs, H. E., & Paulson, R. I. (1996). Racism. In M. A. Mattaini & B. A. Thyer (Eds.), *Finding solutions to social problems: Behavioral strategies for change* (pp. 147–177). Washington, DC: American Psychological Association.

Charles, C. Z., & Massey, D. S. (2003). How stereotypes sabotage minority students. *Chronicle of Higher Education, 49*(18), 10–12.

Corenblum, B., & Annis, R. C. (1993). Development of racial identity in minority and majority children: An affect discrepancy model. *Canadian Journal of Behavioral Science, 25,* 499–521.

Doyo, M. C. (1971). Establishing and changing meaning by means of classical conditioning using the paired-associate method. *Philippine Journal of Psychology, 4,* 117–124.

Gale, E. N., & Jacobson, M. B. (1970). The relationship between social comments as unconditioned stimuli. *Behaviour Research and Therapy, 8,* 301–307.

Grascia, A. M. (2003). White supremacy music: What does it mean to our youth? *Journal of Gang Research, 10*(2), 25–31.

Guerin, B. (2003). Combating prejudice and racism: New interventions from a functional analysis of racist language. *Journal of Community and Applied Social Psychology, 13,* 29–45.

Hall, R. E. (2002). A descriptive methodology of color bias in Puerto Rico: Manifestations of discrimination in the new millennium. *Journal of Applied Social Psychology, 32,* 1527–1537.

Hamilton, J. C., Pinel, E. C., & Roskos-Ewoldsen, D. R. (2002). The effects of a racist act and public counter-demonstrations on race-related behavioral intentions: A natural experiment. *Journal of Applied Social Psychology, 32,* 2611–2620.

Hauserman, N., Walen, S. R., & Behling, M. (1973). Reinforced racial integration in the first grade: A study in generalization. *Journal of Applied Behavior Analysis, 6,* 193–200.

Hennessey, T. M., Rucker, W. B., & McDiarmid, C. G. (1979). Classical conditioning in paramecia. *Animal Learning and Behavior, 7,* 417–423.

Hill, M. E. (2002). Race of the interviewer and perception of skin color: Evidence from the Multi-City Study of Urban Inequality. *American Sociological Review, 67,* 99–108.

Hill, M. E., & Augoustinos, M. (2001). Stereotype change and prejudice reduction: Short- and long-term evaluation of a cross cultural awareness programme. *Journal of Community & Applied Social Psychology, 11,* 243–262.

Hirata, S., & Morimura, N. (2000). Native chimpanzee (*Pan troglodytes*) observation of experienced conspecifics in a tool-using task. *Journal of Comparative Psychology, 114,* 291–296.

Hunter, M. L. (2002). "If you're light you're alright": Light skin color as social capital for women of color. *Gender and Society, 16,* 175–193.

Karuki, Y., & Yanase, T. (1967). Observational learning in the cat. *Annual of Animal Psychology, 17,* 19–24.

Katz, D., & Braly, K. W. (1935). Racial prejudice and racial stereotypes. *Journal of Abnormal and Social Psychology, 30,* 175–193.

Katz, P. A. (2003). Racists or tolerant multiculturalists? How do they begin? *American Psychologist, 58,* 897–909.

Kisilevsky, B. S., Muir, D. W., & Low, J. A. (1992). Maturation of human fetal responses to sound and vibration. *Child Development, 63,* 1497–1508.

Levin, B. (2002). Cyberhate: A legal and historical analysis of extremists' use of computer networks in America. *American Behavioral Scientist, 45,* 958–988.

Locke, J. (1975). *An essay concerning human understanding.* Oxford, UK: Clarendon Press. (Original work published 1690)

Lovelace, V., Scheiner, S., Dohlberg, S., Sergui, L., & Black, T. (1994). Making a neighborhood the *Sesame Street* way. Developing a methodology to evaluate children's understanding of race. *Journal of Educational Television, 20,* 69–77.

Miller, A. W. (1966). Conditioned connotative meaning. *Journal of General Psychology, 50,* 319–328.

Primac, D. W. (1980). Reducing racial prejudice by verbal operant conditioning. *Psychological Reports, 46,* 655–669.

Reeves, S. B., & Nagoshi, C. T. (1993). Effects of alcohol administration on the disinhibition of racial prejudice. *Alcoholism: Clinical and Experimental Research, 17,* 1066–1071.

Rescorla, R. A., & Skucy, J. C. (1969). Effect of response independent reinforcers during extinction. *Journal of Comparative and Physiological Psychology, 67,* 381–389.

Sherman, B. L., & Dominick, J. R. (1986). Violence and sex in music videos: TV and rock 'n' roll. *Journal of Communication, 36,* 79–93.

Skinner, B. F. (1974). *About behaviorism.* New York: Knopf.

Staats, C. K., & Staats, A. W. (1957). Attitudes established by classical conditioning. *Journal of Abnormal and Social Psychology, 57,* 37–40.

Sun, S. W., & Lull, J. (1986). The adolescent audience for music videos and why they watch. *Journal of Communication, 36,* 115–125.

Swim, J. K., Hyers, L. L., Cohen, L. L., Fitzgerald, D. C., & Bylsma, W. H. (2003). African American college students' experiences with everyday racism: Characteristics of and responses to these incidents. *Journal of Black Psychology, 29,* 38–67.

Thyer, B. A. (1996). Behavior analysis and social welfare policy. In M. A. Mattaini & B. A. Thyer (Eds.), *Finding solutions to social problems: Behavioral strategies for change* (pp. 41–60). Washington, DC: American Psychological Association.

Veissier, I. (1993). Observational learning in cattle. *Applied Animal Behavioral Science, 35,* 235–243.

Voelkl, B., & Huber, L. (2000). True imitation in marmosets. *Animal Behavior, 60,* 195–202.

Watson, J. B. (1913). Psychology as the behaviorist views it. *Psychological Review, 20,* 158–177.

CHAPTER 2

From Tragedy to Triumph: The Tulsa Race Riot

Yvonne M. Jenkins

Like my parents, I am a native Oklahoman. I was born and grew up in Tulsa, better known as *T-Town*, my mother's birthplace. Tulsa is the second largest city in Oklahoma and is located in the northeast region of the state. I moved east to attend a historically black university and discovered that some of my peers there, as well as others I have met since undergraduate school, found it unusual to learn that blacks live in Oklahoma. Until the media attention to the Oklahoma City bombing in 1995, introducing myself to others as an Oklahoman was commonly met with "Where?" or with "I didn't know there were black people in Oklahoma!" or by those famous lyrics from the state's musical namesake. I have been amused to discover that, even today, images of Oklahoma are often limited to Hollywood notions of cowboys and Indians, covered wagons, and other cinema representations of the Wild, Wild West. It is as if Oklahoma is perceived as a step back in time, Mars, or some other out-of-this-world entity.

At a more serious level, the black population of Oklahoma has a very proud and distinguished history. Although there is much to celebrate about that history, it is important to acknowledge that it includes "one of the most horrific episodes of racial violence in American history," the Tulsa Race Riot of 1921 (Ogletree, 2003). Aftershocks of that tragedy continue to impact the lives of Oklahomans as well as society at large today.

My personal preoccupation with the Tulsa Race Riot of 1921 has been motivated by (1) a love for my home community, (2) the desire to learn about and acknowledge an important truth about its history, (3) the inspiration "to give back" by making known the enduring traumatic psychological impact of the riot, and (4) an appreciation of the resilience that has enabled its black community to survive, prosper, and triumph over this tragedy.

My introduction to the Tulsa Race Riot of 1921 was gentle, gradual, and without much elaboration. I recall times when my mother mentioned "the riot of 1921" that she had learned about from her mother and maternal grandmother. At the time of the riot, her mother was six months pregnant with her. At the age of nine, my mother lost her own mother after she was refused treatment for a life-threatening illness because of the racial discrimination of Jim Crow laws. When I was around ten years old, I learned of my maternal grandmother's final resting place, an urban cemetery that we often drove by while riding from the segregated black community of north Tulsa to the segregated white areas of Brookside and south Tulsa where my mother worked as a domestic. In retrospect, I recognize that I never even paid attention to the name of that cemetery; rather, it was enough for me to know that it was my maternal grandmother's final resting place. Decades later, I discovered that some believed that many of the riot's victims might have been buried in Oaklawn Cemetery in a mass grave with no headstones to identify who they were, or when they were born or died. Neither was there any marker describing the tragic circumstances of their deaths. While reading an article about the riot in a Boston newspaper in November 1999, I discovered that my grandmother's resting place and Oaklawn Cemetery were the same site.

Given the timing of my mother's comments about the riot, I am sure that some of her memories were triggered by media coverage of the civil rights strife in the United States during the late fifties, including the sit-ins in Tulsa and the race riots that followed during the sixties. I have always been interested in black history. By the time I left home for college, I had studied Oklahoma history as well as Negro history. I also took a course in Negro history at the college level. Yet, I do not recall any formal education about the Tulsa Race Riot of 1921. Initially, I questioned whether my memory was accurate. Could I have simply forgotten an inclusion of this historical event in my studies after so many years, or had there really been such an important omission from those courses? For a while, I even hesitated to check this out with others who had taken both of the courses due to the possibility that my own memory was not intact. When I did, my memories were validated. As Herman wrote in *Trauma and Recovery*,

> In order to escape accountability, the perpetrator does everything in his power to promote forgetting. Secrecy and silence are the perpetrator's first line of defense. (1992, p. 8)

Later, my experience was further confirmed when I read a statement made by Mrs. Eddie Fay Gates, a member of the Tulsa Race Riot Commission. She acknowledged that children in Tulsa did not know about the riot and questioned how they could be expected to learn from it and to improve conditions if not educated about what had happened. More recently, I was stunned but not shocked to learn that information about the riot was banned for many years by book publishers, just as accurate accounts of U.S. and American history that included blacks and slavery had for so many years (Oklahoma Commission to Study the Tulsa Race Riot of 1921, 2001).

During my predoctoral internship at the Center for Multicultural Training in Psychology in Boston, I became interested in the impact of community crisis intervention on social problems. My dissertation research focused on evaluating a training program designed to prepare community mental health workers to intervene in the Boston schools desegregation crisis that occurred in the late 1970s. Several years later, Carmen Fields, a Boston journalist and native Tulsan, produced "Going Back to T-Town," a documentary about the riot of 1921 that aired on PBS in 1992 as part of the *American Experience* series. While viewing the documentary, I was reminded of my mother's comments about the riot. From that point on, my interest in the riot soared. During the fall of that year, I purchased the videotape of the documentary, took it to Tulsa, and viewed it with my mother. My mother has always been a very quiet and gentle soul. Yet, her response to the documentary was enthusiastic and moving. The story of the riot clearly affirmed an important aspect of her experience as she listened to several senior Tulsans, blacks whose faces and stories were familiar to her, recall their experiences of the riot. Their stories probably echoed those she had heard from her mother and grandmother. It suddenly dawned on me afterward that my mother was an immediate descendant of riot survivors even though she had never been formally registered as such.

Since the media paid more and more attention to the riot in the 1990s, during the millennium and beyond I read everything I could get my hands on about the riot. What seemed a bit strange to me was that my circle of friends and other family members who lived in the Tulsa area discussed the riot less than those I knew in other places. I also encountered a similar silence in the aftermath of the Oklahoma City bombing. Later, I discussed this with one of my mentors in the mental health field. During that conversation, it occurred to me that silence, even secrecy, is often present in the aftermath of trauma. My mentor suggested that I write an article about the psychological aftermath of the riot as I struggled to understand the silence. At that time, her suggestion only interested me as a future possibility, since I was preoccupied with learning more facts about this horror that was still a mystery to me.

In 2003, a Harvard-led legal team filed a lawsuit that sought reparations for survivors of the riot and their descendants. In 2004, that lawsuit was defeated on the basis that this injustice was long ago and filing deadlines had passed. Despite this legal setback, the filing of the lawsuit was significant in its own right since it was the first to seek reparations for "the continuing consequences of slavery" (Mansfield, 2003). The lawsuit was an important milestone in the healing of Tulsa's black community in that it acknowledged an ugly secret as an injustice and formally honored the dignity of those who succumbed to and survived the riot as well as their descendants.

TULSA, A MODEL FOR RECOVERY AND HEALING

Like Tulsa's black community, other communities of color across the country have been terrorized by racial violence over the years. Such trauma typically engenders fear, rage, helplessness, and preoccupation with basic survival. This stance is commonly reinforced by shame, silence/secrecy, and denial. To some extent, Tulsa's experience has been consistent with this. Yet, Tulsa's movement toward healing has also been progressive and instructive for community healing, recovery, and the ongoing confrontation of racism. It is hoped that shedding light on this community's experience will promote the recovery and healing of other communities and individuals from violence and trauma rooted in racism and discrimination.

BACKGROUND OF THE RIOT

By 1921, descendants of African slaves who had accompanied Native Americans on the Trail of Tears, children and grandchildren of runaway slaves, and elderly persons who had been born into slavery had migrated to Oklahoma from the South to escape lynching, poverty, and other forms of oppression. However, there was the chilling reality that twenty-three blacks had been lynched in twelve Oklahoma towns in the decade leading up to 1921. None of the perpetrators were punished for these crimes. In fact, the final report of the Oklahoma Commission to Study the Tulsa Race Riot of 1921 (2001) asserts that authority figures even participated in some of the lynchings. Meanwhile, in racially segregated Tulsa, blacks were prohibited from doing business with whites (Moorehead, 2003).

Interracial marriages between blacks and Native Americans led to landownership where oil had already been discovered. Blacks took advantage of the economic boom by establishing their own businesses. These included two newspapers, medical and dental offices, a hospital, a labor union, three groceries, barbershops and beauty parlors, realtors, a branch of the U.S. Post Office, two movie theaters, a hotel, and Dunbar Elementary School. Furthermore, Tulsa County had the second lowest illiteracy rate in the state.

By 1921, blacks had built a "self-sustaining, economically thriving," and progressive community of 10,000 in north Tulsa known as Greenwood (Denniston, 2003). The Greenwood district was referred to as "Black Wall Street" by noted educator Booker T. Washington but disparagingly referred to as "Little Africa" by some in Tulsa's white community. Although black Tulsans were very proud of their community, this was not everyone's sentiment. In fact, some have speculated that it was resentment of this success that fueled the Tulsa riot of 1921 (Moorehead, 2003).

On May 31, 1921, the day before the outbreak of the riot, Dick Rowland, a nineteen-year-old black shoeshine man in downtown Tulsa, took a routine bathroom break by going to the top of the Drexel building, his place of employment, where the only bathroom for "coloreds" was located. It was alleged that, while on that break, he assaulted Sarah Paige, a seventeen-year-old white woman elevator operator. The media was immediately alerted. The headline for the evening edition of the *Tulsa Tribune* read, "Nab Negro for Assaulting Girl," while the editorial promised "[t]o Lynch Negro Tonight." The latter is believed to have initiated the riot, because forty-five minutes after the newspaper went on sale, Tulsans were talking about lynching. That night approximately 2,000 whites gathered outside the Tulsa County Courthouse, which was only about five miles from Tulsa's predominantly black Greenwood.

Armed black war veterans also gathered and offered their help to the local police force after hearing about the white mob and out of concern for Rowland's safety. However, their offer was rejected. Thereafter, according to Ellsworth (1982), as the black veterans were leaving, a white man demanded to know what a tall black veteran armed with an army pistol planned to do with it. The man, who had recently returned from duty in France, replied, "I'm going to use it if I need to." The white man lunged at him, the gun fired, and the riot began.

THE RIOT AND ITS AFTERMATH

Fourteen hours of ensuing violence destroyed an entire community. Mobs were deputized, armed, and spurred on toward violence by city and state officials. In addition, the National Guard was called in by the governor to put an end to what was said to be "an uprising" by blacks. Powerful weapons were used with deadly force against blacks. After running out of ammunition, more than 4,000 blacks were held at the convention hall, other public buildings downtown, and the baseball stadium; or herded into the fairgrounds by torch-bearing whites, beaten, and shot. These sites served as internment camps. Many of the sick and wounded were dumped in front of the convention hall hours before medical attention was provided (Ellsworth, 1982). On June 1, with the aid of the National Guard and the Red Cross, several sites in Tulsa were turned into emergency medical facilities for wounded blacks. Forty-eight whites were also treated at hospitals. Initially, only those blacks who were employed by whites could be released immediately—if their employers vouched for them and assured authorities that the employees would be kept indoors where they were employed.

Although the number of the dead has long been in dispute, the Department of Health's Bureau of Vital Statistics estimated that three hundred blacks and ten whites died in the riot (Ellsworth, 1982). This is thought to be the highest mortality rate ever recorded for a riot on U.S. soil. In addition, 5,000 blacks were left homeless after at least 1,256 houses went up in smoke.

Whites looted 215 black homes, and over $2 million in property damage accumulated over a thirty-five–block area. Many black Tulsans fled the area and found refuge in the Kansas City area, Chicago, cities in the Northeast, and California. Some whites and Maria Morales Gutierrez, a Mexican immigrant, offered their homes as refuge

(Ellsworth, 1982). Meanwhile, Sarah Paige, the alleged victim, pressed no charges and Dick Rowland was later released. Even though a few blacks were charged with riot-related offenses, the impact of racism, prejudice, and discrimination was evident in that not one white person was ever convicted or sent to prison for the murders or arson (Moorehead, 2003).

Authorities refused offers to help black survivors, attempted to con-fiscate land from those who were forced to leave their homes, and buried victims in unmarked graves, according to Kolker (1999). Mean-while, only one block of the original Greenwood business district still stands. That land, which was valued at $13 million in 1921, is currently worth around $65 million.

The report of the Tulsa Race Riot Commission (2000) suggests that two sources of information most accurately corroborate the prop-erty value of the total area of Tulsa destroyed by the riot. First, records of riot-related claims exceeding $1.8 million dollars were filed against the city of Tulsa between June 14, 1921 and June 6, 1922. However, the majority of those claims were disallowed. Yet, a white gunshop owner was compensated for guns that were stolen from his shop.[1] Secondly, the sum of actual damage filed in 193 retrieved court cases against insurance companies and the city of Tulsa equaled $1,470,711.56. This amount bears a close relationship to the range of other estimates that spanned $1.5–1.8 million.

A CHILLING TWIST

Stories about how the remains of the dead were treated after the riot are filled with indignity and horror. For example, at the convention center where many black men were being detained, the body of a dead black man was publicly displayed to frighten and humiliate the group. Funerals and graveside rites for the dead were not permitted in the city. According to Ellsworth (1982), the leader of the National Guard, Adjutant General Charles Barrett, rationalized this action as "military policy, and [necessary because of] the emotional stress which still pre-vailed, and the fact that many churches . . . were being used to shelter the homeless" (p. 67). Ellsworth also revealed that some survivors, including my high school principal, the late Henry C. Whitlow, wit-nessed corpses being piled onto trucks before being driven away. It is believed that some corpses were dumped into the Arkansas River while others were probably buried in a mass grave in Oaklawn Cemetery.

In 1999, the Tulsa Race Riot Commission approved the use of geophysics to look for any existing mass gravesites. In 2002, Clyde Eddie, an eighty-eight-year-old white resident of Tulsa, revealed a poignant memory to the Tulsa Race Riot Commission. At the age of ten, one day he was walking to his aunt's house and saw piano crates just inside the fence at Oaklawn Cemetery. He stopped to peek beyond the fence and saw what he believed to be at least seven corpses inside the crates before being shoved away by some white men. It is now believed that at least 150 bodies were buried in that cemetery under the supervision of a Salvation Army officer.

Early in 2003, state archeologists tested three sites with ground-penetrating radar to find a mass grave and proof of tragedy. Two of those sites, Newblock Park and Booker T. Washington Cemetery, have yielded no appreciable data. However, one subsurface anomaly in Oaklawn Cemetery bears all of the characteristics of a dug pit/trench with vertical walls and an undefined object within the approximate center of the feature. Because this anomaly is visible on electromagnetic induction (EMI) and growth-penetrating radar (GPR), some believe it is authentic even though this is not yet certain.

THE ENDURING PSYCHOLOGICAL IMPACTS OF RACIAL TRAUMA AND PREJUDICE

Despite the secrecy that lingered for decades after the riot, "the physical, psychological and spiritual damage [it imposed] was apparent for years" (Ellsworth, 1982, p. 26). Certainly, since the early 1970s, the media has made the impact of the riot much clearer than ever before. For example, the terrorism inflicted on victims; the incredible loss of life, property, and an entire business community; the displacement of citizens; and other indignities have been revealed in horrific detail.

Some may wonder whether this event that happened so long ago could still have lingering psychological effects. After all, isn't it over? What could an event that happened so long ago have to do with the present? What is the use in dwelling on it? I recall that a similar sentiment about the psychological impact of slavery was debated back and forth by the audience after one of my presentations at the American Psychological Convention several years ago.

In this era where so much is known about posttraumatic stress, it is startling that racial violence and prejudice suffered by blacks are often still paid minimal attention as trauma. Instead, rather than a more comprehensive systems perspective oriented toward social change, the "blame the victim" stance still surfaces as a general explanation for low self- and social esteem, self/community destruction, and other problematic behaviors. In the aftermath of the Tulsa riot, the blame-the-victim stance was perpetuated by distorted newspaper accounts and coverups by the local police; and also by a National Guard motivated by denial and a desire to hold on to an unblemished image, which was always important to socially and politically prominent white Tulsans, since Ku Klux Klan members who held powerful positions in the local government were thought to be criminally involved in the riot. Some black Tulsans felt certain that whites organized efforts to keep that secret. Mainstream allegations that Tulsa's black community was responsible for the riot and other deliberate efforts to conceal the truth within a racist social climate that imposed second-class citizenship on blacks made it difficult to make the truth known for several decades. Despite this, some black Tulsans were brave enough to pass the story on to those who came after them. Others never mentioned it, possibly out of fear, shame, preoccupation with basic survival, and the mental dissociation that is often triggered by trauma.

Since the riot, the black population of Tulsa's movement toward recovery and healing has involved (1) rebuilding the Greenwood community, (2) breaking the silence and commemorating the riot, and (3) filing a lawsuit for reparations.

REBUILDING THE GREENWOOD COMMUNITY

The incredible resilience of those who stayed in Tulsa after the riot is still remarkable in view of the horrific trauma they had endured, the persistence of a hostile environment thereafter, and an uncertain future. Despite the wounding and grief they endured, the survivors rallied around each other in a spirit of collaboration, dignity, and determination. The help offered by the Red Cross and local business-men was readily accepted, and more than 350 tents were erected within the first week after the riot. The local chapter of the National Association for the Advancement of Colored People (NAACP) also made a sizable contribution to the survivors in October 1921. Other contributions in varying amounts came from as far away as California, New York, and New Jersey. By December of that year, efforts had begun to rebuild Greenwood despite obstacles imposed by the Tulsa City Commission and the Chamber of Commerce. Attorney B. C. Franklin, the father of eminent historian John Hope Franklin, and his law partners defeated a city ordinance that blocked the efforts of blacks to rebuild their community.

BREAKING THE SILENCE
AND COMMEMORATING THE RIOT

> Sharing the traumatic experience with others is a precondition of a sense of a meaningful world. (Herman, 1992, p. 70)

Basic to healing the psychological wounds of trauma is breaking—by acknowledging the truth about what has happened—the silence or secrecy that lingers in its aftermath. Recovery can take place only within the context of relationships, not isolation. The awareness gained from sharing also prevents a repetition of the past.

I have often wondered what it was like for my maternal grand-mother and great-grandmother to have experienced the riot and to pass their stories on to my mother. What was it like to bring a child into this world at a time filled with the trauma of so much loss and grief? What was it like to bring a newborn home to a community blemished by the ruins of burned homes, churches, and businesses? What was it like to live such a joyous experience in the midst of homeless families temporarily housed in tents, the sadness and even numbness of over-whelming loss, and the ever-present fear that the embers of racial hatred could ignite again at a moment's notice?

I can only speculate about what my maternal grandmother and great-grandmother experienced, since what my mother passed on to me was without much elaboration. After all, she was only a child when she heard their stories. Her mother and grandmother were both deceased by her mid-teens. I can only imagine that the timing of my mother's birth must have been a bittersweet time for her family and filled with much uncertainty about the future.

Even though I have never had the privilege of knowing my maternal grandmother or great-grandmother, I appreciate the courage and resil-ience they displayed by passing their stories on to my mother. At some level, they must have struggled with the threat or reality of emotional disconnection from one another or from my mother, since this is a fre-quent occurrence among traumatized parents. However, their strong sense of injustice and need for my mother to know about what had hap-pened probably spared her the pain and suffering that such disconnection might have imposed on her as a child. Witnessing in the aftermath of trauma prevents children from becoming silent witnesses to parents' suffer-ing and feeling separated from them, according to Weingarten (2003).

This same author contends that "children do better knowing something rather than nothing" and that dialogue "interrupts transmission of trauma and common shock from one generation to another" (p. 154).

Even though black Tulsans have always acknowledged the reality of the riot more than their white counterparts have, memories of that event gradually seemed to vanish over the years. Eventually it was as if the riot had never occurred at all. Ellsworth (1982) contends that the white community's silence was motivated in part by the need of prominent white Tulsans to maintain an unblemished image of the city. The necessity for blacks to restrict their acknowledgment of the riot to their own community was imperative since it was much harder for them to protest oppression in the absence of laws to protect them from the practices of racism and discrimination in the early nineteenth century. As Seymour Williams, a riot survivor and retired high school teacher, stated in his testimony to the Tulsa Race Riot Commission, "Blacks lost everything. They were afraid it could happen again and there was no way to tell the story. The . . . Negro newspapers were bombed. With the unkept promises, they were too busy just trying to make it . . . killers were still running loose [wearing] blue suits as well as Klan sheets" (p. vii). Williams's view is supported by Herman (1992), who contends that "secrecy and silence are the perpetrator's first line of defense" (p. 9). "Those who are already disempowered . . . are most at risk" (p. 60). Thus, the silence of black Tulsans proved to be adaptive and created a central relational paradox, even though this inadvertently promoted the denial of white Tulsans.[2]

In 1956, Don Ross, then a student at segregated Booker T. Washington High School, was informed of the riot by one of his teachers, W. D. Williams. He could not believe the story because no one he knew had ever mentioned it. It is important to mention here that the irrationality, intensity, and enormity of trauma also make it difficult for those who hear about it to believe that it really happened. A couple of common reactions are "Oh, that couldn't have really happened," "Is he/she really telling the truth?" and "It couldn't have been that bad." Meanwhile, Ross vowed to make the truth known. In 1971, he published the first detailed account of the riot, written by Ed Wheeler, in a magazine called *Impact*. Tulsa's two daily newspapers had rejected Wheeler's article. After Ross, a Democrat, was elected state representative, he proposed legislation for reparations.

On June 1, 1996, the first official commemoration of the anniversary of the riot was held at the Mount Zion Baptist Church in North Tulsa. The original structure, which was brand-new in 1921, was destroyed in the riot. The historic church was filled to capacity. At least 1,200 people attended this moving ceremony, including survivors, descendants, and others from many different backgrounds. According to Gates (2003), dignitaries and powerful speakers participated. In addition, gospel choirs performed, and children sang and read poetry. The commemoration of the riot has since become an annual affair designed "to respect and honor those who survived [the riot], and to share dialogue on how to promote racial healing and harmony" (Gates, 2003, p. 39). This ceremony contributed much to the process of breaking the silence.

In 1997, Don Ross's efforts led to the passage of the bill that created the Tulsa Race Riot Commission and a full investigation into the riot. The media paid much attention to this historic development. By 1999, sixty-five riot survivors had been found (Kolker, 1999), and by 2001, 118 living survivors had been located and 176 descendants registered (Oklahoma Commission, 2001). The survivors' stories are an essential component of the Commission's final report that was issued in 2001. It was that report that officially broke the silence that had prevailed for nearly eighty years.

FILING FOR REPARATIONS

On February 24, 2003, a group of attorneys that included Los Angeles defense attorney Johnnie Cochran; Harvard law professor Charles Ogletree Jr.; and Leslie Mansfield, director of the legal clinic at the University of Tulsa Law School, filed a 139-page lawsuit for reparations. Following completion of the final report of the Commission in 2001, this lawsuit was filed after a yearlong effort to persuade local attorneys to take on the litigation. This was met with rejection.

Therefore, the lawsuit, which was filed on behalf of 200 plaintiffs who included survivors of the riot as well as descendants of victims, demanded reparations for the 300 lives lost during the riot, as well as the losses of homes and businesses. The lawsuit also alleged that state and local authorities failed to stop the riots and even participated in the violence at times (Robertson, 2003). Among those held responsible for the riot are "the current governor of Oklahoma as official successor of the governor in 1921, the current chief of police as the representative of the chief of police at the time of the riot, and the Tulsa Police Department" (Denniston, 2003). Furthermore, efforts will be made to identify at least 100 additional individuals who are believed to have been responsible for the riot.

The lawyers who prepared the lawsuit for reparations believed that it embodied broader themes than those that applied to the Tulsa case. Therefore, it might support a series of preexisting lawsuits that seek reparations for slavery and other forms of racial oppression to be filed in the future. Toward this end, Ogletree believes that the Tulsa case is particularly compelling because "there are identifiable plaintiffs and defendants" and "a fully developed factual record in the form of an official state commission's report issued in 2001" (Denniston, 2003). Finally, this lawsuit will establish whether or not injustices that were committed long ago can be addressed by courts when filing deadlines have passed.

HOW DOES TULSA'S EXPERIENCE INFORM OUR UNDERSTANDING OF WHAT PROMOTES RECOVERY FROM RACIAL TRAUMA?

The immediate support of organizations like the Red Cross and the National Association for the Advancement of Colored People (NAACP), shelter provided by a few white citizens, monetary donations from private citizens from across the country, and the attorneys who freely gave their services to rebuild that community were graciously received by the survivors and descendants of the riot as expressions of concern and compassion after that tragedy. Gestures such as these contributed substantially to reestablishing some semblance of safety and control. This was vital to survivors in the aftermath of trauma. To know that one is cared about at such a devastating time eases the pain of trauma suffered, decreases isolation by facilitating connection to others, and mobilizes hope for a brighter future. It is also important to acknowledge that the faith, prayers for healing, and the church communities of black Tulsans were a continuous source of solace and containment in the wake of relatives and friends who vanished during the riot never to be seen or heard from again, and also in the faces of unbearable sadness and flashbacks of terror.

Other events that continuously promote recovery are annual commemoration ceremonies, the findings of the Tulsa Race Riot Commission in 1997, and the lawsuit for reparations filed in 2003, in that each is an important source of acknowledgment of the injustice suffered. The latter also seeks legal accountability for that injustice. Because of these events, the riot will never be covered up again. At another level, these developments have facilitated a community's movement from remembrance and mourning toward reconnection with ordinary life (Herman, 1992) and broader extensive connection to global world community than ever before. Perhaps Gates (2003) says this best: "The riot has gone from being one of the most covered up events in history to being [common knowledge] all over the world" (p. 39).

Although significant advances in race relations have been made since the Tulsa Race Riot of 1921, in some ways things have not changed more than eighty years later. Prejudice, discrimination, and racially charged disturbances continue to threaten marginalized and disenfranchised communities today. This is evidenced by racially motivated violence, racial profiling, and other discriminatory practices that humiliate, provoke distrust and fear, and result in the maiming and murder of innocent victims. In view of these realities, the following Toolbox for Change is proposed to promote positive relations and to prevent such a tragedy from ever happening again.

Embracing diversity is a lifelong process. This process involves the development of attitudes and behaviors that are informed by and appreciate the racial and cultural dimensions of the self as well as the same in others. Among those factors that facilitate the development of this process are culturally competent education and training, and community mental health practice.

Culturally competent education and training are essential tools for change at individual and community levels. This is imperative from the time of a child's earliest educational experiences in daycare and preschool throughout all subsequent academic levels thereafter over the course of one's lifespan. Exposure to culturally competent curricula prior to and during the college years, integrated with multicultural education, can enhance one's knowledge and appreciation of human diversity. In addition, meaningful and affirmative exposure to others from one's own racial group as well as those from other racial and cultural groups are essential to shaping attitudes and behaviors that reflect acceptance and fairness. Educators must be adequately prepared to provide an inclusive learning environment via diversity training and self-reflection that enables personal as well as professional development in these areas.

In predominantly white school settings, same-race affinity groups for children and adolescents can be effective for promoting positive racial identity development and cultural pride. Such groups benefit children from marginalized and disenfranchised populations as well as children from more privileged backgrounds, since positive racial identity development and cultural pride are essential to the mental and social health of *all* children. Prejudice and discrimination are rooted in ignorance and in isolation from targeted groups. Therefore, multicultural

Toolbox for Change

Tools	Individual	Community	Human services professionals and educators
Culturally competent education and training			X
Multicultural education	X	X	X
Basic crisis Intervention Stress Management			X
Meaningful & affirmative exposure	X	X	X
Intra race affinity groups		X	

discussion and activity groups are also growth enhancing for adolescents who have achieved positive racial identity development and cultural pride via a solid foundation in same-race affinity groups or similar experiences. Like-minded groups for parents of students are also essential for nurturing healthy racial identity development and enabling parents to become effective role models for their children. After all, if positive racial identity development and cultural pride are not reinforced in the home, schools are limited in what they can achieve with children and adolescents in this area.

The preparation of community mental health workers and other human services professionals for intervention in racially charged community crises is also essential. Without this, timely attention to those impacted by such crises may not occur and may lead to needless suffering on multiple levels. Training in crisis intervention stress management (Mitchell & Everly, 1998) or similar intervention that is informed by a particular community's situation could be quite effective in promoting recovery and healing from racially charged community crises. Finally, culturally competent psycho-education and ongoing focus groups that emphasize developing strategies for social change could play a vital role in prevention. Such groups could be conducted in a variety of settings that include but are not limited to places of worship, police departments, city and state government, and corporations.

REFERENCES

Denniston, L. (2003, February 26). Lawyers hope Tulsa case can lay foundation for more claims. *The Boston Globe*, p. 10.

Ellsworth, S. (1982). *Death in a promised land*. Baton Rouge, LA: Louisiana State University.

Gates, E. F. (2003) *Riot on Greenwood*. Austin, TX: Sunbelt Eakin Press.

Herman, J. L. (1992). *Trauma and recovery*. New York: Basic Books.

Kolker, C. (1999, November 7). Unearthing a horror for Oklahoma blacks. *The Boston Sunday Globe*.

Mansfield, L. (2003, February 26). In L. Denniston, Lawyers hope Tulsa can lay foundation for more claims. *The Boston Globe*.

Mitchell, J. F., & Everly, G. S. (1998). *Critical incident stress management: The basic course*. Ellicott, MD: International Critical Incident Stress Foundation.

Moorehead, M. (2003). U.S. ethnic cleaning: The 1921 Tulsa Massacre. Retrieved January 14, 2004, from www.iacenter.org/usethnic.htm

Ogletree, C. T., Jr. (2003, February 26). In L. Denniston, Lawyers hope Tulsa case can lay foundation for more claims. *The Boston Globe*, p. A10.

Oklahoma Commission to Study the Tulsa Race Riot of 1921. (2001, February 28). The Tulsa Race Riot [court report].

Robertson, T. (2003, February 26). Quest for vindication: Survivors of 1921 Tulsa race riots hail suit for reparations. *The Boston Globe*, pp. A1, A17.

Weingarten, K. (2003). *Common shock*. New York: Penguin Group.

CHAPTER 3

Racial and Ethnic Prejudice among Children

Sheri R. Levy
Tara L. West
Luisa F. Ramirez
John E. Pachankis

Pervasive intergroup conflict continues to make national and international headlines, and acts of racial/ethnic discrimination are not limited to adults. For example, in a town on Long Island in New York where some residents were upset about the influx of Mexican immigrant workers, four unprovoked white teenage males set fire to the home of a Mexican family while the family slept inside ("4 teens," 2003). As another example, a group of approximately thirty white teenagers living in an affluent suburb in Las Vegas, Nevada, apparently formed a hate group (311 Boyz) based on Ku Klux Klan principles and have been charged with numerous assaults on minority group members (including two Asian men), even videotaping their vicious acts (Friess, 2003, September 28). Besides such anecdotal evidence, decades of research indicate that racism is a serious problem among children and adolescents in the United States and other countries. Racism appears among children as early as five years of age (Aboud, 1988; Bar-Tal, 1996), suggesting that children often enter school with prejudiced views. With increases in the racial/ethnic diversity of youth in the United States, understanding how prejudice develops and can be changed is urgent. According to the U.S. Census Bureau (2002), non-Hispanic whites will no longer be a numerical majority group in the United States starting in 2060. Thus, children in the United States will increasingly learn, live, and work in racially and ethnically integrated settings.

Researchers, educators, parents, and other concerned individuals have long tried to understand and reduce prejudice among children. The goal of this chapter is to provide a summary of the tremendous strides researchers have made in understanding and reducing racial/ethnic prejudice among children. For decades, researchers have tried to understand the atrocious acts that capture headlines, as reported above, and also those that do not make headlines, for example, when a five-year-old girl refuses to work on a puzzle with a new classmate of a different racial/ethnic group, or when an eight-year-old boy mutters a racial slur under his breath in reaction to a different-race peer.

How do we understand these behaviors? Some might suggest that these acts do not represent the children's true attitudes, but rather reflect their oblivious mimicry of the behavior of others. Thus, there is no prejudice to reduce and the acts should be ignored. In contrast, these behaviors may reflect the children's true attitudes; consequently, children could be taught new, tolerant attitudes. An additional interpretation is that children's attitudes and behaviors in part reflect their lack of social sophistication or ability to be tolerant; thus, reducing their prejudice requires developmentally appropriate training in more sophisticated thought processes. These interpretations reflect some of the main theories of prejudice among children.

In this chapter, we review research on the development and reduction of prejudice among children. We begin by elaborating the main theories of the origins of prejudice among children and discuss the empirical research relevant to these theories. Then, we review and evaluate the prejudice-reduction interventions that have grown out of these theories. Future directions for research on understanding and addressing prejudice among youth are discussed. We will conclude with advice for parents, teachers, policymakers, and others interested in promoting tolerance among youth.

THEORIES OF THE ORIGINS OF PREJUDICE AMONG CHILDREN

In this section, we address the question, Why are children prejudiced? We define "prejudice" as the holding of negative beliefs and feelings toward a group and its members or the exhibiting of hostile or negative treatment directed at a group and its members (Aboud & Levy, 2000; Brown, 1995). Although there are distinctions between race and ethnicity (Ocampo, Bernal, & Knight, 1993; Quintana, 1998), racial and ethnic group memberships appear to have similar implications for prejudice; thus, we will discuss the find-ings of research on racial and ethnic identities together. We focus only on ethnic/racial prejudice because of the combined set of features differentiating it from other prejudices. For example, the category of race is less malleable (for example, people may move in and out of the category of overweight), more visible (for example, people's sexual orientation is not a visible category), and allows for social separation more readily (for example, people may be biased toward members of the other gender, while also engaging in very close relationships with them) than other prejudices. We begin our review by describ-ing traditional theories and then highlighting more contemporary theories.

The Authoritarian Personality

For many years, prejudice among children was considered a minor problem. This is partly due to the limited viewpoint of past theories of prejudice development. An early theory of prejudice among children suggested that it was an outgrowth of abnormal development and thus a rare occurrence. This idea evolved from a psychodynamic frame-work and was articulated by Adorno, Frenkel-Brunswick, Levinson, and Sanford (1950) in their classic book *The Authoritarian Personality*. The term *authoritarian* describes a personality type characterized by excessive conformity, submission to authority, and hostility toward those deviating from conventions (that is, authority-sanctioned stan-dards of behavior). Adorno and colleagues began their studies on the authoritarian personality in an attempt to understand the atrocities of Nazi Germany. They suggested that such personalities resulted from exposure in childhood to threat and punishment in response to expres-sions of unconventional behavior. In an environment that forcefully promotes conventionalism and submission to authority, it was thought that children would need to release their aggressive impulses, but that they would not be able to aggress against their authority figures (their parents). Thus, according to the authors, children projected their anger onto other people. Socially unconventional people were a good target since authority figures approved of aggression toward such social deviants, which could include racial or ethnic minorities in certain contexts. This process was thought to give rise to prejudice toward certain outgroups. However, it is clear that the authoritarian personality is not a reflection of a "German personality." Prejudice is pervasive, and atrocities have occurred all over the world at the hands of many different groups. Prejudiced beliefs are no longer considered an abnormal occurrence (although acts of discrimination are illegal).

The Social Learning Theory

Another traditional approach to prejudice is the social learning theory, which suggests that children learn prejudice by observing and imitating important others (such as parents and teachers), becoming gradually more prejudiced with age. Gordon Allport originally proposed this theory in 1954 in his classic work *The Nature of Prejudice*. Allport suggested that children mimic, and then come to believe, what they are exposed to in their environments. A child who overhears a racial slur from a valued adult will likely repeat that slur, and to the extent that the child understands the meaning behind it, will come to hold the associated negative belief about the group. There is much evidence supporting social learning theory more generally (Bandura, 1977), and very few individuals would claim that we are not influenced by what we are exposed to in our environment. Research, however, has provided inconsistent evidence regarding the relation between children's racial attitudes and the racial attitudes of others in their environment. Much research has investigated the relation between children's racial attitudes and the racial attitudes of their parents. For example, a positive relation was found between the racial attitudes of white fathers and their adolescent sons, but not for black father-son pairs (Carlson & Iovini, 1985). In another study, third-grade children's racial attitudes were not strongly related to their mothers' racial attitudes (Aboud & Doyle, 1996a). Other research has suggested that as black children age, their attitudes toward whites and blacks gradually become more like their parents' attitudes (Branch & Newcombe, 1986). Studies have also examined the relation between children's racial attitudes and the attitudes of their peers. For example, one study found little overlap between black and white ninth graders' racial attitudes and behaviors, and the racial attitudes and behaviors of their peers (Patchen, 1983). Similarly, it was also found that school-aged children and their peers did not generally possess similar racial attitudes, although the children believed that their peers *did* hold attitudes similar to their own (Aboud & Doyle, 1996a; Ritchey & Fishbein, 2001).

These studies examining the relationship between children's racial attitudes and the attitudes of their parents and peers suggest that children may not share their racial attitudes with many of the closest individuals in their lives. Indeed, evidence suggests that parents, particularly members of race-majority groups, rarely discuss prejudice with their children (Kofkin, Katz, & Downey, 1995, as reported in Aboud & Amato, 2001; Knight, Bernal, Garza, Cota, & Ocampo, 1993). Ironically, it appears that more racially tolerant parents may not discuss racial issues with their children for fear of bringing attention to race. Yet, it has been shown that when adults and peers address prejudice, it is decreased (Aboud & Doyle, 1996b). That is, it seems that the lack of strong relation between attitudes of children and their valued adult figures may stem from a lack of discussion, not a lack of influence.

For example, Aboud and Doyle (1996b) found that low-prejudice (as assessed at pretest) white third and fourth graders who discussed their racial attitudes with a high-prejudice peer actually lowered their peer's prejudice. Below are excerpts from the tape recording of a high-prejudice (HP) participant and her low-prejudice (LP) female discussion partner, as they discuss the traits of politeness and bossiness. The children were instructed to discuss various traits as they pertained to descriptions of three groups: Asians, blacks, and whites (Aboud & Doyle, 1996b, p. 170).

LP: You go first.
HP: I think *polite* should go with the White girl.
LP: I think *polite* should go with all of them [*referring to Asians, Blacks, and Whites*], cause like everyone should, they don't have to just because their colour or something.
HP: Listen, most of the time, it's really the dark, most of the time are not really nice.
LP: But they are nice, though. So really all of them are polite.
HP: Yea. So, who's bossy?
LP: All of them.
HP: Let's see if they're all polite and bossy. It's not the same thing. They all have to be.
LP: Sometimes, you could be bossy and polite.
HP: That's kinda weird. It's like you're mean and nice.
LP: Well, it's like [name of classmate]
HP: Yeah.
LP: So, it's possible.
HP: They're all the same.

In this example, a low-prejudice child was able to reduce the prejudice of a high-prejudice peer by pointing out instances of cross-race similarity (how members of all groups can be bossy sometimes) and also within-race trait variability (how whites can exhibit negative and positive traits). Thus, it appears to be possible for significant figures in a child's life to influence his or her racial attitudes through explicit discussion.

Current work on the social learning theory focuses on identifying the most effective types of anti-bias messages. This includes work on multicultural education (providing information about the cultural traditions and customs of groups) and anti-racist teaching (education about historical and contemporary racial/ethnic injustices). This will be discussed in the section describing prejudice-reduction interventions.

The Intergroup Contact Theory

A variant of social learning theory is the intergroup contact theory, also proposed by Gordon Allport (Allport, 1954; Pettigrew, 1998). According to intergroup contact theory, prejudice grows, in part, out of a lack of personal and positive contact among members of different groups. Thus, intergroup harmony can result from increased positive intergroup contact. It became clear after the initial desegregation of American schools that simply providing the opportunity for intergroup contact did not always lead to improved intergroup relations. That is, even though there was racial diversity in the schools, students of the same race tended to sit together in the classroom, in the lunchroom, and on the schoolyard. Unfortunately, schools help create "resegregation" by "tracking" children according to ability. This tracking tends to occur in discriminatory ways, separating children across race lines; this reduces opportunities for positive contact in the classroom, which transfers to the lunchroom and schoolyard (Khmelkov & Hallinan, 1999). As will be elaborated in the section on reducing prejudice, intergroup harmony can be increased when contact is set up to be individualized (one-to-one) and cooperative, when groups are of equal status, and when the contact is sanctioned by authorities.

The Cognitive-Developmental Theory

An important, relatively new, and influential theory is the cognitive-developmental theory of prejudice. This theory starts from the assumption that prejudice is not a minor problem among children and does not necessarily increase with age. The cognitive-developmental theory suggests that children's attitudes toward racial and ethnic groups are influenced by their ability to think about group information in complex ways. For example, a child cannot express empathy for another person until she has the ability to see the world through another person's perspective. Along the same lines, the cognitive-developmental theory suggests that children exhibit prejudice because they are not cognitively sophisticated enough to be open-minded and racially tolerant. With age, presumably all children obtain the cognitive skills that allow for reduced prejudice. These skills are apparently obtained when children are approximately seven to eleven years old. However, prejudice is not perpetually reduced with age. After developing these skills, children may not necessarily use them (as an adult capable of taking another's perspective may not always express empathy [Levy, 1999]). The cognitive-developmental theory was originally articulated by Jean Piaget (Piaget & Weil, 1951) and was applied to the understanding of prejudice by Phyllis Katz (1976), Frances Aboud (1988), and Rebecca Bigler (Bigler & Liben, 1993), among others. According to cognitive-developmental theorizing, prejudice is seemingly inevitable among young children because they lack the skills necessary to view people as individuals. Children tend to focus on surface features and to exaggerate differences among groups (such as assuming that all members of group A do X); only later, as their cognitive systems mature, do they become capable of recognizing similarities across groups (for example, some members of group A do X and some members of group B do X) and differences within the same group (some members of group A do X, and some members of group A do Y). Consistent with these ideas, as early as preschool and kindergarten, race-majority group children exhibit prejudice; examples include prejudice of English-Canadians toward French-Canadians (Doyle, Beaudet, & Aboud, 1988), Euro-Australians toward Aboriginal Australians (Black-Gutman & Hickson, 1996), and Jewish Israelis toward Arabs (Bar-Tal, 1996). Young majority children typically assign more positive and fewer negative attributes to their own groups (*ingroups*) than to other groups (*outgroups*), but show a decline in prejudice at around age seven (Doyle & Aboud, 1995; Doyle et al., 1988; Powlishta, Serbin, Doyle, & White, 1994). Research indeed shows that shifts toward reduced prejudice levels are explained in part by acquisition of the social cognitive skills thought to enable prejudice reduction. That is, as children acquire specific cognitive skills, such as the ability to classify others on multiple dimensions (Bigler & Liben, 1993; Katz, Sohn, & Zalk, 1975), the ability to perceive similarities between members of different groups (Black-Gutman & Hickson, 1996; Doyle & Aboud,

1995), and the ability to perceive differences within the same group (Doyle & Aboud, 1995; Katz et al., 1975), their reported level of prejudice decreases. There is some evidence that these age-related differences cannot be easily explained by increased concerns with appearing prejudiced (Doyle & Aboud, 1995).

The cognitive-developmental theory, despite an impressive body of supportive evidence, is not currently defined in a way that explains individual differences in prejudice among children exhibiting similar cognitive skill levels (Black-Gutman & Hickson, 1996; Levy, 1999; Levy & Dweck, 1999). To address this issue, it may be necessary to consider both environmental and cognitive factors (Black-Gutman & Hickson, 1996). Indeed, some contemporary research is moving toward an integrative approach, combining elements of cognitive development and social learning theories (Aboud, in press; Killen, Lee-Kim, McGlothlin, & Stangor, 2002).

Other research attempting to understand individual differences in prejudice among children who exhibit roughly the same cognitive skill level has examined children's differing "lay theories" of prejudice (Levy, West, & Ramirez, in press). Like scientists, lay people have theories about how the world works. There are many different lay theories available to help individuals understand how the world works and how people should behave. Lay theories are often captured in everyday sayings such as "it's never too late to turn over a new leaf" and "a leopard never changes its spots." These are examples of lay theories that contradict each other. This may in part explain individual differences in social judgment and behavior. For example, children who hold the lay theory that people can change will harbor less prejudice and are more willing to help disadvantaged others than are children who hold the lay theory that people basically cannot change their ways (Karafantis & Levy, 2004; Levy & Dweck, 1999).

Other lay theory work has focused on the "color-blind" principle of ignoring racial and ethnic differences (Neville, Lilly, Duran, Lee, & Browne, 2000; Schofield, 1986). Although laudable in suggesting that surface features like race are superficial, irrelevant, and uninformative bases on which to make judgments of people, the color-blind approach to education is controversial because race and other grouping characteristics *do* affect people's lives, and efforts to assimilate immigrants and ethnic groups into the dominant culture often do not work (Garcia & Hurtado, 1995). In the section on prejudice reduction, we will further discuss the utility of a color-blind teaching approach by discussing an intervention based on the color-blind principle.

Evolutionary Theory

Contemporary theorizing has also begun to focus on an evolutionary account of prejudice. Although given little attention thus far, evolutionary perspectives seem to be gaining a more prominent place in the theorizing of the development of prejudice. According to evolutionary perspectives, prejudice and discrimination are nearly inevitable. Fishbein (1996) argues that the roots of prejudice began in hunter-gatherer tribes and continue universally today because of their success in that period of human evolution. One such proposed evolutionary mechanism relies on a history of related tribe members showing greater preference for each other than for tribe members to whom they are not related, therefore helping and protecting them, which would then maximize the percentage of one's genes that are transmitted to successive generations. Fishbein offers this as evidence that humans are currently predisposed to show favoritism toward individuals who are most similar to themselves. Another such mechanism that may set the stage for prejudice is the human reliance on authority figures to transmit information to their young. This process encourages children to unquestioningly accept what they are told by authority figures, including information about outgroup members. The final mechanism that Fishbein proposes is the hostility that humans have developed in order to protect their children, females, and resources from outsiders. Fishbein argues that the development of prejudice is closely linked to the development of a group identity around ages three or four.

Another evolutionary perspective suggests that children's thinking about social groups is organized according to inherent theories about humans, which guide the way they gather and interpret information about social groups (Hirschfeld, 1995, 2001). These inherent theories help children attend to important group information and ignore unimportant information. According to this perspective, because the concept of race resonates quite well with children's preexisting cognitive structures for differentiating social groups, race becomes a powerful organizing factor for humans.

Despite growing interest in evolutionary theories of racial prejudice, these approaches have generally been criticized for suggesting that prejudice is natural and thus should be condoned. Still, it seems that certain aspects of evolutionary thought overlap with other approaches to prejudice. For instance, similar to the evolutionary mechanism that favors categorization according to similarities to oneself, the aforementioned cognitive theories propose that such categorization helps individuals simplify the wealth of social information that they encounter. Also, there are obvious similarities between sociocultural and evolutionary explanations that suggest that prejudice grows out of limited resources and social forces. Further, the evolutionary emphasis on accepting information from authority figures complements the social learning theory, which suggests that children learn prejudiced views from their parents and other important people in their lives. However, it may be that evolutionary approaches are best suited to explaining the roots of mechanisms currently facilitating prejudice (such as the methods humans use to categorize groups of people), whereas approaches focusing directly on the current mechanisms, such as the social learning theory or cognitive-developmental models, are best suited to understanding the more immediate, and hence most relevant (for our purposes), causes of prejudice.

Summary and Future Directions

In this section, we have reviewed the main theories guiding the understanding of prejudice among children. Research to date suggests that being raised in a prejudiced environment does not necessarily translate into developing prejudiced attitudes, nor does a tolerant environment necessarily lead to tolerant attitudes. It also suggests that prejudice is not exclusively a problem that concerns adult populations. Recent approaches emphasize the importance of integrating research and theorizing from cognitive, developmental, and social (including lay theories) perspectives on prejudice in the attempt to understand its development. For instance, a key finding is that children are more prone to adopt prejudiced attitudes as a result of cognitive-developmental limitations and that they are more capable of incorporating complex information from their environment around the age of seven. This information may be useful for designing interventions to counter prejudiced attitudes that arise from exposure to biased information. More work is still needed on the role of children's lay theories (the ways that they understand their world) in prejudice development.

REDUCING PREJUDICE IN CHILDREN

Interventions to combat prejudice among children have taken many forms. Typically, these interventions are conducted during school and are sometimes integrated into the children's regular curricula. At times, entire schools or districts have adopted interventions as a matter of practice, while others have been the choices of individual teachers. Generally in the United States, prejudice-reducing interventions have focused on the reduction of white children's racial prejudice, given that they have been the dominant majority in society. Although researchers, practitioners, and educators have developed a wide variety of intervention strategies, we limit our discussion to interventions that have been evaluated using quantitative data. We organize our review around the theoretical approaches discussed in the previous section, beginning with interventions derived from traditional theories of prejudice development among children and then turning to interventions based on more contemporary theories.

As noted, the early tendency to explain prejudice as an outgrowth of abnormal development has not proven tenable. Interventions based on this theory suggest that therapy is the appropriate treatment for children who exhibit prejudice. Therapeutic techniques have been used to "treat" prejudice (Cotharin & Mikulas, 1975), but are rarely used today. Relative to other types of intervention strategies, such one-on-one intervention strategies are less than optimal due to the widespread nature of prejudice.

Another core traditional theory is the social learning theory—the idea that children learn, and therefore unlearn, prejudice from their social environment. Intergroup contact theory, originally proposed by Allport, has received an abundant amount of attention in the intervention literature. Intergroup contact that is individualized, cooperative, maintains equal status between individuals, and is sanctioned by authorities appears to be most likely to break down interracial barriers and promote intergroup understanding and friendships. Researchers have successfully shown that intergroup harmony can be promoted by altering features of the classroom environment in accordance with these principles. For instance, Aronson and Gonzalez (1988) designed what is called the *jigsaw classroom*, in which students work cooperatively to learn and teach each other components of an academic lesson. This technique replaces competitive aspects of the classroom with cooperative ones. For example, students in a classroom are divided into six racially and academically mixed groups, each consisting of six students. Each group learns one-sixth of the information that is unique, valuable, and necessary to understand the full lesson. Then, participants in each of the original groups are divided so that new groups are composed of one member of each of the original groups, thereby allowing them to teach each other the entire lesson. Thus, the jigsaw technique promotes interdependence and cooperation, as opposed to competitive attempts to solve the problem. This form of cooperative learning proved to be successful in improving children's relationships with each other and increasing self-esteem, in addition to the fortunate side effect of enhancing students' academic success. Other variations of cooperative learning are successful at increasing intergroup harmony (Johnson & Johnson, 2000; Slavin & Cooper, 1999). These are beyond the scope of this chapter, but include exciting research on bilingual education programs such as the Amigos Two-Way Immersion program in which monolinguistic Spanish- and English-speaking students spend half the day learning in English and the other half of the day in Spanish (Aboud & Levy, 2000; Genesee & Gandura, 1999).

One unfortunate weakness of the cooperative learning strategy in improving intergroup relations is that cross-race friendships may not persist after cooperative learning ends. In general, cross-race friendships tend to decrease with age (Mendelson & Aboud, 1999; Khmelkov & Hallinan 1999). Decreased intergroup friendship with age is somewhat surprising given that there do not appear to be qualitative differences between cross-race and same-race friendships, which would warrant a greater reduction in cross-race friendships (Mendelson & Aboud, 1999). However, some have suggested that cross-race friendships are generally more fragile (Khmelkov & Hallinan, 1999), leaving them more likely to end when peer groups shrink and dating begins. Research on social reasoning by Melanie Killen and colleagues (Killen et al., 2002) suggests that shifts in children's reasoning may in part account for why cross-race friendships decline. Killen's work has shown that, with increasing age, children (such as seventh-graders) think that it is more acceptable to exclude other race peers from friendships because they believe that groups function better when everyone is of the same race (presuming that they share interests). Younger children tend to reason that exclusion based on race is morally wrong; thus reasoning-based interventions might prove fruitful for them. For example, an intervention could challenge the logic suggesting that one's peer group functions better when everyone is of the same race. Finding ways to encourage racially diverse, cooperative group work in middle school, high school, and college, as well as in nonacademic settings, might also prove beneficial.

Multicultural education (teaching about the history of cultural groups) and anti-racist teaching (teaching about historical and contemporary racial/ethnic injustices) represent two anti-bias messages deriving from social learning theorizing, and neither requires that children in the classroom be racially diverse. The most common forms of multicultural education seek to provide knowledge and understanding of diverse groups. Multicultural theory suggests that through learning about cultural groups (for example, being exposed to information about cross-cultural holidays and celebrations), individuals will come to understand and respect different cultures, thereby reducing negative attitudes (Banks, 1995). A criticism of the multicultural theory is that the celebration of differences may increase the likelihood that children and adolescents will place individuals into rigid categories, thereby increasing racial/ethnic stereotyping. This is especially true among children who lack the cognitive sophistication to recognize that individuals fit into multiple categories, for example, based on their age, race, or gender (Bigler, 1999; Kowalski, 1998). Similarly, Rebecca Bigler and colleagues (Bigler, 1995; Bigler, Jones, & Lobliner, 1997) have demonstrated that the use of perceptually salient social categories (such as gender) results in the development of biased attitudes. This occurs, for example, when a teacher uses that group category to differentiate people. Educational curricula that focus specifically on the history of certain racial groups within a racially diverse society may, by highlighting race and racial differences, inadvertently increase children's racial biases. For example, the presentation of race-related educational material during Black History Month differentiates people according to racial group membership. Children exposed to this information may conclude that race is an important dimension along which individuals differ—thus, stereotyping will increase rather than decrease. This work points to the importance of limiting the use of race as a differentiating characteristic in the classroom or, when discussing race, to emphasize the similarities across racial groups and differences within.

Banks (1995) further suggests that effective multicultural education requires that the total school environment be transformed to reflect the racial and cultural diversity of the American society and to help all children experience educational equality. Banks suggests that changes be made in the "values and attitudes of the school staff, curricula and teaching materials, assessment and testing procedures, teaching and motivational styles, and values and norms sanctioned by the school" (p. 329). Banks's multicultural school reform proposal appears less susceptible to some of the concerns raised about proposals that include minimal additions to school curricula (such as inclusion of race-related material only as part of a month-to-month recognition of nonmajority groups).

Often going hand in hand with multicultural education efforts, anti-racist education seeks to provide an in-depth awareness of the history and roots of inequality (Fine, 1995). Thus, anti-racist teaching confronts racism head-on with descriptions of past and contemporary discrimination and inequalities, pointing out the forces that maintain racism. This may increase empathy and at the same time discourage future racism. However, if not done carefully, such teaching could be counterproductive for both perpetrators and targets of racism. By providing insight into the prejudice of the students' ingroup and the students' own prejudiced reactions, students may feel angry or self-righteous (Kehoe & Mansfield, 1993). Yet, a reaction of guilt may have positive outcomes in older adolescents. For example, research with college-age students suggests that guilt can be a motivating force in reducing people's expression of prejudice (Monteith, 1993). It is important to note, however, that discussions of race may be threatening or humiliating to children who are members of the discriminated group (McGregor, 1993). Therefore, although perhaps a powerful intervention, it is necessary that steps be taken to minimize potentially negative side effects of anti-racist education, for example, by providing examples of majority group members who are working to end racism and by pointing out similarities between groups to avoid stereotyping.

Although relatively modern, cognitive-developmental theory has served as a base for several interventions, generally involving skill training. Katz (1973) trained children to perceive differences among members of the same group. This intervention targeted children who were just obtaining this ability (seven-year-olds) and those who likely had already obtained the ability (ten-year-olds). In this brief intervention lasting approximately fifteen minutes, Katz and Zalk taught white children to differentiate among photographs of either black children (experimental condition) or white children (control condition). Two weeks later, children in the experimental condition gave fewer prejudiced responses than those in the control condition, regardless of age. These findings were replicated in a follow-up study (Katz & Zalk, 1978) and extended by Aboud and Fenwick (1999), to be discussed later.

Similar to interventions based on the cognitive-developmental theory, empathy training relies on age-related cognitive skills such as perspective-taking, but includes an additional focus on the understanding and experience of emotions. Presumably, through empathy training, children can place themselves in the shoes of outgroup members who are faced with discrimination, and thus be motivated to alleviate the others' distress as if it were their own—that is, by acting in a less-biased way toward them (Underwood & Moore, 1982). One of the earliest examples of an empathy-inducing intervention was the classroom demonstration devised by Jane Elliot in the late 1960s. In response to the assassination of Martin Luther King Jr., Jane Elliot, a third-grade teacher in a predominately white rural town, taught her students how it would feel to be a target of discrimination. Elliot chose eye color as a characteristic that would differentiate the students, telling students on one day that blue-eyed children were superior, and on the next day, that brown-eyed children were superior. She enhanced the lesson by showing preferential treatment to the "superior" group the entire day, and pointing out the successes and failures of group members as evidence of the group's superior or inferior position. Therefore, for one day, each group of children had a first-hand experience with discrimination on the basis of an arbitrary characteristic. This demonstration is so powerful that it has been captured in two films, *The Eye of the Storm* and *A Class Divided*, which are often shown on public broadcasting stations and in schools. However, actual evidence of the effectiveness of the blue-eyes/brown-eyes simulation is minimal. Weiner and Wright (1973), as an exception, tested a variation of the blue-eyes/brown-eyes simulation with white third graders. In this case, the classroom teacher told children that they were members of "green" or "orange" groups and asked them to wear colored armbands. Like Jane Elliot, the teacher encouraged discrimination against each group for one day. Compared to the control classroom, participants in the simulation reported more willingness to attend a picnic with black children. These results provide encouraging support for the impact of role-playing the target of prejudice on subsequent intergroup behavior.

One caveat with empathy training is that age-related cognitive and affective skills are necessary to adequately benefit from the training. Older children who are more cognitively sophisticated than younger children generally have more sophisticated empathy skills (McGregor, 1993). Thus, it is possible that if children lack the sophistication to engage in perspective-taking, as well as the ability to properly interpret the emotional arousal, empathic activities may not effectively reduce their negative attitudes and behaviors. It is also possible that children who do not know how to interpret or react to the emotional arousal may focus on the negativity of the empathy-inducing experience, resulting in an increased negativity or avoidance of the group with which they are supposed to empathize.

Other research suggests that lay theories relevant to prejudice can be altered, at least temporarily (Levy et al., in press). Research on the color-blind view is encouraging. One way to use the color-blind theory to reduce racial prejudice is to turn people's attention toward the universal qualities of humans instead of racial group membership. Houser (1978), for example, examined whether stereotyping toward several ethnic groups would be reduced among five- to nine-year-old children who watched (versus did not watch) films promoting the message that it is important to focus on universally shared qualities. For example, one film called *The Toymaker* depicted the story of two puppets who were best friends until they looked in the mirror and realized that one had stripes and the other had spots. The toymaker pointed out that they were both created by the same person and were essentially connected to each other (each covering one hand of the toymaker). Although the film clips were brief (approximately ten to fifteen minutes), children who watched them reported a decrease in stereotyping toward several ethic groups from pretest to posttest, relative to children who did not view any films but rather participated in regular classroom activities. Alternatively, the color-blind theory could be used to reduce racial prejudice by redirecting children's focus from racial group membership to the unique internal characteristics of individuals (such as likes and dislikes) (Aboud & Fenwick, 1999; Schofield, 1986). Aboud and Fenwick (1999), for example, found that ten-year-old white children who participated (versus did not participate) in an eleven-week school-based program that trained them to focus on the internal attributes of people demonstrated a decrease in prejudice toward blacks. Throughout the program, children participated in a number of activities in which the theme of each activity was "There is more to me than meets the eye." To illustrate the idea that people possess unique qualities, one activity had participants presented with photographs of different children and then provided with those children's names and individualized trait descriptions, such as the children's likes, dislikes, and unique personality traits.

An interesting aspect of the aforementioned interventions is that they incorporate aspects of cognitive-developmental theory in addition to the color-blind theory. That is, focusing on shared qualities overlaps with the evolving social-cognitive ability of noticing cross-group similarities. Likewise, focusing on unique qualities of individuals is similar to the evolving social-cognitive ability of noticing within-group differences. This overlap is an important one and suggests that social cognitive skills can be taught and strengthened through anti-bias messages.

Summary and Future Directions

Although there is not space to review all of the innovative interventions, it is clear from this selective review that researchers have made tremendous gains in understanding how to reduce prejudice. When the environment is racially diverse, implementing a cooperative learning technique is an effective vehicle for reducing prejudice and also enhancing academic success for all students. Regardless of the racial composition of the environment, other interventions based on social learning theory, such as multicultural education and anti-racist teaching, have much to offer. However, as mentioned, there are some counter-intuitive traps in these interventions that could actually increase prejudice.

Despite impressive progress, there is much that needs to be tested and integrated. This is an exciting time in the field, as abundant findings have begun to amass. It is clear that prejudice is multifaceted and is more likely to be reduced with multiple approaches. For example, it seems worthwhile for schools to consider implementing programs that draw on elements of multicultural education (to appreciate the richness and varying experiences of people from differences cultures) and anti-racist education (to highlight that racism is still a problem), as well as incorporating the color-blind view (to reduce the focus on surface features like race).

It is also important that researchers expand intervention efforts and theorizing. Much research has focused on whites or white-black relations while ignoring other racial/ethnic intergroup relations. It is also clear that children's ages, or social-cognitive skill levels, need to be taken into account rather than employing a "one size fits all" approach.

In addition to directly intervening on children to reduce their prejudice, we might consider intervening on other levels as well (Banks, 1995). We have seen that children's prejudiced attitudes arise from a variety of sources. Thus, we ought to consider a variety of sources through which to counter this prejudice. Indeed, some programs have added a teacher-training component (Verma & Bagley, 1979); and as discussed later, a strong alliance with teachers seems to be a necessity for interventions to succeed.

Another issue in future research is the need to study students at schools with race problems. Not surprisingly, many of the schools that are most willing to participate in interventions are the schools that are already implementing prejudice-reducing strategies and, relative to other schools, have fewer race problems. It is clear that children at participating schools tend to have relatively low prejudice scores even before the interventions (Gimmestad & de Chiara, 1983). This limits the conclusions that can be drawn from the study and fails to accomplish the goal of the interventions—to reduce prejudice. Researchers have lamented the difficulty of securing participation from schools (Verma & Bagley, 1979), an obstacle made even more threatening as the recent emphasis on standardized testing has reduced the time available for nonacademic school-based activities. Thus, future interventions may need to be integrated into the regular lessons. As can be seen, a key to success in the design and implementation of effective interventions is a strong partnership among researchers, educators, and parents.

CONCLUSION

Children exhibit racial and ethnic prejudice from a young age. Prejudice is to some degree inevitable because of limited environmental resources leading to intergroup conflict and because of people's limited cognitive resources. However, we now have a much better understanding of prejudice and potential ways to reduce it. It is clear that prejudice has multifaceted origins; therefore, a multifaceted approach to reducing prejudice is optimal. Drawing on the research reviewed, we offer suggestions for parents, teachers, policymakers, and others interested in promoting tolerance. The suggestions are summarized in the "toolbox for change" below.

Parents, educators, and other important figures in a child's life need to be actively engaged in monitoring and modifying children's exposure to race information (including exposure to negative influences, such as particular movies or television shows). As noted, some evidence suggests that parents (including open-minded, tolerant ones) are not discussing race issues with their children; however, research suggests that discussions about race issues, with an emphasis on anti-bias messages, could reduce children's prejudice levels.

Research on the social-cognitive development of prejudice has shown that children's cognitive skill levels and readiness for learning new skills (such as perspective-taking) influence their interpretations of race-related information. Thus, educators and parents must determine a child's level of social-cognitive development and meet the child at this level with anti-bias messages or influences. Some techniques may be more flexible than others in the extent to which they can be modified to meet the cognitive needs and limitations of children.

However, inducing cooperative and interdependent, as opposed to competitive, learning environments that involve children from different racial backgrounds appears to be beneficial regardless of age.

Educators and policymakers need to make a true commitment to promoting racial tolerance in the schools. This can be accomplished by integrating racial tolerance into school curricula, assessment and testing

Toolbox for Change

For	Images/perceptions of current society	Strategies for change
Individuals	Discussions of race are not needed and could increase prejudice.	Discuss race with children openly and honestly at home and elsewhere at a cognitive-developmentally appropriate level. Promote interracial relations and learning about other groups, but be careful not to overemphasize differences among groups.
Community	Communities are already doing enough to encourage open discussion about race, and racism is not a problem among children.	Provide forums in the community where racism among all age groups is discussed. Institutionalize approval for nonprejudiced attitudes through policies that involve every part of the community.
Practitioners/ educators	School is not the place for prejudice-reduction interventions because time spent on interventions takes away valuable time from fostering academic success.	Integrate multicultural and anti-racist teaching into the basic academic curricula (such as social studies and reading). At racially/ethnically diverse schools, utilize cooperative learning strategies, which also foster academic success.

procedures, teaching styles, and norms sanctioned by the schools. Care needs to be taken that methods do not set other groups apart, for example, by devoting each month to celebrating a different racial or ethnic group, as research has shown that this technique can actually increase prejudice.

In conclusion, prejudice continues to create barriers for the learning and development of children from all racial and ethnic groups. With the increasing diversity of youth in the United States, it is particularly timely and important to make progress toward understanding and reducing racial/ethnic prejudice among children. The research reviewed in this chapter gives us reason to hope that prejudice can be reduced and tolerance can be increased in the near future.

ACKNOWLEDGMENT

This material is based in part upon work supported by the National Science Foundation under Grant No. 0213660 to the first author.

REFERENCES

Aboud, F. E. (1988). *Children and prejudice*. New York: Blackwell.

Aboud, F. E. (in press). The development of prejudice in children and adolescents. In J. F. Dovidio, P. Glick, & L. Rudman (Eds.), *Reflecting on the nature of prejudice*.

Aboud, F. E., & Amato, M. (2001). Developmental and socialization influences on intergroup bias. In R. Brown & S. Gaertner (Vol. eds.), *Blackwell handbook in social psychology, Vol. 4: Intergroup processes*. Oxford, UK: Blackwell.

Aboud, F. E., & Doyle, A. B. (1996a). Parental and peer influences on children's racial attitudes. *International Journal of Intercultural Relations, 20*, 371–383.

Aboud, F. E., & Doyle, A. B. (1996b). Does talk of race foster prejudice or tolerance in children? *Canadian Journal of Behavioral Science, 28*, 161–170.

Aboud, F. E., & Fenwick, V. (1999). Evaluating school-based interventions to reduce prejudice in pre-adolescents. *Journal of Social Issues, 55*, 767–785.

Aboud, F. E., & Levy, S. R. (2000). Interventions to reduce prejudice and discrimination in children and adolescents. In S. Oskamp (Ed.), *Reducing prejudice and discrimination* (pp. 269–293). Mahwah, NJ: Lawrence Erlbaum Associates, Inc.

Adorno, T. W., Frenkel-Brunswick, E., Levinson, D. J., & Sanford, R. N. (1950). *The authoritarian personality*. New York: Harper.

Allport, G. W. (1954). *The nature of prejudice.* Cambridge, MA: Addison-Wesley.

Aronson, E., and Gonzalez, A. (1988). Desegregation, jigsaw and the Mexican American experience. In P. A. Katz & D. A. Taylor (Eds.), *Eliminating racism: Profiles in controversy* (pp. 301–314). New York: Plenum.

Bandura, A. (1977). *Social learning theory.* Englewood, NJ: Prentice-Hall.

Banks, J. A. (1995). Multicultural education for young children: Racial and ethnic attitudes and their modification. In W. D. Hawley & A. W. Jackson (Eds.), *Toward a common destiny: Improving race and ethnic relations in America* (pp. 236–250). San Francisco: Jossey-Bass.

Bar-Tal, D. (1996). Development of social categories and stereotypes in early childhood: The case of "the Arab" concept formation, stereotype and attitudes by Jewish children in Israel. *International Journal of Intercultural Relations, 20,* 341–370.

Bigler, R. S. (1995). The role of classification skill in moderating environmental influences on children's gender stereotyping: A study of the functional use of gender in the classroom. *Child Development, 66,* 1072–1087.

Bigler, R. S. (1999). The use of multicultural curricula and materials to counter racism in children. *Journal of Social Issues, 55,* 687–705.

Bigler, R. S., Jones, L. C., & Lobliner, D. B. (1997). Social categorization and the formation of intergroup attitudes in children. *Child Development, 6,* 530–543.

Bigler, R. S., & Liben, L. S. (1993). A cognitive-developmental approach to racial stereotyping and reconstructive memory in Euro-American children. *Child Development, 64,* 1507–1518.

Black-Gutman, D., & Hickson, F. (1996). The relationship between racial attitudes and social-cognitive development in children: An Australian study. *Developmental Psychology, 32,* 448–456.

Branch, C. W., & Newcombe, N. (1986). Racial attitude development among black children as a function of parental attitudes: A longitudinal and cross-sectional study. *Child Development, 57,* 712–721.

Brown, R. (1995). *Prejudice: Its social psychology.* Cambridge, MA: Blackwell.

Carlson, J. M., & Iovini, J. (1985). The transmission of racial attitudes from fathers to sons: A study of blacks and whites. *Adolescence, 20,* 233–237.

Cotharin, R. L., & Mikulas, W. L. (1975). Systematic desensitization of racial emotional responses. *Journal of Behavior Therapy & Experimental Psychiatry, 6,* 347–348.

Doyle, A. B., & Aboud, F. E. (1995). A longitudinal study of white children: Racial prejudice as a social-cognitive development. *Merrill-Palmer Quarterly, 41,* 209–228.

Doyle, A. B., Beaudet, J., & Aboud, F. E. (1988). Developmental patterns in the flexibility of children's ethnic attitudes. *Journal of Cross-Cultural Psychology, 19*, 3–18.

Fine, M. (1995). *Habits of mind: Struggling over values in America's classrooms.* San Francisco: Jossey-Bass.

Fishbein, H. D. (1996). *Peer prejudice and discrimination: Evolutionary, cultural, and developmental dynamics.* Boulder, CO: Westview Press.

4 teens arrested in firebombing case: Charges in attack on immigrants' Farmingdale home. (2003, July 31). *Newsday.* Retrieved December 10, 2003, from http://www.newsday.com/news/local.longisland/ny-lifirebombing0731jul31.story

Friess, S. (2003, September 28). A gang (or is it?) afflicts upscale Las Vegas area: Youth attacks appear to lack usual motives. *The Boston Globe.* Retrieved December 10, 2003, from http://www.boston.com.news/nation/articles/2003/09/28/a_gang_or_is_it_afflicts_upscale_l

Garcia, E. E., & Hurtado, A. (1995). Becoming American: A review of current research on the development of racial and ethnic identity in children. In W. D. Hawley & A. W. Jackson (Eds.), *Toward a common destiny* (pp. 163–184). San Francisco: Jossey-Bass.

Genesee, F., & Gandura, P. (1999). Bilingual education programs: A cross-national perspective. *Journal of Social Issues, 55*, 627–643.

Gimmestad, B. J., & de Chiara, E. (1983). Dramatic plays: A vehicle for prejudice reduction in the elementary school. *Journal of Educational Research, 76*, 45–49.

Hirschfeld, L. A. (1995). Do children have a theory of race? *Cognition, 54*, 209–252.

Hirschfeld, L. A. (2001). On a folk theory of society: Children, evolution, and mental representations of social groups. *Personality and Social Psychology Review, 5*, 107–117.

Houser, B. B. (1978). An examination of the use of audiovisual media in reducing prejudice. *Psychology in the Schools, 15*, 116–122.

Johnson, D. W., & Johnson, R. T. (2000). The three Cs of reducing prejudice and discrimination. In S. Oskamp (Ed.), *Reducing prejudice and discrimination.* Mahwah, NJ: Lawrence Erlbaum Associates.

Karafantis, D. M., & Levy, S. R. (2004). The role of children's lay theories about the malleability of human attributes in beliefs about and volunteering for disadvantaged groups. *Child Development, 75*, 236–250.

Katz, P. A. (1973). Stimulus predifferentiation and modification of children's racial attitudes. *Child Development, 44*, 232–237.

Katz, P. A. (1976). Attitude change in children: Can the twig be straightened? In P. A. Katz (Ed.), *Towards the elimination of racism.* New York: Pergamon.

Katz, P. A., Sohn, M., & Zalk, S. R. (1975). Perceptual concomitants of racial attitudes in urban grade-school children. *Developmental Psychology, 11*, 135–144.

Katz, P. A., & Zalk, S. R. (1978). Modification of children's racial attitudes. *Developmental Psychology, 14*, 447–461.

Kehoe, J. W., & Mansfield, E. (1993). The limitations of multicultural education and anti-racist education. In K. A. McLeod (Ed.), *Multicultural education: The state of the art* (pp. 3–8). Toronto, Canada: University of Toronto.

Khmelkov, V. T., & Hallinan, M. T. (1999). Organizational effects on race relations in schools. *Journal of Social Issues, 55*, 627–645.

Killen, M., Lee-Kim, J., McGlothlin, H., Stangor, C. (2002). How children and adolescents evaluate gender and racial exclusion. *Monographs of the Society for Research in Child Development, 67*, 1–119.

Knight, G. P., Bernal, M. E., Garza, C.A., Cota, M. K., & Ocampo, K. A. (1993). Family socialization and Mexican American identity and behavior. In M. E. Bernal and G. P. Knight (Eds.), *Ethnic identity: Formation and transmission among Hispanics and other minorities.* Albany, NY: SUNY Press.

Kofkin, J. A., Katz, P. A., & Downey, E. P. (1995). *Family discourse about race and the development of children's racial attitudes.* Paper presented at Society for Research in Child Development, Indianapolis, Indiana.

Kowalski, K. (1998). The impact of vicarious exposure to diversity on preschoolers' emerging ethnic/racial attitudes. *Early Child Development and Care, 146*, 41–51.

Levy, S. R. (1999). Reducing prejudice: Lessons from social-cognitive factors underlying perceiver differences in prejudice. *Journal of Social Issues, 55*, 745–766.

Levy, S. R., & Dweck, C. S. (1999). The impact of children's static versus dynamic conceptions of people on stereotype formation. *Child Development, 70*, 1163–1180.

Levy, S. R., West, T., & Ramirez, L. (In press). Lay theories: Unitary and dual implications for intergroup relations. In W. Stroebe & M. Hewstone (Eds.), *The European Review of Social Psychology.*

McGregor, J. (1993). Effectiveness of role playing and anti-racist teaching in reducing student prejudice. *The Journal of Educational Research, 86*, 215–226.

Mendelson, M. J., & Aboud, F. E. (1999). Measuring friendship quality in late adolescents and young adults: McGill friendship questionnaires. *Canadian Journal of Behavioural Science, 31*, 130–132.

Monteith, M. (1993). Self-regulation of prejudiced responses: Implications for progress in prejudice-reduction efforts. *Journal of Personality and Social Psychology, 65*, 469–485.

Neville, H. A., Lilly, R. L., Duran, G., Lee, R. M., & Browne, L. (2000). Construction and initial validation of the color-blind racial attitudes scale. *Journal of Counseling Psychology, 47*, 59–70.

Ocampo, K. A., Bernal, M. E., & Knight, G. P. (1993). Gender, race, and ethnicity: The sequencing of social constancies. In M. E. Bernal &

G. P. Knight (Eds.), *Ethnic identity: Formation and transmission among Hispanics and other minorities* (pp. 47–59). Albany, NY: SUNY Press.

Patchen, M. (1983). Students' own racial attitudes and those of peers of both races, as related to interracial behavior. *Sociology & Social Research, 68,* 59–77.

Pettigrew, T. F. (1998). Intergroup contact theory. *Annual Review of Psychology, 49,* 65–85.

Piaget, J., & Weil, A. M. (1951). The development in children of the idea of the homeland and of relations to other countries. *International Social Science Journal, 3,* 561–578.

Powlishta, K. K., Serbin, L. A., Doyle, A., & White, D. (1994). Gender, ethnic, and body type biases: The generality of prejudice in childhood. *Developmental Psychology, 30,* 526–536.

Quintana, S. M. (1998). Children's developmental understanding of ethnicity and race. *Applied and Preventive Psychology, 7,* 27–45.

Ritchey, P. N., & Fishbein, H. D. (2001). The lack of an association between adolescent friends' prejudices and stereotypes. *Merrill-Palmer Quarterly, 47,* 188–206.

Schofield, J. W. (1986). Causes and consequences of the colorblind perspective. In J. F. Dovidio & S. L. Gaertner (Eds.), *Prejudice, discrimination, and racism* (pp. 231–253). Orlando, FL: Academic Press.

Slavin, R. E., & Cooper, R. (1999). Improving intergroup relations: Lessons learned from cooperative learning programs. *Journal of Social Issues, 55,* 647–663.

Underwood, B., & Moore, B. (1982). Perspective taking and altruism. *Psychological Bulletin, 91,* 143–173.

U.S. Census Bureau. (2002). Population division, population projects branch. Retrieved December 5, 2003, from http://www.census.gov/population/www/projections/natsum-T5.html

Verma, G. K., & Bagley, C. (1979). Measured changes in racial attitudes following the use of three different teaching methods. In G. K. Verma & C. Bagley (Eds.), *Race, education and identity* (pp. 133–143). New York: St. Martin's Press.

Weiner, M. J. & Wright, F. E. (1973). Effects of undergoing arbitrary discrimination upon subsequent attitudes toward a minority group. *Journal of Applied Psychology, 3,* 94–102.

CHAPTER 4

Racism, Racial Stereotypes, and American Politics

Frederick Slocum
Yueh-Ting Lee

PREJUDICE, NEGATIVE STEREOTYPES, AND POLITICS

Out of the many stories illustrating the influence of racial animosities in American politics, the steady movement of white, working-class voters of Macomb County, Michigan (near Detroit), from solidly Democratic in 1964 to solidly Republican in 1984 surely would, on the surface, rank as neither the most relevant nor the most dramatic. Indeed, this two-decade shift in presidential voting in one Michigan county would probably be no more than a footnote in history books had not national Democratic Party officials set out to study why so many Macomb County voters had abandoned the party in presidential voting. Macomb County was a largely working-class area, with a very high concentration of current and retired auto workers, and with strong union ties, which tend to favor Democratic voting. In 1960, Macomb voters supported Democrat John F. Kennedy over Republican Richard Nixon by a 60 percent to 37 percent margin. But in 1984, Republican Ronald Reagan carried the county 67 percent to 33 percent over Democrat Walter Mondale. Reagan, in cruising to a forty-eight–state sweep, benefited from similarly high levels of support among working-class whites in suburban Chicago, Cleveland, Philadelphia, and other midwestern and northeastern cities (Edsall & Edsall, 1992).

In early 1985, national Democratic Party officials sponsored a series of focus groups to determine why so many working-class whites had so thoroughly repudiated the party. Pollster Stanley Greenberg summarized the results this way:

> These white Democratic defectors express a profound distaste for blacks, a sentiment that pervades almost everything they think about government and politics. . . . Blacks constitute the explanation for . . . almost everything that has gone wrong in their lives; not being black is what constitutes being middle class; not living with blacks is what makes a neighborhood a decent place to live. These sentiments have important implications for Democrats, as virtually all progressive symbols and themes have been redefined in racial and pejorative terms. The special status of blacks is perceived by almost all of these individuals as a serious obstacle to their personal advancement. Indeed, discrimination against whites has become a well-assimilated and ready explanation for their status, vulnerability and failures. . . . (Greenberg, 1985, pp. 13–18, 28)

These conclusions indicate the central roles of *racial prejudice* and *negative stereotyping* in explaining the movement of these white voters away from the Democratic Party's candidates in presidential voting.

The apparent preference for all-white neighborhoods probably owes to negative *stereotyped* views that when blacks move into an all-white neighborhood, poverty, crime, drug trafficking, illegitimate births, decrepit homes and lawns, and ultimately declining property values, will probably result. The seismic political shift in Macomb County, then, reveals the central role of racial animosities and racial stereotyping in U.S. politics. Unfortunately, it is only one of many such cases.

A cautionary note and some definitions are in order here. Research on stereotypes and prejudice has yielded complex but fruitful results when accuracy (accurate versus inaccurate stereotypes) and valence (positive versus negative stereotypes) are addressed (Corrigan, Watson, & Ottati, 2003; Fiske, 1998; Lee, Albright, & Malloy, 2001; Lee, Jussim, & McCauley, 1995; Lee, McCauley, & Draguns, 1999; Olson, 1994). The racial stereotypes addressed throughout this chapter are mostly inaccurate and negative. By definition, *prejudice* is a negative attitude toward some members of a group or things of a category (Corrigan & Penn, 1999; Tajfel, 1981; Lee & Ottati, 1993, 1995). By definition, *stereotypes* are the "ascribing [of] characteristics to social groups or segments of society" (Lee et al., 1995). Examples of ethnic and racial stereotypes include the views that blacks are lazy, that Asian

Americans are hardworking, and that Jews are prone to engage in shady financial dealings. The stereotype then is applied to varying degrees to individual encounters with a Jewish person, a black person, and so on. Not all stereotypes are negative—but many are. In this chapter, we concern ourselves with how *negative* racial and ethnic stereotypes intrude into American politics.

This chapter examines the centrality of racism and racial stereotyping in American politics and the nature of that influence as well. We refer to both historical and recent cases and data. The chapter will show that in the political arena, racism and negative racial stereotypes have a frequent and continuing presence in American political campaigns and public policy.

We begin by examining two sets of historical cases: first, the blatantly antiblack appeals found in the American South before the civil rights era and their political consequences; and second, anti-immigrant appeals made against Asian and other immigrants during the nineteenth and early twentieth centuries. Next, we consider modern issues and controversies in U.S. politics, specifically examining prejudice against new immigrants, in campaign appeals, in public pronouncements made by government officials, and in voting. Throughout, we will examine our cases and controversies through the lens of psychological theories and research findings on the nature and consequences of racial prejudice and stereotyping. We conclude with some suggestions on how the information presented here can be used to combat racial prejudice and discrimination.

RACISM, PREJUDICE, AND POLITICS: HISTORICAL CASES

This section examines some cases illustrating the impacts of racism and racial prejudice in American political history. We focus especially on how prejudice and racial stereotypes are translated into electoral rules and public policies that suppress racial minorities and define them as less-than-welcome actors in the political community.

Racism, Prejudice, and Politics in the Pre–Civil Rights South

There can be no doubt that until the 1960s, southern politics was organized around ensuring white domination and the subordination and oppression of blacks in every walk of life. As Marion D. Irish

(1942) concluded, "The elementary determinant in Southern politics . . . is an intense Negro phobia which has scarcely abated since Reconstruction." Most Southern whites were highly prejudiced against blacks, and elected officials themselves held similar racial views, felt forced to become hard-line segregationists just to survive politically, or some combination of both. Southern senators like Strom Thurmond (SC) and James Eastland (MS); and governors such as Orval Faubus (AR), George Wallace (AL), and Ross Barnett (MS) were at the forefront of resistance against federal civil rights laws and decisions, even personally attempting to block the carrying out of federal court-ordered integration in some cases. The racist rhetoric of long-time Sen. Theodore Bilbo of Mississippi was so raw that even his fellow segregationists were embarrassed to associate with him too closely.[1]

Armed with negative stereotypes of blacks as lazy, intellectually inferior, lacking in thrift, sexually promiscuous, prone to violence, and unfit for leadership positions, the dominant white majority in the South constructed social and political arrangements that perpetuated white domination and black suppression (Black & Black, 1987). As of the Supreme Court decision *Brown v. Board of Education* (1954), seventeen Southern and border states legally mandated segregated public schools; various state laws banned blacks from working in certain occupations altogether; and state laws and local ordinances enforced rigid racial segregation in wide swaths of society.[2] In electoral politics, discriminatory poll taxes, literacy tests, the white primary, the grandfather clause, administrative delays and barriers for blacks registering to vote, the creative drawing of at-large electoral districts (to dilute black voting power), and threatened and actual violence combined to render blacks politically powerless in the Deep South, and to severely weaken their political power elsewhere in the South.[3] By law, blacks were relegated to separate and inferior facilities in every public arena—bus and train stations, law schools, drinking fountains, and many others.

Government-enforced racial discrimination was an unmistakable result of prejudice and racial stereotypes. The negative stereotype of blacks as unclean led whites to enforce segregated public places; the stereotype of black children as slow to learn, disruptive, and prone to violence led to segregation in the public schools; the stereotype of black men as sexual predators bent on sullying the virtue of white women led to antimiscegenation laws[4] as well as extremely harsh treatment of any black male suspected of sexually assaulting a white woman. The stereotype of blacks as naturally lazy and unfit for leadership served to justify laws barring them from certain occupations and reserving public office for whites only. Government agencies even got into the act of reinforcing and maintaining these systems of white privilege and domination. The Mississippi Sovereignty Commission (1956–1977), a state-created and state-funded agency, spied on and harassed civil rights workers and activists, worked to preserve a segregated society, and launched public relations campaigns extolling Mississippi and its "way of life."

White southerners' resistance to racial integration in public schools was as fierce as in other arenas. The Supreme Court had ruled that school desegregation must be undertaken "with all deliberate speed." However, southern state and local officials responded with far more deliberation than speed—and far more defiance than compliance. Nineteen senators and seventy-seven representatives from southern states signed the "Southern Manifesto" (1956), which criticized *Brown v. Board of Education* and commended the motives of those states that had declared the intention to resist forced integration by any lawful means. Prince Edward County, Virginia, shut down its public schools from 1959 to 1964 rather than integrate, reopening only in response to a federal court order. During those five years, state funds supported private, segregated schools for the district's 1,550 white students, while 1,800 black students were locked out of an education, save those sent away from home to attend school elsewhere.[5] During the 1964–1965 school year, a full ten years after the *Brown* decision, 97.8 percent of the South's black schoolchildren still attended all-black schools (Southern Education Reporting Service, 1967).

For blacks in the South, the criminal justice system provided no refuge from racism and white domination. All-white juries were routine; blacks accused of crimes, especially those involving white victims, were speedily convicted, often with little regard to evidence and/or actual involvement in the alleged crime, and routinely received harsh sentences. Whites accused of crimes against blacks sometimes got off scot-free; in many other cases they received light punishment. In 1955, Emmett Till, a black youth from Chicago who was visiting relatives in Mississippi, reportedly whistled at a white female store clerk after buying candy. That same evening, he was kidnapped and brutally murdered. The store clerk's husband and brother-in-law stood trial for the grisly killing, but an all-white jury acquitted them. The two messages were unmistakable. First, any black person who accused a white person of a crime in Mississippi would probably fail. Second, potentially violent reprisals awaited those who even tried.[6]

The 1964 murders of three civil rights workers near Philadelphia, Mississippi (later dramatized in the 1988 movie *Mississippi Burning*, partially based on real-life events) did result in state trials for murder and conspiracy; some of the suspects were law enforcement officers. The men were acquitted of murder in their state trials, but later were tried and convicted in federal court on civil rights violations. In 1963, civil rights activist and NAACP field secretary Medgar Evers was shot to death in the driveway of his own home in Jackson, Mississippi. In 1964, Byron de la Beckwith, an avowed white supremacist, was tried twice for the killing (both times with all-white juries), but both trials resulted in hung juries. de la Beckwith remained a free man until 1994, when new evidence surfaced and prosecutors reopened the case against him. He was tried a third time, convicted, and sentenced to life in prison, this time by a jury with eight blacks and four whites. In January 2001, he died in prison.

Through 1965, southern history in general, and these examples in particular, richly document that southern politicians sought to harness the machinery of government to maintain racial segregation and white domination of the economy and polity. Virtually everywhere in the South, the Democratic Party was the vehicle for ensuring these outcomes. As Black and Black noted,

> Early in this century, most white Southerners looked upon the rest of the nation . . . with abiding hostility and suspicion. Unable to forget or forgive the nightmare of war, defeat and occupation, most whites shared the conviction that non-southerners must never again be allowed to interfere with southern racial practices. Acting almost as if it were an independent nation, the South pursued deterrence of outside intervention in race relations as the paramount objective of its 'foreign' policy. White southerners needed a political organization capable of maximizing their leverage on national politics, and the Democratic Party became that device. (1987, p. 233)

In short, politics in the pre–civil rights South was first and foremost a struggle to translate the white majority's prejudice and antiblack stereotypes into legally mandated segregation and many other discriminatory public policies. Prejudice and racism clearly manifested themselves in political campaigns and had wide-ranging public policy consequences.

RACISM, PREJUDICE, AND THE HISTORY
OF ANTI-IMMIGRANT APPEALS

In 220-plus years of U.S. history, almost nothing has been more politically charged or laden with racial bias than the immigration and naturalization process of the United States. Unfortunately, in social science and humanities studies, little attention has been paid to how U.S. immigration and naturalization policies systematically relate to ethnic contact, social identity, and racial power. According to Takaki (1989), Asian Americans experience much prejudice and discrimination in the United States because they differ from Europeans in three ways—geographically (region of origin), culturally/religiously, and physically/racially. There was much evidence of historical discrimination and prejudice against Chinese Americans (see Dinnerstein, Nichols, & Reimers, 1996; Dinnerstein & Reimers, 1999; Lee, Quinones-Perdomo, & Perdomo, 2003). In the mid-nineteenth century, Chinese immigrants began coming in ever-larger numbers to the United States. The Chinese came to the United States for three major reasons: European powers had intruded in China, resulting in internal turmoil and emigration; gold was discovered in California; and the industrial development of the United States required a large labor force. With respect to the latter, by the end of the nineteenth century, Chinese laborers worked long hours and received less pay than their competitors—Irish immigrants who themselves were mistreated. Many Caucasians considered the Chinese to be "yellow devils" who should be driven into the Pacific Ocean (Joshi, 1999). Personal accounts of Chinese immigrants give witness to their special experiences (Rico & Mano, 2001). Although Ellis Island in New York was seen as a symbol of freedom for Europeans, Angel Island in San Francisco was seen as a place of imprisonment, where Chinese immigrants were jailed. This was evident in *The Gold Mountain Poems*, anonymous works written by early Chinese immigrants to the United States (Rico & Mano, 2001, p. 261). Here is one of the poems.

> So, liberty is your national principle;
> Why do you practice autocracy?
> You don't uphold justice, you Americans,
> You detain me in prison, guard me closely.
> Your officials are wolves and tigers,
> All ruthless, all wanting to bite me.
> An innocent man implicated, such an injustice!
> When can I get out of this prison and free my mind?

The above poem expresses the hardship and discrimination the Chinese immigrants faced when arriving in America.

American immigration policy has been racist, or at a minimum, racially biased. The first anti-immigration law in the history of America was the 1882 Chinese Exclusion Act. This act was not repealed or abandoned until 1943. A 1901 "gentleman's agreement" slowed the immigration of Japanese laborers. In other words, while millions of Europeans immigrated to the United States of America, very few Asians were allowed the same privilege (Cao & Novas, 1996; Takaki, 1989).

In innumerable other cases, immigration, naturalization, and citizenship policies were based on ethnic identity and white dominance (Aguirre & Turner, 2001; Hu-DeHart, 2000; Lee et al., 2003). That is, only whites were allowed to naturalize ethnic nonwhites. Consistent with Roger Smith's research on politicians who create citizens, the first famous case was *Dred Scott v. Sandford* (U.S. Report, 1997).[7] Scott, a slave, escaped from the South to the North and asked the Supreme Court to grant him freedom. However, access to the courts was predicated on citizenship. Dismissing Scott's claim, Chief Justice Roger Taney declared in 1857 that Scott and all other blacks, free or enslaved, were not and could never be citizens because they were "a subordinate and inferior class of beings" (Lopez, 2002, p. 8). A more blatant case of judicial reasoning based on a racial stereotype can scarcely be imagined.

In the early twentieth century, there were two other famous cases concerning Asians and citizenship. In *Ozawa v. United States* (1922), Takao Ozawa petitioned for U.S. citizenship, but was turned away. He appealed and argued that Japanese people should be considered "white" (Fong & Shinagawa, 2000, p. 17). The Supreme Court unanimously ruled against him on two grounds: the existing law simply did not include the Japanese as part of a legitimate category, and "white" meant "a person of the Caucasian race." The Court dismissed Ozawa's argument that he was more "white" than other darker-skinned "white" people such as some Italians, Spanish, and Portuguese (Fong & Shinagawa, 2000, p. 17).

After the Ozawa case, the Court considered *United States v. Thind* in 1923. This time the Supreme Court ruled that Bhagat Singh Thind could not be a citizen because he was not "white," even though Asian Indians were classified as Caucasians. The Court stated, "It may be true that the blond Scandinavian and the brown Hindu have a common ancestor in the dim reaches of antiquity, but the average man knows perfectly well that there are unmistakable differences between them today" (Fong & Shinagawa, 2000, p. 17). In other words, only "white" Caucasians were considered eligible for U.S. citizenship. In short, American citizenship and immigration policies have been strongly influenced by ethnic and racial identity, white dominance, and white power.

The cases of white racial domination in the South and immigration policy each furnish strong evidence of the influence of racial prejudices and stereotyping in American political history. But to what extent do racism, prejudice, and racial stereotypes influence American politics *today?* The next section examines this question closely.

Racism, Prejudice, and American Politics: Modern Issues and Controversies

A close reading of post-1960s American politics raises suspicion that racism, prejudice, and racial stereotyping hold an active and continuing sway in American politics. Indeed, we contend that even today, race remains the "800-pound gorilla" of American politics. Racial issues have become a central division between the Democratic and Republican parties (Carmines & Stimson, 1989). The nature of some racial issues has changed from conflicts centering on equal opportunity (such as integration of schools and public places, and workplace discrimination) to those centering on equal outcomes (affirmative action, language instruction in schools, etc.). Racial conflicts have also evolved away from black–white dynamics alone and toward the multiple racial and ethnic interactions and dynamics found in an increasingly diverse nation. The September 11, 2001, terrorist attacks hastened this process; since then, complaints of discrimination against Arab Americans and Middle Eastern nationals by airlines and government alike have surfaced.[8] Recent psychological research has further confirmed this discrimination (Lee, Takaku, Ottati, & Yan, 2004).

The impacts of prejudice and negative stereotyping in politics have evolved, but they remain potent even today. We support this conclusion by examining the roles of prejudice and stereotyping in, first, immigration politics; second, election campaign rhetoric; third, noncampaign rhetoric by government officials; and fourth, in voting and elections.

Prejudice against and Stereotyping of New Immigrants: The Case of California's Proposition 187

California's Proposition 187 (1994) offers a case study of recent government action against illegal immigrants. California's direct initiative process allows voters to decide policy questions directly (by-passing the conventional policymaking route of enactment by the state legislature). Proposition 187 would have deprived illegal immigrants of welfare benefits, education, and all but emergency medical care. In addition, teachers, police officers, and welfare workers would have been required to report any knowledge of illegal immigrants to the Immigration and Naturalization Service (INS). After organizers gathered the needed number of signatures, the proposition was placed on the ballot for the 1994 general election. In the heated election campaign that followed, Republican Governor Pete Wilson highlighted his support for Proposition 187 and attacked his Democratic opponent, Kathleen Brown, for opposing it. Pro-Wilson ads emphasized the campaign's racial overtones, showing blurry, sinister images of illegal immigrants crossing the Mexican border into California as a sinister voice intoned "they keep on coming." The effect, if not the intent, was to foster a sense of California under siege, being overrun by hordes of illegal immigrants, and to intimate that Wilson would protect the state against this menace. Wilson won reelection, and the voters passed Proposition 187. But it was never implemented because the courts struck it down.

Lee and his colleagues (Lee & Ottati, 2002; Lee, Ottati, & Hussain, 2001) performed a series of studies after Proposition 187 by presenting a scenario to various American participants. The participants read the following scenario (written in English), supposedly from a U.S. newspaper, about "Carlos Suarez's life and work in America."

In 1985, Mr. Carlos Suarez emigrated from Mexico City to California (United States) without proper legal documents. He is considered an illegal alien. The reason for his immigration was to escape poverty, homelessness, and unemployment. Mr. Carlos Suarez found a manual job as a part-time worker in a small California town. In 1986, he returned to Mexico City to marry. When he returned to the United States a few months later, he brought his new wife with him. Since then, they have had three children. The eldest child is seven years old and ready for elementary school. The family lives in a tiny, inexpensive home in the barrio section of town. Carlos still works long hours for below-minimum wage and remains ineligible for social and welfare benefits.

In 1994, California approved Proposition 187, which deprives illegal immigrants of welfare benefits, education, and all but emergency medical care. In addition, California teachers, police, and welfare workers are required to report any knowledge of illegal immigrants to the Immigration and Naturalization Services for the purpose of deportation.

After reading the foregoing scenario, participants were asked various questions, including whether or not they supported Proposition 187. Of the white respondents, 70 percent voted in favor of Proposition 187, compared to 12.6 percent of the black and Asian Americans and 3.5 percent of the Latinos. Dropping abstaining participants produced a strongly significant ethnicity effect, $\chi^2(2, N = 240) = 125.20, p < .001$. Overall, there was a statistically significant difference among ethnic voters. But how were they different? When a comparison was performed between any two groups, it was found that the whites significantly differed from the Latinos, $\chi^2(1, N = 140) = 80.15, p < .001$, and from the black and Asian Americans, $\chi^2(1, N = 186) = 87.53$, $p < .001$. There was no significant difference between black and Asian Americans, and Latinos did not achieve significance, $\chi^2(1, N = 154) = 3.45, p > .10$. In other words, the minority Americans displayed the same voting behavior or attitudes toward Proposition 187 (that is, much less in favor of it than white Americans) based on what Lee and his colleagues found (Lee & Ottati, 2002; Lee, Ottati, & Hussain, 2001).

Lee and his colleagues (Lee & Ottati, 2002; Lee, Ottati, & Hussain, 2001) also assessed prejudice toward Mexicans as "illegal" or "undocumented" immigrants. Prejudicial attitudes toward Mexicans were then assessed using Westie's (1953) Interpersonal Prejudice Scale. This contained six items, all beginning with the phrase "I would be willing to have a Mexican (or Chicano) as. . . ." For the six items, the remainders of the sentence were "a close personal friend," "a dinner guest in my house," "a person I might often visit with," "an acquaintance," "someone I might say hello to" and "someone I might see on the street," respectively. For each item, subjects responded on a scale ranging from 1 (strongly agree) to 7 (strongly disagree). These six items were summed to produce a total "interpersonal prejudice" score. Higher scores on this index reflect greater prejudice against Mexicans.

Regression analysis revealed that both perceptions of economic threat ($b = -.61, p < .0001$) and interpersonal prejudice ($b = -.35$, $p < .0001$) operated as highly significant (and unique) predictors of attitudes toward immigrants generally and toward Proposition 187 specifically. An analogous analysis was used to predict the "children's education" item. Again, both perception of economic threat ($b = -.33, p < .001$) and interpersonal prejudice ($b = -.43, p < .0001$)

operated as highly significant (and unique) predictors. Importantly, perceptions of economic threat and interpersonal prejudice were essentially unrelated ($r = -.13, p > .10$). Thus, these two indices function as relatively distinct and nonoverlapping predictors (Lee & Ottati, 2002; Lee, Ottati, & Hussain, 2001).

These results demonstrate that perceived national economic threat and prejudice against Mexicans operate as distinct predictors of white attitudes toward Proposition 187 and "illegal" immigration. Importantly, perceived economic threat and anti-Mexican prejudice were relatively independent predictors. This discounts the possibility that perceptions of economic threat simply function to justify prejudiced attitudes toward Mexicans. If this were the case, perceptions of economic threat and prejudice toward Mr. Carlos Suarez and other "illegal" Mexicans should have served as redundant predictors (Lee & Ottati, 2002; Lee, Ottati, & Hussain, 2001).

Prejudice and Negative Stereotyping in Political Campaign Rhetoric

The 1960s federal civil rights laws put an end to the most egregious government acts of segregation and discrimination. However, they did not halt ambitious politicians' use of racial prejudice and stereotypes in campaigns. Even in the 1990s, campaign messages that appealed to white prejudices against, and stereotypes of, minorities were not difficult to find, despite the "norm of racial equality" that prohibits the too-explicit use of racial appeals in campaigns (Mendelberg, 2001).

One of the most explicitly racial campaign ads in recent American politics was aired in the 1990 North Carolina Senate race between Republican Jesse Helms and his Democratic opponent, former Charlotte mayor Harvey Gantt, a black. The Helms campaign aired a television commercial showing a white hand crumpling a job rejection letter as an announcer intoned, "You wanted that job, and you were the best qualified. But they had to give it to a minority because of a racial quota." The ad went on to trumpet Helms' position against affirmative action, implying that Gantt supported racial quotas. The ad was aired only during the final days of the campaign and apparently boosted Helms to a narrow victory in a campaign that had been a dead heat one week before the election.

The issue of violent crime has provided opportunities for politicians to bait white stereotypes about violent young black males. The Willie Horton television ads (run on George Bush's behalf during the 1988 presidential election) featured a menacing image of Horton, a black escapee from Massachusetts who fled to Maryland and broke into a couple's home and attacked them, raping the woman and stabbing her husband. The ads, sponsored by a group supporting George Bush's presidential bid with the Bush campaign's apparent endorsement (Mendelberg, 2001), showed a menacing, scowling head shot of Horton. The ads highlighted Horton's crimes and attacked Democratic presidential candidate Michael Dukakis (then governor of Massachusetts) for the weekend release program under which Horton had fled the state. The Willie Horton TV ads were widely criticized for fueling white stereotypes of violent and criminal tendencies among young black men. Mendelberg shows that Republican political operatives had planned the Horton campaign as a means of winning white support by making implicitly racial appeals.[9] Mendelberg summarizes the role of Bush campaign manager Lee Atwater in endorsing implicit racial appeals:

> Atwater concluded, based on his experience in southern campaigns, that a Republican candidate for the presidency had to make appeals to race but mask them. Atwater did not arrive at this strategy from scratch, nor did he acquire it in 1988. It was already considered a tried-and-true method by the top echelons of the Republican Party. (2001, p. 144)

The Willie Horton ad was a textbook implicitly racial campaign appeal—and by no means has it been the last. In other campaigns, implicitly racial issues (especially welfare) have figured prominently. In his 1989 bid for a Louisiana U.S. Senate seat and his 1991 campaign for governor of Louisiana, Republican candidate and former Ku Klux Klan leader David Duke made blatantly racial appeals. Duke attacked the "welfare underclass" and decried "welfare systems that encourage illegitimate births" and "set-asides to promote the incompetent" (Anti-Defamation League, 2004). Even though Duke lost both races, he received 44 percent of the overall vote—and 60 percent of the white vote—in his 1989 Senate bid. In 1991, Republican (and political unknown) Kirk Fordice won the Mississippi governor's race by using implicit racial appeals: opposing quotas, saying that welfare recipients should be forced to work, and attacking policies for coddling criminals. In the 2003 Mississippi governor's race, Republican Haley Barbour issued a veiled racial appeal by using the term "welfare" in criticizing state social spending.[10]

Arguments that these are legitimately race-neutral appeals are questionable at best, in light of numerous research findings on racial coding and implicit racial appeals. A number of studies indicate that *welfare* and *crime* are both racially loaded terms (Tursky, Lodge, & Reeder, 1979; Gilens, 1999; Hurwitz & Peffley, 1997; Slocum, 2001). These terms, and related ones like *underclass* and *welfare queen*,[11] activate whites' preexisting racial stereotypes about the "typical" welfare recipient (a black or Latina single mother), the violent criminal or crack cocaine user (a young black male), or the inner city resident (a black or Latino person), for political gain.

Campaign appeals that activate white stereotypes about blacks and Latinos are not the only manifestations of racial prejudice in campaign rhetoric. The 1983 Chicago mayor's race exposed extraordinary racial divisions, pitting black Democrat Harold Washington against white Republican Bernard Epton in a city that previously had never elected a black mayor. The campaign featured bare-knuckled and nonsubtle racial appeals. The campaign slogan "Epton: Before it's too late" was viewed widely as a masked racial appeal—to vote for Epton lest Washington, and by extension Chicago's black community, take over City Hall. More explicit still were the pro-Epton bumper stickers that proclaimed, "Vote right, vote white."

Negative racial stereotypes can also be injected into the congressional redistricting process—always an intensely political exercise. Every ten years, the U.S. Census Bureau must seek an accurate count of the U.S. population and that of each state—the latter determines how many U.S. House of Representatives members a state will have. States may gain one or even two House seats if their population growth exceeds national population growth; conversely, slower-growing states may lose House seats. States that gain or lose one or more House seats following a census *must* redraw their House districts; other states *may* redraw them. State legislatures are responsible for redrawing districts; the majority party there naturally seeks to draw districts for political advantage. Thus, a state may choose to redraw districts in response to a shift in party control in the state legislature. In Texas, the 2002 elections swept Republicans into control of both chambers of the state legislature. At the behest of U.S. Representative and House Majority Leader Tom DeLay, Republicans in the Texas legislature pushed through an unprecedented mid-decade redrawing of the state's U.S. House districts. Normally, redrawing takes place only once per decade, following the release of population data from the U.S. Census.

The 2003 Texas redistricting, if it survives court challenge, may set up a situation of near-complete racial polarization by party in the state's congressional delegation—and perhaps not by accident. In October

2003, Texas Republicans, in control of both houses of the state legislature and holding all twenty-nine statewide elected offices, redrew the state's U.S. House districts to elect more Republican U.S. House members from the state. Currently, there are sixteen Democratic and sixteen Republican House members from Texas (following Rep. Ralph Hall's January 2004 party switch from Democratic to Republican). The redistricting would probably yield a seven-seat Republican gain, with a House delegation of twenty-three Republicans and nine Democrats from Texas after the 2004 elections. Depending on who runs and the election results, Texas's U.S. House delegation may become near-completely polarized by party and race combined. A likely outcome is that the twenty-three Republicans will include twenty-two whites and one Latino, while all nine Democrats will be black or Latino. This effectively would stamp a "black or brown" face on the Texas Democratic Party in terms of its congressional delegation, as white Democrats are driven into extinction. It seems reasonable (at least) to speculate that Texas Republicans intend exactly this result: to define the Texas Democratic Party as beholden to "black and/or brown" interests, and thus to lock up the lion's share of the majority white vote and extend its current dominance into the foreseeable future. Through redistricting, Texas may have an effort to create a congressional delegation that will either give birth to a negative stereotype among Texas voters that Democrats serve black and Latino interests only, to reinforce any existing such stereotype, or some combination of both. This is not an implausible scenario; in 2002, Texas Democrats ran a Latino candidate (businessman Tony Sanchez) for governor and a black (former Dallas mayor Ron Kirk) for U.S. Senate—a "dream team" that fell flat; both candidates lost by wide margins in an election dominated by national security issues and President George W. Bush's popularity.

Clearly, political campaign rhetoric has at times contained racially coded appeals, and even the redrawing of congressional districts can carry racial overtones. Overall, there is substantial evidence of the use of covert (implicit) racial appeals in U.S. elections (Glaser, 1996; Mendelberg, 2001). These appeals do not create new white racial stereotypes; instead, they activate already-existing ones for political gain. In addition, the Texas redistricting may be an effort to create new (and/or reinforce existing) stereotypes, this time about the opposition party, also to secure a political advantage.

Interestingly, efforts by a party or candidate (usually Republican) to define the (usually Democratic) opposition as beholden to "black" interests seem commonplace; similar efforts targeting "Latino" interests are rarer but still can be found; similar efforts targeting Asian American or Native American interests appear virtually nonexistent. This probably owes to the more positive stereotype of Asian Americans as a "model minority," distinguished more by studiousness and a strong work ethic, rather than the often-negative stereotypes attached to blacks and, to a lesser extent, Latinos. Also, only a handful of Asian Americans hold statewide or federal public office, most notably Gary Locke, the governor of Washington state, and several U.S. House members from California and Hawaii. For Native Americans, their numbers almost everywhere are too small for them to elect one of their own to statewide or federal office. Still, one U.S. senator (out of 100) and one U.S. representative (out of 435) are Native American. Also, Americans' views of Native American are probably less influenced by negative stereotypes than they are for blacks and Latinos, in part because Native American are much less numerous, so fewer people have had direct contact with them.

PREJUDICE AND STEREOTYPING IN ELECTED OFFICIALS' STATEMENTS

Since the September 11, 2001, terrorist attacks, several lawmakers, all white, southern, conservative Republicans have made comments widely regarded as insensitive to various racial or ethnic groups. On December 5, 2002, Republican Senator Trent Lott of Mississippi (then-Senate majority leader) addressed a crowd attending the 100th birthday party of then-Senator Strom Thurmond (R-SC):

> I want to say this about my state. When Strom Thurmond ran for president (1948), we voted for him. We're proud of it. And if the rest of the country had followed our lead, we wouldn't have had all these problems over all these years, either.

In 1948, Thurmond had run as the Dixiecrat Party's candidate for president under a segregationist platform.[12] Lott's words provoked gasps from the party guests—and a firestorm of nationwide criticism that subsided only when Lott resigned his position as Senate majority leader. Lott's remarks were by no means the first time he had faced charges of racially insensitive speech.[13]

Since the September 11, 2001 terrorist attacks, several U.S. House members also have offered racially insensitive remarks. In a radio interview (September 17, 2001), then-Representative John Cooksey

(R-LA) implied that someone appearing Middle Eastern should expect to be questioned in the investigation of the attacks:

> If I see someone who comes in that's got a diaper on his head and a fan belt wrapped around the diaper on his head, that guy needs to be pulled over. When you've got a group of people who are not American citizens, who are of Arab descent and they were involved in killing 5,000 Americans . . . I think we can and should scrutinize people who fit that profile until this war on terrorism is over. (McKinney, 2001)

Cooksey later added, "[T]hat gets back to something called racial profiling." After Sikh Americans (many of whom wear turbans) and Arab Americans expressed outrage over these stereotyped comments, Cooksey apologized, admitting a "poor choice of words."

Similarly, then-U.S. Representative (now Senator) C. Saxby Chambliss (R-GA) told a November 2001 gathering of Georgia law enforcement officers that an appropriate response to terrorism would be to "turn the sheriff loose and have him arrest every Muslim that crosses the state line" (CNN Crossfire, 2002). Chambliss later expressed regret and apologized for the comment.

Three Republican U.S. representatives from North Carolina, Cass Ballenger, Howard Coble, and Sue Myrick, also made comments widely seen as racially insensitive. During an interview with the *Charlotte Observer* on December 19, 2002, Ballenger said that "in some areas of the South . . . there are people who get rubbed the wrong way and think, 'We've got to bend over backwards; we've got to integrate' and things like that" (Morrill, 2002). During the same interview, he disclosed a "segregationist feeling" toward Democratic then-Representative Cynthia McKinney of Georgia (who is black) and referred to her as "a bitch." Ballenger later apologized as well.

In a radio talk show (February 4, 2003), Coble defended as "appropriate at the time" President Franklin D. Roosevelt's decision to send Japanese Americans to internment camps during World War II. Coble said the internment helped protect Japanese Americans against a fearful, often intolerant public, and helped ensure national security. "Some [Japanese Americans] were probably intent on doing harm to us. Just as some of these Arab Americans are probably intent on doing harm to us," Coble said. In 1988, Coble had opposed the congressional bill providing monetary reparations to survivors of the internments.

Myrick, in a speech to the conservative Heritage Foundation on domestic terrorism (January 28, 2003), referred to Arab Americans and said, "Look who runs all the convenience stores across the country" (Morrison, 2003). Myrick defended her remarks by saying she simply wanted to remind communities of the threat of terrorism, including "the illegal trafficking of food stamps through convenience stores for the purpose of laundering money to countries known to harbor terrorists." Myrick later said she did not intend to insult any ethnic group.

The comments by Lott, Cooksey, Chambliss, Ballenger, Coble, and Myrick can be brushed off as unrelated, isolated incidents. However, this view strains credulity; there is a disturbing pattern here. Lott's statements appear to condone an openly segregationist philosophy; Ballenger's seem to imply support for segregation twice over, once in referring to a black lawmaker and once again in implying that integration "[rubs] people the wrong way" and means "bending over backward," as if racial segregation were a more comfortable alternative. The statements of Chambliss, Coble, Cooksey, and Myrick all reflect ethnic stereotyping of people of Arab and/or Middle Eastern ancestry. Chambliss' suggestion that law officers "arrest every Muslim that crosses the state line" and Coble's "just as some of these Arab Americans are probably intent on doing harm to us" needlessly amplify some people's fears that in light of 9/11, Arabs and/or Middle Easterners pose a security threat. Cooksey's gratuitous indulgence in ethnic stereotyping was evident in his reference to Arab Americans, coupled with the offensive "diaper on his head" remark, a crude reference to the turbans worn by some Sikh Americans (who are not Middle Eastern but South Asian, and who are racially and religiously distinct from most Arabs and Middle Easterners). His remarks also indicated approval of ethnically targeted racial profiling of Arab and/or Middle Eastern individuals. Myrick's statement lent credence to two other stereotypes: the curious one that Arab Americans own convenience stores and the far more offensive implication that they use those stores to channel funds overseas to support terrorist activities.

These remarks are even more disturbing considering that they came from the mouths of U.S. lawmakers. Individuals in such high office represent districts with thousands of people. They have an obligation to represent all their constituents—including blacks, Asian Americans, and those of Arab or Middle Eastern ancestry. These insensitive and/or stereotypical remarks surely call into question these lawmakers' credentials to represent diverse constituencies, and they leave reason to wonder whether at heart, these lawmakers harbor prejudices that ultimately could not resist expression, however inadvertent. The knowledge that all six of these lawmakers represent conservative, southern districts does little to dispel these suspicions.

These comments furnish striking evidence of varying combinations of racism, racial insensitivity, and/or racial/ethnic stereotyping by people elected to high public office (the U.S. Congress) and altogether outside the heat of an election campaign. If these lawmakers—a highly educated group—truly harbor the views suggested by their statements, one can only wonder about the racial and ethnic attitudes harbored by at least some of their constituents—in particular, the white majorities in Trent Lott's Mississippi and the other lawmakers' House districts.

Recent research on white southerners' racial attitudes has used an unobtrusive "list experiment" methodology that allows individuals to report prejudiced views without the interviewer knowing them (Kuklinski, Cobb, & Gilens, 1997). The results, though tentative because they are based on small sample sizes, are disturbing, if not appalling. The list experiment methodology yielded an estimate that 10 percent of non-southern whites, but fully 42 percent of southern whites, would be angry or upset at "a black family moving in next door." Similarly, an estimated 11 percent of non-southern whites, but 63 percent of southern whites, would be angry or upset at "interracial dating, with black teenagers taking out white teenagers" (Kuklinski et al., 1997; Kuklinski & Cobb, 1998). Although further research is needed, these stunning results suggest that white southerners' racial attitudes may be far less positive than usually reported in nationwide surveys that use direct, overt measures of racial attitudes.

Trent Lott and the other five lawmakers, all white, conservative southerners, may be reflecting racial attitudes that are widespread among the whites who comprise majorities of their constituencies.

Overall, racial and/or ethnic stereotyping is highly evident in a sampling of recent (post–9/11) comments made by elected officials. Indeed, racial animosities and stereotypes have scarcely disappeared from either campaign or noncampaign rhetoric. We now consider the extent to which racism and prejudice are apparent in voting.

PREJUDICE AND STEREOTYPING IN VOTING

Voting rights are one element that distinguishes a democratic state from a totalitarian one. However, the right to vote is meaningful only to the extent that qualified would-be voters are actually allowed to vote. To vote in federal elections, a person must be eighteen years old, a U.S. citizen, and not institutionalized or a convicted felon. The

Voting Rights Act of 1965, the 24th Amendment (abolishing poll taxes), and several Supreme Court decisions combined to effectively abolish most racially discriminatory voting practices. However, some reports of more subtle forms of voting discrimination, possibly based on race, continue to surface.

We consider prejudice and stereotyping in voting in two senses. Our first concern lies in the voting process itself: efforts to suppress minority voting may contribute to an election win for the candidate supported by most white voters—usually, the more conservative candidate is the beneficiary. Our second concern lies in the potential role of prejudice and stereotyping in an individual's vote choice itself, especially in elections pitting a white candidate against a minority candidate. In both cases, there is much reason to suspect that hidden prejudices influence efforts to suppress minority voting and the individual voting decision in elections where white and minority candidates face off.

Racial Prejudice and Stereotyping in Voting Procedures

Voting is more available to all voting-eligible Americans, regardless of race or ethnicity, as a result of the Voting Rights Act (1965) and other government actions and court decisions. However, there are a number of alleged cases of racially targeted voter suppression efforts that were done to influence the results of hotly contested elections. Here we consider some examples of this phenomenon, as well as one allegation that never was proven true.

When they surface, allegations of racially motivated voter suppression efforts often come from southern states, where blacks make up sizable shares of state populations—up to 36 percent in Mississippi. In Louisiana's 2002 U.S. Senate runoff election, there were allegations of efforts (presumably by Republican supporters) to suppress black voter turnout. According to the reports, flyers were distributed at mostly black public housing complexes in New Orleans, telling residents they could vote on December 10 if the weather was bad on Election Day (which was December 7). This was a complete fallacy, as the election ended when polls closed December 7. Democratic Sen. Mary Landrieu, with overwhelming support from Louisiana's black voters, won reelection to a second term, despite these voter suppression efforts targeting blacks. In a somewhat "cleaner" tactic in the same election, Louisiana's Republican Party paid for political signs in black neighborhoods that read, "Mary, if you don't respect us, don't expect us"—an attempt to emphasize complaints by some blacks that Landrieu had not paid enough attention to their issues.

In the 2003 Kentucky governor's race, there were complaints of a different method of suppressing black turnout: stationing Republican election observers at polling places in largely black Louisville neighborhoods. On October 23, 2003, the *Louisville Courier-Journal* reported on Republican plans to place Election Day challengers in fifty-nine voting precincts in mostly black Louisville neighborhoods. Republican leaders defended the plans as a legitimate means of enabling challenges to people suspected of being ineligible to vote. However, leaders of the National Association for the Advancement of Colored People (NAACP) called the plans "blatant intimidation" and "an effort to suppress the African American community." The chairperson of the Jefferson County Democratic Party said, "[They] have only one purpose: to intimidate and suppress votes in the West End and other minority areas."

Although not illegal, Kentucky Republicans' poll-watching efforts do seem vulnerable to charges that they are targeting black voters in hopes of suppressing black turnout. However, a race-neutral objection could be raised: that the Republican goal is to reduce turnout in Democrat-rich neighborhoods and the fact that many are heavily black is mere coincidence. In the face of these competing claims, divining actual motives is difficult. Claims that Republicans deliberately set out to prevent people from voting because of their race are thus difficult to verify empirically.

Although most voter suppression efforts seem aimed toward suppressing black turnout, more subtle means can be used to suppress turnout among Latinos and/or immigrants from elsewhere. A 1975 amendment to the Voting Rights Act requires the use of bilingual ballots in voting districts with low voter turnout and where 5 percent or more of residents have a first language other than English. A county where 4 percent of residents are Hmong (for example) may choose to, but is not required to, provide bilingual ballots for Hmong residents. A decision not to print bilingual ballots may save the county money, but it would probably lower voter turnout among the Hmong minority. In general, the decision to provide or not provide ballots, voting instructions, and/or translators for citizens whose first language is not English sends (intentionally or unintentionally) an unmistakable symbolic message about how welcome these citizens are in the electoral arena—and in society more generally.

One additional, never-proven allegation of racially targeted voter suppression came from Ed Rollins, campaign manager for Christine

Todd Whitman, the Republican candidate in the 1993 New Jersey governor's race. Rollins initially stated that Republican officials had distributed $500,000 in "walking around money" to black ministers who agreed to help suppress the black vote. Rollins later recanted this testimony, but it nonetheless ruined his political career. The charges were never proven, and the New Jersey Democratic Party, which initially had contested the election in court, dropped its challenge, realizing that there was no proof that the alleged actions alone had swung the election Whitman's way.

The Louisiana and Kentucky examples show that efforts to suppress black turnout are very real. Since blacks vote Democratic by a lopsided margin (for example, 90 percent for Al Gore and 8 percent for George W. Bush in the 2000 presidential election), Republicans benefit to the extent that they can engineer lower turnout among black voters. Efforts to suppress voter turnout among other racial or ethnic minorities are rare because the party loyalties of Latinos, Asian Americans, and Native Americans are more divided than those of blacks. Latinos of Mexican or Puerto Rican origin tend to favor the Democratic Party (not as lopsidedly as blacks do), but those of Cuban origin (found mostly in Florida) are heavily Republican. Asian Americans vary by nationality, but a large share, up to 35 percent of some groups, identify as independents. Native American party loyalties vary by tribe, and trend Democratic overall—but again, not by lopsided margins. The fact that most blacks are visually identifiable as such makes it easier to seek ways to dampen turnout. In contrast, heavily Republican constituencies, such as business executives and evangelical Christians, are not visually identifiable: it is impossible to simply look at a person and identify him or her as an evangelical. This helps explain why voter suppression efforts, when they occur, often are racially targeted, and are more often attributed to conservative and/or Republican causes or supporters.

Racial Prejudice and Stereotyping in Individual Vote Choices

Here we consider the role of racial prejudice in individuals' vote choices. In an election pitting a minority candidate against a white opponent, race and/or ethnicity is especially likely to affect voting. In such cases, racially polarized voting is common: white voters tend to vote for white candidates, while minority voters prefer minority candidates. This pattern was evident in the 1983 Chicago mayor's race between Harold Washington and Bernard Epton; in the 1990 and 1996 North Carolina Senate races between Jesse Helms and Harvey Gantt; and in the Philadelphia mayoral races of 1987, 1999, and 2003.[14] However, racial-bloc voting is not inevitable when a white candidate and a minority candidate contest an election. In the 1983 Charlotte, North Carolina mayor's race, Harvey Gantt, a black, defeated a white opponent with a biracial voting coalition combining overwhelming black support with significant white support.

All these elections involve a white candidate opposing a black candidate—the most common scenario. Elections in which a white candidate opposes a Latino, Asian American or Native American candidate can be found, but are far rarer. Most winning Latino candidates hail from districts where Latinos make up a majority or near-majority of residents (seen in parts of California and the Southwest, in some South Florida districts, and in a few congressional districts in the Chicago area and other urban areas). In the rarer cases where an Asian American wins elective office, there usually is a notable Asian American presence in the electorate (seen in Hawaii, the San Francisco area, other portions of California, and the Seattle area in Washington state). The same holds true for Native Americans; the only U.S. House member of Native American ancestry hails from near Tulsa, Oklahoma, in a congressional district with a sizable Native American presence. Invariably, a winning minority candidate benefits from strong voter mobilization among members of the minority group in question. When a minority candidate loses (for example, Tony Sanchez, the Latino candidate for the Texas governorship), the loss often can be attributed to factors other than the candidate's race or ethnicity. In Sanchez's case, the Republican trend among Texas whites coupled with an unfavorable national political trend favoring Republicans probably doomed his electoral prospects and would have done so regardless of his race or ethnicity.

Racially polarized voting usually damages the prospects of minority candidates, because most voting districts have a white majority. The mere presence of racially polarized voting, however, does not demonstrate *per se* that white voters fail to support minority candidates *because of their race*. Establishing such a proposition requires that potential other (race-neutral) reasons for vote choice be ruled out. Determining with certainty the motives behind voting decisions is difficult and probably impossible without individual interviews or extensive survey research. In the 1990 and 1996 North Carolina Senate races, Gantt enjoyed overwhelming black support, but his white support was short of what he needed to win. White Helms supporters may have had race-neutral reasons for preferring Helms, who had close ties to social and religious conservatives. In North Carolina, as elsewhere in the South, conservative whites outnumber liberal whites (Black & Black, 1987), and many white voters may have preferred Helms because of his more conservative views, not because of his race.

One case in which we can more reasonably suspect racial motives behind racially polarized voting is the 1989 Virginia governor's race. L. Douglas Wilder, a black Democrat and descendant of slaves, faced a white Republican opponent, Marshall Coleman. Preelection polls consistently showed Wilder leading Coleman by 4 to 11 percentage points; yet Wilder won by a far narrower margin, with only 50.1 percent of the vote. The polls tracked opinion right up to Election Day, meaning they should have detected across-time changes in the candidates' relative support.

The most likely explanation for the discrepancy between the preelection poll results and the election outcome is Wilder's race. Some poll respondents (almost certainly, heavily white) probably told the pollster they would support Wilder, but insincerely; in the privacy of the polling booth they voted for Coleman out of discomfort over the prospect of a black governor. Here, hidden prejudices loom large, and race-neutral alternative explanations are less convincing: if perhaps 5 percent of poll respondents who said they would support Wilder later changed their minds in Coleman's favor, why did other polls taken up to Election Day still show Wilder comfortably ahead and not detect this shift?

The claim that these white voters preferred Coleman for a race-neutral reason (such as his conservatism) rather than his race also is unconvincing. Elections commonly involve two candidates of the same race, one relatively more liberal, the other relatively more conservative. But they rarely witness a sudden Election Day shift in the conservative's favor that goes undetected in preelection polls. The Wilder-Coleman election, however, involved a black against a white—a situation ripe not only for racial-bloc voting, but also for some (unknown) fraction of whites to insincerely report their voting intentions so that the white candidate suddenly wins a larger share of the white vote than preelection polls showed. We cannot say we have conclusively ruled out other factors explaining this curious result. However, the strange disconnection between the election outcome and the poll results, and the fact that polls did not reveal it, are entirely consistent with the pattern we would expect if some white respondents told the pollster they would vote for Wilder, only to vote for Coleman instead—and it is hard to conceive of any reason for this other than Wilder's race.

The 1989 Virginia governor's race, moreover, is not alone. In the 1989 New York City mayor's race, David Dinkins, a black, won the election narrowly even though preelection polls showed him leading by 5 to 15 percentage points. Here again, Dinkins's actual victory margin was far less than the polls suggested. In sum, these elections suggest that hidden prejudices may still work against the election of minority candidates in local and statewide races. Although racial stereotypes are commonly attributed to many racial and ethnic minorities, those attached to blacks (including laziness/lack of work ethic, violence, and lack of sexual restraint) are probably more negative overall than those attached to other groups, especially Asian Americans, who as a "model minority" are stereotyped in more positive terms. Thus, black candidates especially face a disadvantage in an election against a white opponent, owing to the widespread nature of racial stereotypes among the white majority, coupled with the especially negative nature of black stereotypes.

Overall, there is evidence suggesting that racial prejudice and stereotyping continue to play a significant role in voting in U.S. elections—both in the voting process, through efforts to suppress voter turnout among minority groups, and in the vote choice exercised by the individual voter, through hidden but electorally potent discomfort among some whites at the prospect that a minority candidate, and especially a black candidate, might win elective office.

CONCLUSION

In this chapter, we have examined both historical and current issues and cases of racial stereotyping, prejudice, and discrimination in political arenas. The issues we have examined include historical legal discrimination, anti-immigration politics, campaign and noncampaign rhetoric, and voting. If politics is related to power and control, American politics cannot be separated from race and ethnicity. There are at least two major contributors to racial and ethnic elements in American politics. One is identity (who we are culturally or racially); the other is contact, which often leads to conflict. Racial identity and contact are interrelated. Based on this, social conflict (including negative stereotypes and prejudice) occurred in the past, continues to occur today, and has notable and wide-ranging consequences in American politics. Politics would have been much simpler if there were just one ethnic or racial group. According to the integrative model of ethnic contact, identity, and conflict (CIC) (Lee, Quinones-Perdomo, & Perdomo, 2003), the seeds of complicated group relations and intergroup conflict (for example, negative attitudes, prejudice, and discrimination) were planted on the day when Europeans came to this land and contacted Native Americans. The arrival of black slaves and Chinese Americans brought here as "coolies" only intensified political conflicts between racial and ethnic groups.

As can be seen in Myrdal's research (1944), Americans have faced an unresolved dilemma that holds true today and tomorrow. On one hand, Americans want to maintain democratic values, human rights, and civil rights. On the other hand, there are realistic conflicts of group interest (in terms of values and political and economic interests)—as seen in contemporary conflicts over language policies and affirmative action.[15] Immigration, racially polarized voting patterns, and events since September 11 further confirm this tension.

Two psychological notes are in order before we conclude. First, past racial appeals in politics have been directed mostly toward the white majority, and have targeted (sought to arouse and exploit hostility toward) black candidates and interests. Any future racial appeals may also target other minority groups: Latinos, Asian/Pacific Americans, Native Americans, and others. Future research should attend to this possibility. Psychologists have demonstrated that people show a common preference for ingroup members (called *ingroup favoritism*), and prejudice against outgroup members, especially during any competition (Brewer, 1979; Lee, McCauley, Moghaddam, & Worchel, 2004). Second, this chapter has considered only *negative* racial stereotypes and their impacts on U.S. politics. This does not mean all stereotypes (racial or nonracial) are negative or inaccurate (Lee, Jussim, & McCauley, 1995). But negative stereotyping probably facilitates racial appeals during political campaigns. Perhaps understanding and appreciating human differences may help us to reduce intergroup conflict and racial appeals, as shown in the "toolbox for change" below. In any event, it is important that covert racial appeals, when made, be exposed publicly. When that happens, covert racial appeals lose their effectiveness, owing to the prevalent "norm of racial equality" in the United States (Mendelberg, 2001).

In sum, hidden prejudices play a central role in American politics. They influence the campaign messages that parties and candidates deliver (by promoting covert racial appeals and racially laden symbolism), and the noncampaign messages provided by elected officials, which

Toolbox for Change

For	Images/perceptions	Strategies for change
Individuals	Learn positive attitudes toward immigrants and minority candidates.	To be exposed to different cultural and racial groups and gain knowledge and information about them.
Community	Be more receptive to immigrants and more aware of and fair-minded to minority candidates.	Help new immigrants to settle into communities; expose and protest racial appeals and discrimination.
Practitioners/ educators	*Campaign managers:* Be aware of covert racial appeals; commit to "fair" (race-neutral) campaign messages and strategies. *Educators/counselors:* Understand and appreciate ethnic and cultural differences by studying stereotypes.	Candidates, activists, and voters should speak out immediately when a racial appeal is made in political campaigns. Educators and practitioners should participate in diversity-related workshops and training in combating racism and discrimination, and interact with different racial and ethnic groups.

at times reveal racial and ethnic stereotypes. Hidden prejudices also affect strategies of voter mobilization and suppression (as shown in racially targeted voter suppression efforts), and voting patterns, especially those of whites, when a white candidate and a minority candidate run against each other.

Though we may not resolve the tension between Americans' support for democratic values and human rights and the realistic group conflicts that underlie racial divisions in society, we are not hopeless or pessimistic about the future. We know there are differences wherever and whenever there are human beings. Over the long term, education, coupled with a commitment to understanding and appreciating differences, may help reduce negative stereotypes, racial prejudice, discrimination, and their consequences in the political and social arenas.

NOTES

1. In 1934, Bilbo won his first Senate race by further ratcheting up his already notable racist rhetoric. He advocated deporting blacks to Africa, called U.S. Representative Claire Booth Luce a "nigger lover" and in 1938 praised Adolf Hitler on the floor of the Senate. In attacking interracial marriage, Bilbo opined that "one drop of Negro blood placed in the veins of the purest Caucasian destroys the inventive genius of his mind and strikes palsied his creative faculty" (Anonymous, 1997).

2. Some of the segregation ordinances were sublimely absurd in their wide scope. In 1922, Mississippi passed a law mandating segregated taxicabs; a 1932 Atlanta, Georgia, ordinance required that black and white baseball teams play at least two blocks apart; Birmingham, Alabama, had a law on the books prohibiting interracial domino playing.

3. In Mississippi, the state in which racially hostile voting practices were most effective in suppressing black registration and voting, only 6.7 percent of blacks, but 69.9 percent of whites, were registered to vote as of March 1965; in Alabama, the corresponding figures were 19.3 percent for blacks and 69.2 percent for whites. Regionwide in 1960, 61 percent of whites were registered to vote, but only 29 percent of blacks were.

4. Antimiscegenation laws were laws banning interracial marriage and/or sexual relations. In *Loving v. Virginia* (1967), the Supreme Court ruled such laws unconstitutional.

5. See Donald P. Baker, "Shame of a nation." *The Washington Post* (2001, March 4), p. W08.

6. The two men charged in Emmett Till's murder were Roy Bryant, the store owner and the husband of the clerk, and J. W. Milam, his brother-in-law. At trial, the prosecution had trouble finding witnesses willing to testify against them. Finally, Emmett's sixty-four-year-old uncle, Mose Wright, stepped forward, and several other blacks joined him in identifying Bryant and Milam as the two men who had kidnapped Emmett. For their own protection, all of them had to be hurried out of the state after their testimony. In his closing statement, the defense lawyer told jurors, "Your fathers will turn over in their graves if [Milam and Bryant are found guilty], and I'm sure that every last Anglo-Saxon one of you has the courage to free these men in the face of that [outside] pressure." The all-white jury then returned not guilty verdicts after deliberating less than an hour.

7. Regarding Smith's work, see Smith (1997).

8. For example, ethnic or nationality-based profiling of people perceived as Arab or Middle Eastern has led airlines to force some such individuals off airplanes even after they cleared stringent security checks. These involuntary removals have been justified, supposedly, because the pilots or other passengers felt uncomfortable flying with someone of Arab or Middle Eastern descent on board. Source: Sasha Polikow-Suransky, "Flying while brown." *The*

American prospect 12(20) (2001, November 19). The federal government itself has been party to some arguably discriminatory actions against Arabs and Middle Easterners. A report from the U.S. Department of Justice's inspector general concluded that the department's roundup of hundreds of illegal immigrants in the months after the September 11 attacks was riddled with "significant problems, that forced many people with no connection to terrorism to languish in jails in unduly harsh conditions." The same report added that FBI officials "'made little attempt to distinguish' between immigrants who had possible ties to terrorism and those swept up by chance in the investigation." Source: Eric Lichtblau, "U.S. report faults the roundup of illegal immigrants after 9/11" (*The New York Times*, 2003, June 3).

9. Lee Atwater, a native South Carolinian and Bush's campaign manager, got his start in politics in the 1970s as an aide to Strom Thurmond, the Dixiecrat-turned Republican who was an early pioneer of implicit racial appeals. Atwater considered Richard Nixon's 1968 "Southern strategy" of appealing to racially resentful white southerners "a blueprint for everything I've done in the South." Early in 1988, Atwater told the press, "The Horton case is one of those gut issues that are values issues, particularly in the South, and if we hammer at these over and over, we are going to win." Source: Andrew Rosenthal, "Foes accuse Bush campaign of inflaming racial tension" (*The New York Times*, 1988, October 24).

10. Barbour also highlighted his opposition to affirmative action and favored a voter identification requirement strongly opposed by black legislators in his state. Barbour's veiled racial messages included not only words but also imagery. During the campaign, Barbour wore on his lapel a pin featuring the Mississippi state flag, which includes the Confederate stars and bars emblem. In Mississippi's 2001 referendum on whether or not to retain the Confederate emblem in the state flag, voters supported keeping the Confederate emblem, 65 percent to 35 percent, in an intensely racially polarized vote. In two 80 percent-black counties, the vote was 83 percent to 17 percent in favor of removing the Confederate insignia; in two 85 percent–white counties, the vote was 90 percent to 10 percent in favor of retaining it.

11. The pejorative and racially loaded term *welfare queen* found its way into national political discourse due to Ronald Reagan's liberal use of the term during his 1976 and 1980 presidential campaigns. In 1976, Reagan often recited the story of a woman from Chicago's south side who was arrested for welfare fraud. "She has eighty names, thirty addresses, twelve Social Security cards, and is collecting veteran's benefits on four nonexisting deceased husbands. And she is collecting Social Security on her cards. She's got Medicaid, is getting food stamps, and she is collecting welfare under each of her names," Reagan said. Variants of the tale had other details, including that she drove a Cadillac to pick up her welfare check, and that she used food stamps to buy vodka. The "welfare queen" Reagan spoke of was a myth,

but it did serve as a lightning rod for white resentments over paying taxes that supported welfare programs that presumably allowed such cheating. The "welfare queen" stereotype centers on a black woman, probably a single mother, who prefers to collect welfare checks rather than work, and who has one or more children born out of wedlock—a toxic stew of noxious white stereotypes of black laziness, sexual promiscuity, illegitimacy, and devil-may-care irresponsibility.

12. In 1948, Strom Thurmond led a walkout from the Democratic Party by white segregationists in the Deep South who bitterly opposed President Harry S. Truman's support of modest racial reform in the United States. The most recalcitrant segregationists in Southern politics—Theophilus Eugene "Bull" Connor of Alabama, Roy V. Harris of Georgia, and Leander Perez of Louisiana—led Thurmond's Dixiecrat Party. On the evening of his nomination for president at a convention in Birmingham, Thurmond's supporters celebrated by lynching President Truman in effigy. During his campaign for president, Thurmond said, "I want to tell you, ladies and gentlemen, that there's not enough troops in the army to force the southern people to break down segregation and admit the Negro race into our theaters, into our swimming pools, into our homes, and into our churches."

13. In 1999, reports surfaced that Lott several times had addressed meetings of the Council of Conservative Citizens (CCC), a group whose bias against blacks and other minorities is scarcely concealed. Lott has been photographed in at least one CCC meeting. The CCC has ties to more openly white supremacist groups, and it inflames racial fears and resentments using issues like black-on-white crime and nonwhite immigration. In addressing a 1992 CCC meeting in Mississippi, Lott commented, "The people in this room stand for the right principles and the right philosophy. Let's take it in the right direction and our children will be the beneficiaries."

14. In the initial 1999 matchup between white Republican Sam Katz and black Democrat John Street, Katz carried 97 percent of the 742 voting divisions with white majorities, while Street carried 98 percent of the 750 voting divisions with black majorities. "The level of racially polarized voting is nowhere as high as it is in Philadelphia," said David Bositis, a scholar with the Joint Center for Political and Economic Studies, an urban affairs think tank in Washington.

15. The recent Supreme Court decisions on affirmative action in public colleges and universities (*Gratz v. Bollinger* and *Grutter v. Bollinger*, both in 2003) will probably only enhance public debates over the value and fairness of race-based affirmative action and the acceptable limits of its application.

REFERENCES

Aguirre, A., Jr., & Turner, J. (2001). *American ethnicity: The dynamics and consequence of discrimination.* New York: McGraw-Hill.

Anonymous. (1997, July–August). Death of a demagogue. *American Heritage*, 99–100.

The Anti-Defamation League. (2004). *Extremism in America: David Duke.* Retrieved July 19, 2004, from www.adl.org/learn/ext_us/duke.asp

Black, M., & Black, E. (1987). *Politics and society in the South.* Cambridge, MA: Harvard University Press.

Brewer, M. B. (1979). Ingroup bias in the minimal intergroup situation: A cognitive-motivational analysis. *Psychological Bulletin, 86,* 307–324.

CNN Crossfire (2002). *Is the U.N. being unfair or does Israel have something to hide? Is privacy dead in public places?* (aired April 30, 2002). Transcript accessed July 20, 2004 at http://www.cnn.com/TRANSCRIPTS/0204/30/cf.00.html

Cao, L., & Novas, H. (1996). *Everything you need to know about Asian American history.* New York: Plume.

Carmines, E., & Stimson, J. (1989). *Issue evolution: Race and the transformation of American politics.* Princeton, NJ: Princeton University Press.

Corrigan, P. W., & Penn, D. L. (1999). Lessons from social psychology on discrediting psychiatric stigma. *American Psychologist, 54,* 765–776.

Corrigan, P. W., Watson, A. C., & Ottati, V. (2003). From whence comes mental illness stigma? *International Journal of Social Psychiatry, 49*(2), 142–157.

Dinnerstein, L., Nichols, R. L., & Reimers, D. M. (1996). *Natives and strangers: A multicultural history of Americans.* New York: Oxford University Press.

Dinnerstein, L., & Reimers, D. M. (1999). *Ethnic Americans: A history of immigration.* New York: Columbia University Press.

Edsall, T., & Edsall, M. (1992). *Chain reaction: The impact of race, rights and taxes on American politics.* New York: W. W. Norton and Company.

Fiske, S. (1998). Stereotyping, prejudice and discrimination. In D. T. Gilbert, S. T. Fiske, & G. Lindzey (Eds.), *Handbook of social psychology* (4th ed., Vol. 2, pp. 357–411). New York: McGraw-Hill.

Fong, T. P., & Shinagawa, L. H. (2000). *Asian Americans: Experiences and perspectives.* Upper Saddle River, NJ: Prentice Hall.

Gilens, M. (1999). *Why Americans hate welfare.* Chicago: University of Chicago Press.

Glaser, J. (1996). *Race, campaign politics and the realignment in the South.* New Haven, CT: Yale University Press.

Greenberg, S. B. (1985, April 15). *Report on Democratic defection.* Washington, DC: The Analysis Group, pp. 13–18, 28.

Hu-DeHart, E. (2000). Rethinking America. In V. Cyrus (Ed.), *Experiencing race, class, and gender in the United States* (pp. 168–171). Mountain View, CA: Mayfield Publishing Company.

Hurwitz, J., & Peffley, M. (1997). Public perceptions of race and crime: The role of racial stereotypes. *American Journal of Political Science, 41*(2), 375–401.

Irish, M. D. (1942, February). The Southern one-party system and national politics. *Journal of Politics, 4*, 80.

Joshi, S. T. (1999). *Documents of American prejudice: An anthology of writings on race from Thomas Jefferson to David Duke.* New York: Basic Books.

Kuklinski, J., Cobb, M., & Gilens, M. (1997). *Racial attitudes and the "New South." Journal of Politics, 59*(2), 323–349.

Kuklinski, J., & Cobb, M. (1998). When white Southerners converse about race. In J. Hurwitz & M. Peffley (Eds.), *Perception and prejudice: race and politics in the United States.* New Haven, CT: Yale University Press.

Lee, Y.-T., Albright, L., & Malloy, T. (2001). Social perception and stereotyping: An interpersonal and intercultural approach. *International Journal of Group Tension, 30*(2), 183–209.

Lee, Y.-T., Jussim, L., & McCauley, C. (1995). *Stereotype accuracy: Toward appreciating group differences.* Washington, DC: American Psychological Association.

Lee, Y.-T., McCauley, C., Moghaddam, F., & Worchel, S. (2004). *The psychology of ethnic and cultural conflict.* Westport, CT: Praeger Publishers.

Lee, Y.-T., McCauley, C., & Draguns, J. (1999). *Personality and person perception across cultures.* Mahwah, NJ: Erlbaum.

Lee, Y.-T., & Ottati, V. (1993). Determinants of ingroup and outgroup perception of heterogeneity: An investigation of Chinese-American stereotypes. *Journal of Cross-Cultural Psychology, 24*, 298–318.

Lee, Y.-T., & Ottati, V. (1995). Perceived ingroup homogeneity as a function of group membership salience and stereotype threat. *Personality and Social Psychology Bulletin, 21*, 612–621.

Lee, Y.-T., & Ottati, V. (2002). Attitudes toward American immigration policy: The role of ingroup-outgroup bias, economic concern, and obedience to law. *Journal of Social Psychology, 142*(5), 617–634.

Lee, Y.-T., Ottati, V., & Hussain, I. (2001). Attitudes toward "illegal" immigration into the U.S.: California Proposition 187. *Hispanic Journal of Behavioral Sciences, 23*(4), 430–443.

Lee, Y.-T., Quinones-Perdomo, J., & Perdomo, E. (2003). An integrative model of ethnic conflict, identity, and conflict (CIC): Application to U.S. immigration and naturalization. *Ethnic Studies Review, 26*, 57–80.

Lee, Y.-T., Takaku, S., Ottati, V., & Yan, G. (2004). Empirical research on perception of terrorism, justice and peace. In Y-T. Lee, C. McCauley, F. Moghaddam, & S. Worchel (Eds.), *The Psychology of Ethnic and Cultural Conflict* (pp. 217–234). Westport, CT: Praeger Publishers.

Lopez, I. F. H. (2002). Racial restrictions in the law of citizenship. In A. A. Kromkowski (Ed.), *Race and ethnic relations* (12th ed., pp. 7–12). Guilford, CT: McGraw-Hill/Dushkin.

Mendelberg, T. (2001). *The race card: Campaign strategy, implicit messages and the norm of equality.* Princeton, NJ: Princeton University Press.

McKinney, J. (2001). Cooksey: Expect racial profiling. *The Advocate* [online edition]. Retrieved July 19, 2004, from members.tripod.com/ocssa/turban.htm

Morrill, J. (2002, December 19). Myrick calls for Sen. Lott to step aside; Ballenger agrees but says he's also had 'segregationist feeling.' *The Charlotte Observer* [online]. Retrieved July 20, 2004, from www.charlotte.com/mld/observer/news/4779957.htm

Morrison, P. (2003, February 28). Two N.C. Republicans draw fire for "outrageous" ethnic comments. *The National Catholic Reporter Online.* Retrieved July 20, 2004, from www.natcath.com/NCR_Online/archives/022803/022803k.htm

Myrdal, G. (1944). *An American dilemma: The Negro problem and modern democracy.* New York: Harper & Row.

Olson, J. (1994). *The psychology of prejudice: Ontario symposium on personality.* Hillsdale, NJ: Erlbaum.

Rico, B. R., & Mano, S. (2001). *American mosaic: Multicultural readings in context.* New York: Houghton Mifflin Company.

Slocum, F. (2001). White racial attitudes and implicit racial appeals: An experimental study of "race coding" in political discourse. *Politics and Policy, 29*(4), 650–669.

Smith, R. M. (1997). *Civic ideals: Conflicting visions of citizenship in U.S. history.* New Haven: Yale University Press.

Southern Education Reporting Service. (1967). A statistical summary, state by state, of school segregation-desegregation in the southern and border area from 1954 to the present. Nashville, TN: Southern Education Reporting Service, pp. 2, 43–44.

Tajfel, H. (1981). *Human groups and social categories.* Cambridge, UK: Cambridge University Press.

Takaki, R. (1989). *Strangers from a different shore: A history of Asian Americans.* Boston, MA: Little Brown.

Tursky, B., Lodge, M., and Reeder, R. (1979). Psychophysical and psychophysiological evaluation of the direction, intensity and meaning of race-related stimuli. *Psychophysiology, 16,* 452–462.

U.S. Report. (1997). Opinion of the Supreme Court, December term, 1956. (Original work published 1856)

Westie, F. R. (1953). A technique for the measurement of race attitudes. *American Sociological Review, 18,* 73–78.

CHAPTER 5

The African Diaspora and Culture-Based Coping Strategies

Edward Stephenson

> Dominating all the complex systems which drive Western societies, white racism singled out Africa and Africans of the Diaspora for a holocaust of five hundred years and more one which shows no sign of letting up. On the eve of the twenty-first century, white racism threatens Black people with continued exploitation, degradation, social confinement, and marginalization and, failing that, extermination.
>
> (Munford, 1996, p. 3)

The problem of the twentieth century, W. E. B. Du Bois (1969) prophetically proclaimed, would be the problem of the color line. As we embark upon a new millennium and witness the technological advances that have represented the hallmark of our civilized progress, we must ask ourselves whether such progress has been accompanied by improvements in our social relations, particularly as this relates to the treatment of racial and cultural minorities. Although such treatment has historically been determined by a host of social and cultural factors, perhaps the most important of these factors is the experience of prejudice and discrimination. Consequently, in determining the relevance of Du Bois's prophetic proclamation to the quality of our social relations, we must then ask ourselves whether racism is a thing of the past. Should we no longer take heed to the cry of the prophets, given that slavery has long ended and the American creed of equality and justice stands at the forefront of the moral and ethical consciousness of most Americans? If on the other hand, racism is indeed alive and well, the relevant question then becomes, how is racism manifested in postmodern, multicultural, and multiethnic America? Are people's en-counters with racism the same for everyone, or are there inter-ethnic variations? How are the various ethnic groups impacted by racism, and in what ways do they cope?

The present chapter attempts to answer the above questions by using the concept of the African Diaspora as a conceptual guide for interpreting and analyzing both inter- and intra-group differences in relation to African American blacks' and West Indians' encounters with racism in the United States. Because ethnic labels such as *black*, *African American*, and *West Indian* are often used interchangeably, it is important that, for the purpose of conceptual clarity, these terms be operationally defined. Thus, *African American*, in the present context, refers to blacks whose heritage is contained within the geo-graphic boundaries of the United States, while *black American* is used as a more all-inclusive concept to refer to both indigenous blacks and those who originated from the West Indies but who presently reside in the United States. Historically, the terms *West Indies* and the *Caribbean* have been used interchangeably, since the West Indies are a group of islands stretching from the north coast of Venezuela to the south coast of Florida, situated in the Caribbean Sea (Gopaul-McNicol, 1993). The term *West Indian* is thus used here to refer to individuals from the Caribbean.

THE AFRICAN DIASPORA AND INTRA-ETHNIC VARIATIONS IN THE EXPERIENCE OF RACISM

The African Diaspora refers to "the global dispersion (voluntary and involuntary) of Africans throughout history; the emergence of a cultural identity abroad based on origin and social condition; and the psychological or physical return to the homeland, Africa" (Harris, 1993, p. 3). As a mode of intellectual inquiry, the African Diaspora concept originated in 1965 when the International Congress of African Historians convened in Tanzania and included in its program a ses-sion titled "The African Abroad or the African Diaspora" (Harris, 1993). Since that time, scholars from various disciplines have con-ducted research about the African Diaspora in Asia, the Americas, and

Europe; thus expanding our understanding of the presence and contributions of people of African descent outside the continent (Harris, 1996).

The concept of the African Diaspora is posited here as a useful conceptual tool discussing intra-ethnic variations in the experience of racism. Not only does the concept acknowledge the shared experience of racism, it more importantly alerts us to the varied nature of this experience and the fact that such variations result from black people having been dislocated and decentered from their core African selves and cultures.

Therefore, when we consider the impact that racism has had on the lives of blacks in the United States, it is important that we keep in mind the heterogeneous nature of the group and, in so doing, make distinctions with regard to their ethnicity. Such interethnic variations have, however, been ignored by researchers, whereby most of the research on blacks in the United States has focused primarily on them while ignoring other Diaspora ethnicities. In concurring with this view, Rogers (2001) asserts the following:

> In much of the influential scholarship on racial and ethnic politics in the United States, there has been a longstanding tendency to treat the Black population as if it were a homogeneous lot. Many studies routinely ignore intra-group differences, tensions, and conflicts within Black politics. Such treatments simplistically assume or imply an undifferentiated Black community bound by common experience and wedded to some unitary vision of a political agenda. (p. 164)

Consequently, even though an extensive body of research attests to blacks' continued exposure to racial discrimination (Kessler, Mickelson, & Williams, 1999) and the deleterious impact that it has on their psychological and physical well-being (Jackson et al., 1996; Salgado de Snyder, 1987; Browman, 1996; Murrag, Khatib & Jackson, 1989; Plummer & Slane, 1996), we however know very little in terms of intra-group and inter-group variations in black people's experience of racism and the differential impact it may have on their lives.

The rapid increase in blacks from Latin America and the West Indies necessitates social scientific inquiry into the ways in which these groups are similar to and different from their black counterparts, particularly regarding their encounters and experiences with racism and prejudice. What is race like in such contexts? How does racism affect such groups, and how do they cope with racism upon migrating to a culture where race is often the "master" status marker that defines and shapes, more than anything else, people's humanity and their relations with each other? Furthermore, do West Indians share the same firm sense of racial identity as blacks, and does this shared identity serve to unite both groups? On the other hand, do ethnic differences between the groups override the influence of racial identity to the point of being responsible for divergences in attitudes and behaviors? That is, is ethnicity superordinate to race in structuring the nature of black and West Indian social relations?

These are some of the questions that will be addressed in subsequent sections of this analysis. While racism continues to be an integral part of the black experience, people are affected differently depending on the particular type of racism involved. Thus, before proceeding to discuss intra-group variations in the experience of racism, we will examine the various types of racism, doing so in a manner that considers the relevance that these typologies have for describing the experiences of not only blacks but West Indians as well.

TYPOLOGY OF RACISM: INDIVIDUAL, INSTITUTIONAL, AND CULTURAL

Perhaps the most comprehensive typology of racism to have been developed thus far is that offered by Jones (1991), whose conceptualization includes three dimensions: individual, institutional, and cultural. The first type, individual racism, refers to "the belief that black people as a group are inferior to whites because of physical (that is, genotypical and phenotypical) traits. He or she [the black individual] furthermore believes that these physical traits are determinants of social behavior and of moral and intellectual qualities, and ultimately presumes that this inferiority is a legitimate basis for that group's inferior social treatment" (Jones, 1998, p. 417). Because of being experienced on a personal level, individual racism may be more easily recognizable than the other two forms. For instance, many blacks have had the experience of walking into a store and being perceived with suspicion or ignored while standing in line. Examples such as these represent the more subtle forms of individual racism, what Pierce (1995) refers to as "micro-aggressions." Pierce notes that an individual may have numerous encounters of this type, most of which, while being overlooked, may contribute to one's overall level of stress. The pervasive nature of individual racism is reflected in a study by Landrine and Klonoff (1996), who found that 98 percent of the 153 people who participated in their study reported experiences with racial discrimination in the previous year. More significant, one third of the sample reported instances of the more overt forms of individual racism, including being hit, shoved, picked on, and threatened with harm. While West Indians share with blacks the experience of individual racism, there is, however, a difference in terms of the degree and severity of this experience. Blacks, unlike West Indians, were exposed to the harsher and more blatant forms of American racism that existed prior to the 1960s civil rights era. These earlier forms of racism were more visible and were expressed more openly and with greater animosity than they are today. Such "old-fashioned" or "dominative" (Kovel, 1970) forms of racism manifested themselves in such behavior as lynching and were institutionalized in the forms of slavery, segregation, and in social norms and customs. Such overt forms of individual racism were a product of the white supremacist mind-set that characterized the period, a mind-set in which blacks were perceived in negative stereotypical terms: as hyperaggressive, hypersexual, superstitious, lazy, happy-go-lucky, ignorant, and musical. Such stereotypical views were the basis of white contempt for blacks and resulted in a desire to maintain social distance (Bogardus, 1925). It is no wonder then, that given their historical legacy of racism, some blacks possess a large degree of race-based hostility and resentment toward white Americans. Furthermore, perhaps it is because of not sharing in this historical legacy that West Indians have traditionally been known to have more optimal and harmonious relations with whites compared to their black counterparts.

The second form of racism put forth by Jones (1997) is institutional racism: policies and procedures that are used to exclude blacks from full participation in the institutional spheres of life. An example of institutional racism is the use of culturally biased assessment procedures that result in blacks having more negative outcomes compared to their white counterparts. For instance, in the mental health area, according to Sue and Sue (1999), white therapists are inclined to assess black clients as nonverbal, paranoid, angry, and most likely to have character disorders or to be schizophrenic. In addition, intelligence tests have often been used to argue that blacks are intellectually inferior to whites (Jensen, 1969; Herrnstein & Murray, 1994).

While both West Indians and blacks are presently exposed to institutional discrimination in various spheres of life—education, media, occupation, etc.—the impact that such discrimination has in shaping attitudes and behavior is mediated by the historical nature of their encounters. It is indeed the case that blacks have had a longer history of being excluded from equal participation in American life than the relatively recent West Indian arrivals. By virtue of their immigrant status, West Indians were not subjected to the dehumanizing effects of legally mandated segregation. They therefore did not have to attend segregated schools, drink at separate water fountains, sit in the back of the bus, or live in particular neighborhoods as did blacks. It is perhaps because of not having such experiences that West Indians tend to be more optimistic in their relations with whites and that they feel that their aspirations are ultimately realizable. For blacks, on the other hand, their historical experience of institutionalized discrimination may be responsible for inculcating within the group a sense of limited social mobility, truncated aspirations, and an overall negative outlook on their perceived social and economic possibilities.

The last form of racism, cultural racism, is defined as "the individual and institutional expressions of the superiority of one race's cultural heritage over that of another race" (Jones, 1998, p. 15). Cultural racism, that which is ultimately responsible for devaluing various aspects of black culture, is pervasive in its influence, affecting all aspects of life. According to Ramseur (1998), three major themes emerge in the literature on cultural racism: (1) blacks as unattractive and not socially valuable, (2) blacks as unable to be effective and to achieve in the world, and (3) blacks as characterized by identification-based stereotypes: being sexually and aggressively impulsive and uncontrolled.

While being exposed to cultural racism, the cultural background of West Indians mediates and restructures their experience of such forms of racism. West Indians are often distinguished from blacks on the basis of culture. While American blacks are generally perceived as inferior cultural entities, West Indians are perceived in a more positive light by virtue of their cultural attributes. It is indeed the case that in explaining the differences that exist between themselves and blacks, West Indians often point to their perceived cultural superiority.

Consequently, West Indians attribute their relative success in American society to such cultural attributes as hard work, high motivation and perseverance, and the ability to delay gratification, virtues that are thought to be absent in their black counterparts. One consequence of this perceived cultural difference is the tendency among some West Indians to distance themselves from blacks. As Waters (2001) puts it, "Indeed, one finds cultural distancing from black Americans among the immigrants we interviewed. They argued that West Indians merited inclusion in American society because of their strong work ethic, the value they placed on education, and their lack of pathological behaviors. By asserting a cultural identity as immigrants and as members of a model minority, West Indians make a case for cultural inclusion in American society" (p. 212).

A CLOSER LOOK AT INTRA-GROUP VARIATIONS IN THE RACISM EXPERIENCE

The overriding themes of this chapter are that black people's encounters with racism, the impact it has on their lives, and the manner in which they cope are determined in part by their particular ethnic backgrounds. Blacks in the United States constitute a heterogeneous group, many of whom are West Indian or from West Indian backgrounds. West Indians are, themselves, a heterogeneous group whose customs have been influenced by African, Spanish, British, French, Dutch, Asian, and American cultures. With the exceptions of Trinidad and Guyana, people of African heritage make up 90 percent of the population in most of the region's islands. European and American whites make up about 5 percent, and Chinese and biracial individuals make up the remaining 5 percent (Gopaul-McNicol, 1993). Demographically, in 1990 there were over one million foreign-born people residing in the United States who identified themselves as black with Caribbean origin. Approximately 230,000 Haitians and 334,000 Jamaicans composed the majority of non-Latino Caribbean black immigrants (U.S. Bureau of the Census, 1993), who were concentrated in a few states, including 50 percent in New York and 17 percent in Florida.

FACTORS RESPONSIBLE FOR THE DIFFERENT PERCEPTIONS OF RACE AND RACISM BETWEEN BLACKS AND WEST INDIANS

West Indians' De-Emphasis of Race

In addressing the West Indians' encounter with racism and the impact that it has on their lives, it is important that their ethnic and racial statuses be considered, particularly in terms of how the status characteristics distinguish them from their black counterparts. There are identifiable differences between West Indians and blacks in their perceptions of race and racism. A dominant perception of West Indians regarding race is that while racism exists to a certain degree in the United States, it is not a problem in the West Indies, this being attributable to a number of factors. First, there are demographics: the fact that in many West Indian societies, black members constitute the majority of the population and occupy a variety of roles. Vickerman (1999) contends that blacks' occupation of high-status roles is commonplace and understandable. Race is detached from notions of success and failure, because within the same race one may observe many individuals covering a full spectrum of social possibilities. Unlike in the United States, a correlation is not routinely made between race and success: failure is not viewed as "black," and success is not viewed as "white." In the United States, however, race is very much seen as a determinant of success. With power resting in the hands of the white majority, racial discrimination is pervasive and real in its effects, penetrating all aspects of life—institutional, cultural, and interpersonal.

A second factor responsible for the lack of importance West Indians place on race is ideology. Within many West Indian societies, the prevailing ideology is multiracialism, which is often interpreted to mean nonracialism: the belief that everyone is the same regardless of race and that race makes no difference in the scheme of social relations. In Jamaica, the ideology of nonracialism has achieved penetrating power through institutionalization by the educational and political systems. The former has tried to substitute alternative criteria for achieving upward mobility. It has included the following core assumptions: (1) upward mobility is possible for all regardless of race, (2) education is the means of achieving this, (3) because the system is meritocratic, whether individuals rise or fall depends on how hard they work, and (4) as more than mere acquisition of knowledge, "education" means adhering to such values as law and order and speaking "properly" (that is, standard English) (Vickerman, 1999).

A third factor that explains the different perceptions that West Indians and American blacks have regarding the importance of race is the culture associated with immigration. The notion of voluntary and involuntary minorities is one that was originally made by Ogbu (1990). Voluntary minorities have chosen to move to a society to improve their well-being, while involuntary minorities were initially brought into the society through slavery, conquest, and colonization. This distinction becomes crucial, Ogbu argues, in explaining the different responses that both groups have toward the experiences of racism and discrimination. Specifically, because they use their home country and culture as a frame of reference, voluntary immigrants do not react to discrimination in the same manner as involuntary minorities, thinking that it is something that they can overcome. Consequently, immigrants have a more positive view of white Americans and their institutions than do blacks.

Involuntary minorities, because of not having a homeland with which to compare their current treatment nor to root their identities in, tend not to see discrimination against them as a temporary barrier to be overcome. Instead, recognizing that they belong to a disparaged minority, they compare their situation with that of their white counterparts. The prejudice against them seems permanent and institutionalized, leading involuntary minorities to conclude that solidarity and challenges to the rules of the dominant society are the only ways to improve their situation, this manifesting itself in what Ogbu terms "oppositional identities" (Waters, 1999). These oppositional identities mean that involuntary minorities come to define themselves in terms of their opposition to the dominant group. For blacks in America, Ogbu (1990) asserts, the very meaning of being black involves not being white. A strong value is placed on solidarity and opposition to the rules perceived as being against them; when a member of the group is seen as cooperating with the dominant society's institutions, his very identity is called into question.

THE IMPORTANCE OF RACIAL IDENTITY

One of the most useful theoretical constructs that we may use to describe the different experiences of race between American blacks and West Indians is that of racial identity. The development of racial identity, in terms of how it has been conceptualized, is thought to occur in a stage-wise fashion. While several models of racial identity now exist, one of the earliest of these models is the negrescence model of Cross, Parham, and Helms (1998), which consists of five stages: preencounter, encounter, immersion-emersion, internalization, and internalization commitment. In the preencounter stage, the individual views the world from a white frame of reference and behaves in ways that devalue or deny his or her blackness. In the encounter stage, the individual experiences events that challenge his or her previous mode of thinking. For instance, a black person who views his or her race as not important and wishes to be accepted just as a human being is denied access to living in an exclusive neighborhood because of skin color. In the third stage, immersion-emersion, the individual withdraws from the dominant culture and immerses himself or herself in black culture. Black pride begins to develop, but internalization toward one's own blackness is minimal. The fourth stage, internalization, is characterized by inner security as conflicts between old and new identities are resolved. Global antiwhite feelings subside as the person becomes more flexible, more tolerant, and more bicultural.

The manner in which West Indian and American blacks negotiate the above stages depends on a number of factors, one of which is the manner in which identity is constructed. American blacks have traditionally adhered to the "one-drop" rule in their construction of race. That is, they have defined themselves as either black or white. Thus, while a light-skinned black person is seen as black here in the United States, in the West Indies, he or she may be seen as "West Indian white." West Indians, therefore, define race broadly enough to give the individual some latitude for negotiating identity. Color distinctions range from dark-skinned African black at one end of the spectrum to light-skinned European white at the other, with many gradations in between. Thus, phenotypically light-skinned persons who migrate from the West Indies and who are suddenly told that they are black because American society does not recognize the existence of physically intermediate positions, find themselves in a dilemma (Gopaul-McNicol, 1993).

Many West Indians, both phenotypically black and white, tend to discover race upon entry into the United States. Most come with an absence of racial awareness and may be thus characterized as being at the preencounter stage of development. Predictably, such West Indians may attempt to assimilate into white society while denying their blackness.

Moreover, they may attempt to distance themselves from other American blacks to avoid the imposition of a more restrictive and less affirming identity. This was confirmed in a study by Waters (1999), who found that many of her West Indian respondents adopted a very strong ethnic identity, which involved distancing themselves from American blacks. These individuals tended to agree with parental judgments that there were strong differences between Americans and West Indians. This often involved a stance that West Indians were superior to American blacks in their behavior and attitudes. The fact that Jamaicans and other West Indians claim to have discovered their "blackness" only after migrating to America appears puzzling, but only until it is realized that they are referring to the social meanings attributed to skin color, rather than skin color itself. As Vickerman (1999) explains it,

These social meanings differ significantly between the West Indies and the United States. In America, Blackness signifies a whole continuum of negative attributes, ranging from low intelligence to criminality. In the West Indies, negative attributes have, also, long been attached to Black skin, but significantly, these have tended to be less all pervading and have not acted as an absolute bar to upward mobility. Because of this relative difference, Black West Indian immigrants can, in migrating, discover the full implications of anti-black stereotyping. They learn what it means to be Black because in the transition from one country to another, the social expectations of those having African ancestry and/ or Black skin become much more constrained. (p. 26)

In many instances, continued exposure to racial experiences causes many West Indians to enter the encounter stage of racial identity. By this, one means that West Indians (1) come to understand that race permeates all facets of American life, (2) expect to have unpleasant encounters because of race, and (3) often become pessimistic that the United States will become "color-blind" anytime soon (Vickerman, 1999). One of the major factors in the transition that West Indians make to the encounter and immersion stages of racial identity centers on their experiences of interpersonal racism. Because of such experiences, their openness and willingness to respond to whites as individuals eventually erode. As Waters (1999) says, "The suspicion that any individual white might treat one badly because of skin color begins to shape every encounter between black and white. Interpersonal racism ultimately undermines the ability of blacks and whites to ever forget race. The ghost of past bad encounters influences current encounters. The immigrant learns to expect race to permeate every potential encounter with a white American" (p. 169). In addition to encounters with interpersonal racism, West Indians have also been subjected to institutional racism, including residential segregation. For instance, in studying West Indians in New York, Crowder (1999) found that these West Indians, in being denied access to white neighborhoods, were concentrated in largely black tracts within the metropolitan area.

In being subjected to such forms of discrimination, there may be a greater tendency for West Indians to identify and bond with their black counterparts. In discussing these black-identified West Indians, Waters (1999) suggests that they do not see their ethnic identities as important to their self-image. When their parents and friends criticized American blacks, these individuals disagreed. They instead tended to downplay an identity as Jamaican or Trinidadian and described themselves as American.

Finally, there are some West Indians who adopt more of an immigrant attitude toward their identities than either their black-identified or ethnic-identified counterparts do. These individuals have strong identities as Jamaican or Trinidadian but do not distance themselves from American blacks. Instead, their identities are strongly linked to their experiences in the islands, and they do not worry about how they are seen by other Americans, white or black (Waters, 1999).

COPING WITH PERCEIVED RACISM: THE ROLES OF CULTURAL RESOURCES AND ADAPTIVE BEHAVIORS

Even though there is a growing body of knowledge that informs us of racism's effects, we know very little about how blacks and other minorities cope with racism (Clark, Anderson, Clark, & Williams, 1999). The particular style with which blacks cope with racism depends on the particular context in which it occurred (Feagin, 1991). For example, racial hostility encountered in the street is most likely met with withdrawal, resigned acceptance, or verbal retort. In situations in which blacks experience racism in public accommodations, the response is generally verbal counterattack or feigned acceptance.

West Indians, like their American black counterparts, utilize a range of strategies to deal with racism, the most important of these being an increasing consciousness of race. In his study of West Indians in the United States, Vickerman (1999) described the types of racial encounters and coping strategies used by West Indians in dealing with racism. Vickerman describes four types. The first are confrontation-situations in which racial agents approach West Indians in an overt, aggressive manner. The latter perceive this to be the case and respond in kind. Examples include situations in which West Indians perceive themselves as being physically attacked, threatened, or insulted. Assertion, the second type, involves situations in which racial agents, while not approaching West Indians in an overt way, nevertheless affect them adversely because of their race or ethnicity. West Indians perceive these situations in a negative manner and act assertively. Examples include situations in which racial agents (usually whites) refuse to serve West Indians or to promote them on the job. The third type is resignation. This is similar to assertion in that racial agents do not overtly approach West Indians but, nevertheless, affect them negatively. The latter, while understanding this, nevertheless choose to avoid confrontation. A preeminent example of this are situations where whites deliberately avoid blacks in public. The final category, pragmatism, describes situations in which racial agents approach West Indians aggressively, but the latter, fearing the consequences of a similar response, opt for a subdued reply. Encounters with the police are the main examples of this type of situation (Vickerman, 1999).

One of the most dominant and mutually shared strategies used by American blacks and West Indians in coping with discrimination is the tendency to minimize their personal experience of discrimination.

In elaborating on the use of such a coping strategy by second-generation West Indians, Bashi Bobb and Clarke (2001) contend,

> Second-generation West Indians seemed to be well aware of racism's existence and unanimously declared it to be a big problem for Blacks, detailing the way it negatively affects the level and shape of Blacks' participation in economic and social life. However, they varied as to whether they felt it had affected them personally. While some felt that they had been treated unfairly by the system in general or by particular White persons, others felt that they had not encountered unfair treatment. Still others thought that, although they had encountered racism, they were able to ignore, circumvent, or counteract the expected negative consequences. (pp. 225–226)

The tendency to minimize one's personal experience of discrimination is not unique to West Indians but rather is a phenomenon that applies to minorities in general. Known as the "person-group discrimination discrepancy phenomenon" (Taylor, Wright, Moghaddam, & Lalonde, 1990), such behavior may be adaptive in terms of bestowing certain psychological benefits for the individual. This was demonstrated by Ruggiero and Taylor (1997), who found that when blacks attributed negative events to discrimination directed at them personally, these attributions resulted not only in a loss of self-esteem but also a loss of perceived control over personal events.

While some individuals tend to minimize the experience of discrimination, there are others for whom discrimination is perceived as an integral part of their lives. What are the factors that determine individual differences in people's perceptions of discrimination? One factor is the individuals' level of identification with groups (Crocker & Major, 1989). In exploring this idea in relation to blacks, Shelton and Sellers (2003) found that group members for whom race was a central component of their identity were more likely to attribute an ambiguous discriminatory event to race than were blacks for whom race was a less central component of their identity.

Although there exist similarities in how both West Indians and blacks cope with racism, there are differences that are worth noting. One major difference is the way identity is constructed and expressed. For West Indians, the transnational dimensions of their identity (characterized by the belief that returning home is always an open and viable possibility) allow them to see their experience of discrimination as temporary and one from which they can always escape. Rogers (2001) describes this exit option available to West Indian immigrants:

> Afro-Caribbean immigrants have an exit option for responding to American racism. If the immigrants find their mobility blocked by insuperable racial barriers, they will likely maintain their transnational attachments and keep the "myth of return" alive. In such instances the myth of return becomes an option for escape or exit, which coincidentally may dampen the immigrants' interest in political participation in general, or radical political action or systemic reform more specifically. Rather than make costly political demands for reform, the immigrants can simply exit the political system. (p. 183)

In the second instance, West Indians have the option of constructing their ethnic identity in a manner that emphasizes their unique West Indian cultural orientation, one that makes them visibly different from their black counterparts. In fact, those who construct their identity this way tend to distance themselves from blacks so as to avoid racial stigmatization (Reid, 1969; Bryce-Laporte, 1972; Waters, 1999).

THE CONCEPT OF PROACTIVE COPING

When applied to blacks in the Diaspora, the concept of coping may best be considered proactive in nature. That is, coping not only involves protecting oneself from the negative effects of perceived racism; but in a proactive sense also involves utilizing one's creative and productive capacity to transcend oppressive circumstances and, in doing so, to realize one's potential as a complete and whole human being.

The African Diaspora model presented here assumes that the development of proactive coping competencies is based on the degree to which one's self-orientation is grounded in and affirms an African-centered cultural orientation. As Kambon (1998) describes it, ". . . for African people, our psychological-spiritual health, our energy and our strength comes from our cultural foundation; our customs and practices which symbolize and reaffirm our ancestral linkage . . . hence, African mental health depends on our closeness to or the continuity with what we Africans maintain to our cultural origins . . ." (p. 47).

What this suggests, therefore, is that when we consider the adaptive and proactive behaviors used by blacks and West Indians in coping with racism and other negative life events, perhaps the best place to look is in the culture. Contained within culture are "cultural resources": those resources that facilitate and contribute to the survival of the group. An important cultural resource for most cultural minorities, blacks and West Indians in particular, is their worldview—values and beliefs that, among other things, give meaning to and determine the manner in which they define themselves in relationship to their world. The adherence of black youth to a particular worldview or to certain cultural orientations may contribute to their level of vulnerability and/or resistance to race-related sources of stress, such as discrimination (Harrell, 2000).

THE AFRICAN-CENTERED WORLDVIEW AS THE BASIS OF PROACTIVE COPING AMONG AFRICAN AMERICANS AND WEST INDIANS

The major components of an African-centered worldview have been described by Myers (1987) as constituting the deeper dimensions of culture, the dimensions of which include the following: ontology, axiology, and epistemology. Ontology is concerned with the manner in which reality is constituted. Within African ontology, the self is conceived as a spiritual entity or essence. Parham (2002) articulates this point quite succinctly: "Self as essence refers to the ontological belief among African people that the fundamental basis of human beingness is spirit. What makes one a human being is the presence of a spirit-based essence. One form of this spirit essence, referred to as the soul, is thought to be the spark of the divine, God" (p. 79). Religion has historically played an important role in the lives of Africans (Taylor, Thornton, & Chatters, 1987; Browman, 1996). The baseline rates of religious involvement for blacks are generally higher than those of the general population. For example, blacks have been found to (a) report higher levels of attendance at religious services than whites, (b) read more religious materials and monitor religious broadcasts more than whites, and (c) seek spiritual comfort through religion more so than whites (Chatters, Taylor, & Lincoln, 1999). Moreover, because of its significance with the broader black culture, religion may serve as an effective coping mechanism, as some studies have shown (Christian & Barbarin, 2001).

For instance, in an earlier study, Browman (1985) examined coping resources among black fathers and found that religious orientation had a much stronger positive effect on the level of life happiness among black fathers than did family cohesion or any other informal resource investigated. Some researchers have found that religious affiliation and frequency of spiritual practice positively affected black students' adjustment to college; higher levels of adjustment then contributed to better academic success. For example, Neighbors, Jackson, Browman, and Gurin (1983) found prayer to be the most common coping response to worries or stressful episodes for blacks. In particular, black women have been found to use prayer in response to physical health as well as interpersonal, emotional, and death problems (Browman, 1996).

A second dimension of worldview is axiology: those things that are most valued within a culture. Within an African-centered framework, what is most valued is the extended self or tribe that operates under rules geared toward collective survival. Family is thus conceptualized beyond the nuclear family and encompasses distant relatives and "fictive kin," or members who are not blood relatives. Family values among blacks include a strong sense of responsibility for each other, respect for elders, sharing material needs, and caring for each other (Billingsley, 1992). These adaptive behaviors are learned within the context of the family. Family, in addition, has been found to be an effective means of coping with negative life events, such as domestic violence (Coley & Beckett, 1988).

One of the adaptive behaviors that is learned within the family context and that serves as an important cultural resource in coping with racism is that of racial socialization: "What Black parents communicate to Black children about what it means to be a Black American, what they may expect from Black and white persons, how to cope with it [racism and discrimination], and whether or not the disparaging messages of the broader culture are true" (Green, 1990, p. 209). Racial socialization has been found to be an effective means by which blacks cope with acculturative stress (Thompson, Anderson, & Bakeman, 2000). Needed, however, are studies that examine the role that racial socialization plays in coping with perceived racism and discrimination.

As with blacks, family for West Indians is also an important cultural resource used in coping with perceived discrimination. West Indian family has historically served as the primary social unit and central survival strategy for its members. Family survival depends on a social network that exists both in the United States as well as on the island of origin. Relatives help provide financial assistance that allows the individual to migrate as well as care for his or her children while they are away. Upon arrival, family members serve as an important mechanism in providing financial, emotional, and social support, thus easing the stress of migration (Basch, 2001).

A third dimension of worldview is epistemology, the basis upon which knowledge is derived. Within an African-centered epistemology, emphasis is placed on self-knowledge as the primary means of knowing. It is assumed that the self is a microcosm of the external reality, and we thus come to know the world by first knowing the self. What this suggests is that one of the ways that blacks may cope with racism is by coming to know themselves and their culture. Knowledge of culture, furthermore, "grounds" the individual within the group and contributes to developing a positive group identity. This group-derived ego strength can then mediate against assaults on the self from the wider society.

The tendency for blacks to be grounded in their culture and to affirm themselves may best be operationalized within the theoretical framework of "African self-consciousness" (Baldwin & Bell, 1985). African self-consciousness (ASC) is attitudes and behaviors that comprise four attitude-behavior dimensions: (a) awareness-recognition, which affirms black identity and African cultural heritage; (b) establishment of survival priorities, which recognizes survival of blacks as a priority and values the role institutions play in achieving that; (c) self-knowledge affirmation, which supports active participation in behaviors that promote the survival and liberation of black people and active defense of their dignity and integrity; and (d) resistance to oppression, which recognizes racial oppression as an obstacle to meeting the action goals described above. African self-consciousness, because of its potential for enhancing self-esteem, may serve as a valuable mechanism for coping with discrimination. The ASC is believed to be responsive to affirmative cultural experiences. That is, blacks from more African-affirming environments will have higher ASC scores. Correlational research shows a relationship between subjects' ASC scores and their parents' membership in black organizations (Baldwin, Brown, & Rackley, 1991), Afrocentric values in heterosexual relationships (Bell, Bouie, & Baldwin, 1990), and attendance at a historically black institution (Baldwin, Duncan, & Bell, 1987).

CONCLUSION

Racism will only be eliminated through the development and enactment of comprehensive policies that center around both attitudinal

Toolbox for Change

For	Images/perceptions	Strategies for change
Individual	Negative intragroup and intergroup racial and ethnic self-perceptions.	Development of positive racial and ethnic identities through critical self-inquiry and cultural affirmation.
	Cultural encapsulation: the inability to see beyond the confines of one's own culture.	Development of intercultural understanding, particularly those dimensions that are shared by American blacks and West Indians.
	Sociopolitical blindness: lack of awareness and understanding of the dynamics of prejudice and discrimination.	Development of political awareness: understanding the dynamics of prejudice and discrimination and how one is affected by such forces.
	Conflicting, antagonistic, stereotypic, and ethnocentric attitudes and behaviors between West Indians and American blacks.	Diversity training that emphasizes the commonalities in the cultural and social experiences among American blacks and West Indians.
Community	Negative racial and ethnic images projected by the media.	Organized community campaigns aimed at ensuring media accountability.
	Conflicting social relations between American blacks and West Indians.	Community events, particularly of a cultural nature in which conflicting groups come together under conditions of (a) equal status, (b) superordinate goals, and (c) the sanction of authority.

For	Images/perceptions	Strategies for change
Practitioners/ educators	Cultural incompetence: lack of knowledge of how culture shapes attitudes and behavior.	The development of cultural competence: an awareness, knowledge, and skill in integrating cultural factors into one's practice. For instance, having knowledge of one's own culture as well as the culture of another. In the case of American blacks and West Indians, it involves having knowledge of the shared cultural and historical experiences of both groups. Competence also includes both groups being aware of their own biases and prejudices in relation to the other. Finally, competence involves having the skill to participate effectively in productive intercultural relations.
	Ineffective coping strategies	The development of proactive, culture-based coping strategies that include the use of spirituality, family, community, and knowledge of self and culture.

and structural changes. In the first instance, efforts should be made to change the racial attitudes of white Americans. This involves enhancing their levels of social awareness in a manner that facilitates growth and development of their racial and ethnic identities.

Structural changes involve addressing the various sources of economic and cultural inequality in American life, particularly its urban centers, where a large number of American blacks and West Indian blacks reside. In discussing the nature of this inequality as it applies to West Indian immigrants, Waters (2001) contends, "The erosion of first generation optimism and ambition that occurs in the second generation could be stopped if job opportunities were more plentiful, inner city schools were nurturing and safer. Decent jobs, effective schools, and safe streets are not immigrant-oriented or race-based policies. They are universal policies that would benefit all urban residents. . . . Policies that benefit immigrants would be policies that benefit all Americans" (p. 209).

Structural inequalities may also be addressed through policies that ensure that reparations be made for past and continuing injustices. In *Race and Reparations: A Black Perspective for the 21st Century*, Munford (1996) describes his vision of reparation. He writes, "I envisage large scale reparations programs transferring the capital to fuel black corporate ownership, combined with comprehensive affirmative action, parity, minority set-asides, as well as race-conscious quotas" (p. 430).

The responsibility for change also resides among blacks themselves. Black Americans and West Indians are confronted with the challenge of developing positive and constructive interethnic relations. This is only possible by each group coming to know the other and, in so doing, affirming those things that they share as Diaspora people while respecting those things that are sources of difference. Last, change also involves both groups developing positive racial identities characterized by an enduring sense of love and respect for self and each other.

REFERENCES

Baldwin, J. A., & Bell, Y. R. (1985). The African self-consciousness scale: An Africentric personality questionnaire. *The Western Journal of Black Studies, 9*, 61–68.

Baldwin, J., Brown, R., & Rackley, R. (1991). Some socio-behavioral correlates of African self-consciousness in African-American college students. *Journal of Black Psychology, 17*, 1–17.

Baldwin, J., Duncan, J., & Bell, R. (1987). Assessment of African self-consciousness among students from two college environments. *Journal of Black Psychology, 13*, 27–41.

Basch, L. (2001). Transnational social relations and the politics of national identity: An eastern Caribbean case study. In N. Foner (Ed.), *Islands in the city: West Indian migration to New York*. New York: University of California Press.

Bashi Bobb, V., & Clarke, A. (2001). Experiencing success: Structuring the perception of opportunities for West Indians. In N. Foner (Ed.), *Islands in the city: West Indian migration to New York.* New York: University of California Press.

Bell, Y. R., Bouie, C. L., & Baldwin, J. A. (1990). Africentric cultural consciousness and African-American male-female relationships. *Journal of Black Studies, 21,* 162–189.

Billingsley, A. (1992). *Climbing Jacob's ladder: The enduring legacy of African American families.* New York: Simon and Schuster.

Bogardus, E. S. (1925). Measuring social distance. *Journal of Applied Sociology, 9,* 299–308.

Browman, C. L. (1996). The health consequences of racial discrimination: A study of African Americans. *Ethnicity and Disease, 6,* 148–153.

Browman, P. (1985). Black fathers and the provider role: Role strain, informal coping resources and life happiness. In A. W. Boykin (Ed.), *Empirical research in black psychology* (pp. 9–19). Washington, DC: National Institute for Mental Health.

Bryce-Laporte, R. (1972). Black immigrants: The experience of invisibility and inequality. *Journal of Black Studies, 3,* 29–56.

Chatters, L., Taylor, R., & Lincoln, K. (1999). African American religious participation: A multi-sample comparison. *Journal of the Scientific Study of Religion, 38,* 132–145.

Christian, M. D., & Barbarin, O. A. (2001). Cultural resources and psychological adjustment of African American children: Effects of spirituality and racial attribution. *Journal of Psychology, 27,* 43–63.

Clark, R., Anderson, N., Clark, V., & Williams, D. (1999). Racism as a stressor for African Americans. *American Psychologist, 54,* 805–816.

Coley, S., & Beckett, J. (1988). Black battered women: Practice issues. *Social Casework, 69,* 483–490.

Crocker, J., & Major, B. (1989). Social stigma and self-esteem: The protective function. *Psychological Review, 96,* 608–630.

Cross, W. E., Parham, T. A., & Helms, J. E. (1998). Negrescence revisited: Theory and research. In R. Jones (Ed.), *African American identity development.* Berkeley, CA: Cobb & Henry Publishers.

Crowder, K. (1999). Residential segregation of West Indians in the New York/New Jersey metropolitan area: The roles of race and ethnicity. *International Migration Review, 33,* 79–113.

Du Bois, W. E. B. (1969). *The souls of black folk.* New York: New American Library. (Original work published 1903)

Feagin, J. R. (1991). The continuing significance of race: Anti-black discrimination in public places. *American Sociological Review, 56,* 101–116.

Gopaul-McNicol, S.-A. (1993). *Working with West Indian families.* New York: The Guilford Press.

Green, B. A. (1990). The role of African American mothers in the socialization of African American children. *Women and Therapy, 10,* 205–225.

Harrell, S. P. (2000). A multidimensional conceptualization of racism-related stress: Implications for the well-being of people of color. *American Journal of Orthopsychiatry, 70*(1), 42–57.

Harris, J. (1993). *Global dimensions of the African diaspora*. Washington, DC: Howard University Press.

Harris, J. (1996). The dynamics of the global diaspora. In J. Alusine & S. Maizlish (Eds.), *The African Diaspora*. Texas A&M University Press.

Herrnstein, R., & Murray, C. (1994). *The bell curve: Intelligence and class structure in American life*. New York: Free Press.

Jackson, J. S., Brown, T. N., Williams, D. R., Torres, M., Sellers, S., & Brown, K. (1996). Racism and the physical and mental health status of African Americans: A thirteen year national panel study. *Ethnicity and Disease, 6*, 132–147.

Jensen, A. (1969). How much can we boost IQ and achievement? *Harvard Educational Review, 39*, 1–123.

Jones, A. (1991). Psychological functioning in African Americans: A conceptual guide for use in psychotherapy. In R. Jones (Ed.), *Black psychology*, 3rd ed. Berkeley, CA: Cobb and Henry.

Jones, R., ed. (1998). *African American mental health: Theory, research and intervention*. Hampton, VA: Cobb and Henry Publishers.

Kambon, K. (1998). An African-centered paradigm for understanding the mental health of Africans in America. In R. Jones (Ed.), *African American mental health: Theory, research and intervention*. Hampton, VA: Cobb and Henry Publishers.

Kessler, R., Mickelson, K., & Williams, D. (1999). The prevalence, distribution, and mental health correlates of perceived discrimination in the United States. *Journal of Health and Social Behavior, 40*, 208–230.

Kovel, J. (1970). *White racism: A psychohistory*. New York: Random House.

Landrine, H., & Klonoff, E. A. (1996). *African American acculturation: Deconstructing race and reviving culture*. Thousand Oaks, CA: Sage Publications.

Munford, C. J. (1996). *Race and reparations: A Black perspective for the 21st century*. Trenton, NJ: Africa World Press.

Murrag, C. B., Khatib, S., & Jackson, M. (1989). Social indices of the black elderly: A comparative life cycle approach to the study of double jeopardy. In R. L. Jones (Ed.), *Black adult development and aging* (pp. 167–187). Berkeley, CA: Cobbs and Henry.

Myers, L. (1987, September). The deep structure of culture: Relevance of traditional African culture in contemporary life. *Journal of Black Studies, 18*(1), 72–85.

Neighbors, H., Jackson, J., Browman, P., & Gurin, G. (1983). Stress, coping, and black mental health: Preliminary findings from a national study. *Prevention in Human Services, 2*, 1–25.

Ogbu, J. (1990, Spring). Minority status and literacy in comparative perspective. *Daedelus, 119*(2), 141–168.

Parham, T. (2002). *Counseling persons of African descent: Raising the bar of practitioner competence.* Thousand Oaks, CA: Sage Publications.

Pierce, C. M. (1995). Stress analogies of racism and sexism: Terrorism, torture, and disaster. In C. V. Willie, P. P. Reiker, B. M. Kramer, & B. S. Brown (Eds.), *Mental health, racism and sexism* (pp. 277–293). Pittsburgh, PA: University of Pittsburgh Press.

Plummer, D., & Slane, S. (1996). Patterns of coping racially stressful situations. *The Journal of Black Psychology, 22,* 302–315.

Ramseur, H. (1998). Psychologically healthy African American adults. In R. Jones (Ed.), *African American mental health: Theory, research and intervention.* Hampton, VA: Cobb and Henry Publishers.

Reid, I. (1969). *The Negro immigrant: His background, characteristics, and social adjustments, 1899–1937.* New York: Columbia University Press. (Original work published 1939)

Rogers, R. (2001). "Black like who?" Afro-Caribbean immigrants, African Americans, and the politics of group identity. In N. Foner (Ed.), *Islands in the city: West Indian migration to New York.* London: University of California Press.

Ruggiero, K. M., & Taylor, D. M. (1997). Why minority group members perceive or do not perceive the discrimination that confronts them: The role of self-esteem and perceived control. *Journal of Personality and Social Psychology, 72,* 373–389.

Salgado de Snyder, V. N. (1987). Factors associated with acculturative stress and depressive symptomatology among married Mexican immigrant women. *Psychology of Women Quarterly, 11,* 475–488.

Shelton, J., & Sellers, R. (2003). The role of racial identity in perceived racial discrimination. *Journal of Personality and Social Psychology, 84*(5), 1079–1092.

Sue, D. W., & Sue, D. (1999). *Counseling the culturally different: Theory and practice.* John Wiley & Sons.

Taylor, D. M., Wright, S. C., Moghaddam, F. M., & Lalonde, R. N. (1990). The personal/group discrimination discrepancy: Perceiving my group, but not myself, to be a target for discrimination. *Personality and Social Psychology Bulletin, 16,* 254–262.

Taylor, R., Thornton, M., & Chatters, L. (1987). Black Americans' perceptions of the socio-historical role of the church. *Journal of Black Studies, 18,* 123–138.

Thompson, C., Anderson, L., & Bakeman, R. (2000). Effects of racial socialization and racial identity on acculturative stress in African American college students. *Cultural Diversity and Ethnic Minority Psychology, 6,* 196–210.

United States Bureau of the Census. (1993). *Statistical abstract of the United States: 1993.* Washington, DC: The Reference Press, Inc.

Vickerman, M. (1999). *Crosscurrents: West Indian immigrants and race.* Oxford, UK: Oxford University Press.

Waters, M. (1999). *Black identities: West Indian immigrant dreams and American realities.* Cambridge, MA: Harvard University Press.

Waters, M. (2001). Growing up West Indian and African American: Gender and class differences in the second generation. In N. Foner (Ed.), *Islands in the city: West Indian migration to New York.* Berkeley: University of California Press.

CHAPTER 6

The Aversive Form of Racism

Gordon Hodson
John F. Dovidio
Samuel L. Gaertner

Prejudice has traditionally been viewed largely as a psychopathology affecting particular individuals. Proposed solutions were historically aimed at identifying and treating individuals (such as high authoritarians) who are prone to express prejudice openly (Dovidio, 2001). Influenced by the cognitive revolution in social psychology, subsequent theorizing swung drastically in the opposite direction, arguing that *basic* and *normal* cognitive mechanisms were responsible for stereotyping and prejudice (Fiske & Taylor, 1991; Hamilton, 1981). From this more cognitive perspective, the fundamental manner in which humans perceive, think, and reason makes people prone to stereotype members of other groups and to display attitudes and behaviors that favor one's own group (ingroup) over other groups (outgroups).

Whereas these intrapersonal processes contribute to a general predisposition toward prejudice, social factors also play a role by shaping norms and influencing personal ideals. In particular, contemporary norms in North America and Western Europe strongly support egalitarian values (Dovidio & Gaertner, 1998; Schuman, Steeh, Bobo, & Krysan, 1997) and encourage personal ideals and motivations to be nonprejudiced (Plant & Devine, 1998). Thus, many individuals in contemporary society experience psychological ambivalence—a conflict between the almost unavoidable consequences of normal cognitive processing that facilitates prejudicial thinking on the one hand, and nonprejudiced values and self-images on the other. Because of this ambivalence, discrimination currently tends to be expressed in very subtle, and often rationalizable, ways. One form of contemporary bias is aversive racism (Kovel, 1970).

AVERSIVE RACISM

As a form of contemporary prejudice, aversive racism represents a subtle form of bias typically expressed by well-intentioned, liberal, well-educated individuals (Dovidio & Gaertner, 1998; Dovidio & Gaertner, in press; Gaertner & Dovidio, 1986), in contrast to other forms of modern prejudice, such as modern racism (McConahay, 1986) and symbolic racism (Sears, 1988), which focus more on political conservatives. From the aversive racism perspective, culturalization practices and normal cognitive biases form the basis of negative feelings that exist "under the surface" of consciousness and conflict with more deliberative and consciously held beliefs regarding the positive value of equality and justice among racial groups. The end result can be a rather subtle, albeit insidious, form of racism: the aversive racist discriminates primarily when features of the situation allow him or her to maintain a positive (that is, nonprejudiced) view of the self.

In this chapter, we examine two basic propositions of the aversive racism perspective. One proposition is that aversive racists are most likely to express prejudice and discrimination under conditions of situational ambiguity, when the attitude or behavior that disadvantages blacks can be attributed to causes other than prejudice or can be justified along nonracial grounds. The other proposition is that, because it is less recognizable as *prejudice against* another group, bias may often be expressed more in terms of pro-ingroup bias (that is, favoring one's own group) than anti-outgroup bias (that is, derogating the outgroup).

Aversive Racism and Attributional Ambiguity

Consistent with the notion that contemporary racial bias is more likely to be expressed under conditions of situational ambiguity—when identification of prejudice is rendered less obvious—Gaertner and Dovidio (1977) conducted a study examining helping behavior in an interracial setting. White participants were led to believe that an individual in another room was in need of emergency assistance. The researchers manipulated whether the person in need of help was portrayed as white or black. In addition, participants were led to believe that they were either the sole witnesses to the emergency situation (a clear-cut situation, in terms of providing help) or were in a situation where two other people were also present (a more ambiguous situation in terms of future action, as others could be expected to help).

Consistent with the aversive racism framework, when they were placed into a clearly defined situation in which failure to help a black person could be easily construed as racist behavior (the "only witness" condition), white bystanders did not discriminate against blacks: whites were helped 83 percent of the time, whereas blacks were helped 95 percent of the time. However, when the situation was made more ambiguous, by the introduction of other white bystanders who could also potentially provide assistance (Darley & Latané, 1968), white participants were less likely to help black (38 percent) than white (75 percent) victims. Bias against blacks therefore emerged not when the situation was unambiguous and could be directly attributed to the individual, but rather under conditions under which a failure to help could be attributed to factors *other* than prejudice (for example, the belief that someone else was helping the victim).

In the larger society, this type of subtle bias influences the personal and economic welfare of blacks in fundamental and pervasive ways. In a study on hiring decisions (Dovidio & Gaertner, 2000), white college student participants were asked to make decisions about prospective white and black job candidates with strong or weak credentials (unambiguous situation) or marginal credentials (ambiguous situation). Supportive of the aversive racism perspective, no discrimination against black applicants emerged when applicants presented clearly strong or weak credentials. Such bias would clearly indicate racism. That is, to deny a strong black candidate, or to accept a weak white candidate over a black candidate, would be a strong and obvious indication of overt prejudice.

As illustrated in Table 6.1, discrimination against blacks emerged when applicants possessed marginal credentials and hiring decisions that could be attributed to nonracial factors, such as the potentially questionable credentials of the applicant. Whites with marginal credentials, however, were given the benefit of the doubt and were more likely to be hired than similarly qualified blacks. Furthermore, this pattern of results was found in both a 1989 sample and again in another 1999 sample. In contrast, white participants exhibited significantly lower levels of self-reported prejudice against blacks across this ten-year

Table 6.1
Recommendations and attributions of personal characteristics and interpersonal orientation as a function of candidate qualifications and race (Dovidio & Gaertner, 2000)

	Strength of recommendation*			Percent recommended		
Condition	1988–1989	1998–1999	Both	1988–1989	1998–1999	Both
Strong qualifications						
White	6.74	6.21	6.52	89%	79%	85%
candidate	(1.41)	(2.09)	(1.72)			
Black	7.32	7.00	7.18	95%	87%	91%
candidate	(1.67)	(1.60)	(1.62)			
Moderate qualifications						
White	6.05	5.69	5.91	75%	77%	76%
candidate	(1.73)	(1.60)	(1.67)			
Black	5.06	4.53	4.82	50%	40%	45%
candidate	(1.39)	(1.64)	(1.51)			
Weak qualifications						
White	3.05	2.42	2.81	5%	8%	6%
candidate	(1.65)	(1.68)	(1.66)			
Black	3.29	3.77	3.50	12%	15%	13%
candidate	(1.69)	(1.69)	(1.68)			

*Means with standard deviation presented in parentheses.

period. Thus, with increasingly prevailing egalitarian norms in society, people may report lower levels of personal prejudice while continuing to exhibit subtle discrimination, primarily in normatively ambiguous situations or in situations in which behavior that disadvantages blacks may be attributable to nonracial factors.

These effects have been found in samples of well-educated college students. In general, students tend to be less prejudiced than the general population (Schuman et al., 1997). For example, in a pilot study (Hodson, Dovidio, & Gaertner, 2002, p. 462), white college students in the United States were more favorable ($M = 71$) toward blacks on a feeling thermometer, ranging from 0 (extremely unfavorable) to 100 (extremely favorable), than was the general public ($M = 63$, $p < .03$). In another study, most college students (90 percent) believed themselves to be nonprejudiced in *absolute* terms (Hodson, Dovidio, & Gaertner, 2000); that is, they did not simply believe that they were less prejudiced than the general population, but they also felt that they were not prejudiced at all. Thus, the overwhelming majority of white college students in this sample, *irrespective of their level of prejudice*, perceived themselves as nonprejudiced. These findings are consistent with the possibility that aversive racism may characterize the racial attitudes of college students generally.

With these findings in mind, we expanded upon the previous hiring decisions study (Dovidio & Gaertner, 2000) in a recent university admissions study and considered the role of individual differences in self-reported prejudice. Hodson and colleagues (2002) asked white participants to evaluate white and black applicants with strong or weak credentials (that is, candidates with unambiguous qualifications) or mixed credentials (candidates with ambiguous qualifications). Those with mixed credentials were characterized by either strong high school achievement and weak standardized test scores or weak high school records and strong standardized test scores. Applicants were experimentally matched, such that white and black applicants with similar qualifications, differing only in terms of racial category, could be compared. Participants were asked to make recommendations on university admissions, with those recommendations being passed on to the admissions board to serve as student feedback to be considered for the following year's admissions.

No discrimination emerged for those scoring low in prejudice on the "Attitudes toward Blacks" scale (Brigham, 1993), regardless of applicants' credentials. That is, individuals low in prejudice did not exhibit bias against blacks in any of the experimental conditions. High prejudice-scoring participants also expressed no racial discrimination in their recommendations for applicants with clearly strong or weak credentials, when the expression of bias would be overt and obvious. However, consistent with the findings of Dovidio and Gaertner (2000), relatively high prejudice-scoring students (who regard themselves as nonprejudiced) discriminated in favor of white applicants when a candidate's credentials were ambiguous (mixed). Moreover, these participants who discriminated systematically against blacks engaged in differential weighting of the criteria that they claimed to use in making their decisions, rating the *weaker* aspect of the applicant's credentials as *more important* for admissions decisions when the candidate was black than when the candidate was white. For instance, individuals high in prejudice weighed standardized test scores as low in importance when presented with black applicants with high standardized test scores but weak high school grades, yet they tended to rank high school grades lower in importance when presented with black applicants with strong high school records but weak standardized test scores. This represents systematic discrimination that is not very obvious and can be "justified" or rationalized along nonracial grounds (that is, "the individual did not have the necessary qualifications").

The impact of subtle racial discrimination also extends to legal decisions, which involve decisions about personal freedom (incarceration) and life and death (capital punishment). Compared to whites, blacks in the United States are more likely to be pronounced guilty of crimes (Fairchild & Cowan, 1997) and are issued longer prison sentences (Robinson & Darley, 1995). Although several factors can contribute to such findings, the subtle nature of prejudice is likely to blame for some of the discrepancy between the outcomes of white and black defendants. Exploring this possibility, Johnson, Whitestone, Jackson, and Gatto (1995) conducted a simulated jury experiment in which the researchers manipulated the race of the defendant (white versus black). In instances when all evidence heard was allowed to be used by the participant jurors, no bias against blacks emerged. Yet when information damaging to the defendant was presented and then retracted due to its supposedly unsuitable nature, this inadmissible information was actually used, resulting in decisions against black defendants significantly more often than against white defendants. Consistent with the aversive racism framework, participants were not aware of this bias. In fact, contrary to their action, they reported that the inadmissible information was *less* influential on their decisions when the defendant was black than white.

In another study of juridic decisions, Dovidio, Smith, Donnella, and Gaertner (1997) found that aversive racists did not issue more death penalty verdicts for blacks than whites in general. However, the presentation of a single black juror voting for a black defendant's death penalty introduced enough social ambiguity to increase the likelihood of blacks being found guilty of capital offences. Consistent with aversive racism, a guilty verdict presumably appears less racist in its origins when it is supported by an independent black individual and thus is more likely to be adopted under such conditions.

Across a variety of studies, therefore, support has emerged for the notion that prejudice is more likely to emerge when the motivation for behavior that disadvantages blacks is not directly attributed to the individual's racial biases, but rather can be attributed to or rationalized by nonracial factors (Dovidio & Gaertner, 1998; Dovidio & Gaertner, in press). This feature of contemporary racial bias makes it particularly subtle and less recognizable than the traditional, more overt form of prejudice.

Aversive Racism and Ingroup Favoritism

A second aspect of the aversive racism framework is that contemporary racial prejudice is more likely to be expressed in terms of thoughts and actions reflecting pro-ingroup biases than anti-outgroup sentiment (Gaertner & Dovidio, 2000; Gaertner et al., 1997). It is well recognized that people prefer groups to which they belong (ingroups) over groups to which they do not belong (outgroups) (Brewer, 1979; Mullen, Brown, & Smith, 1992). For instance, Perdue, Dovidio, Gurtman, and Tyler (1990) tested preference for items associated with "we" versus "they" at a very basic and unconscious level in a series of experiments. In one experiment that demonstrated differential evaluations of ingroups and outgroups, nonsense words (for example, *jof, giw*) that were paired with ingroup pronouns (for example, *we, us*) were rated more positively than nonsense words paired with outgroup pronouns (such as *they, them*). In another experiment, subliminal primes of *we* resulted in more rapid response times to positive person descriptors (such as *kind*) than when these descriptors were paired with *they* or with a control prime such as *xxx*. This pattern of response times indicates that ingroup primes are more closely associated with positive than negative associations. The reverse, however, was not true; that is, presentation of the pronoun *they* did not lead to faster reaction times for negative-person descriptors. In these studies, then, *we* was associated with greater positivity, but *they* was not more closely linked to increased negativity, suggesting that pro-ingroup biases are generally more prominent than anti-outgroup biases. In resource allocation research, response asymmetries in behavior have also been noted. In particular, group members are more likely to give rewards to ingroup members than punishments to outgroup members (Hodson, Dovidio, & Esses, 2003; Mummendey & Otten, 1998).

These pro-ingroup biases are a dominant feature in research examining aversive racism. For example, in the emergency helping study mentioned previously (Gaertner & Dovidio, 1977), consistently high levels of helping whites, regardless of the presence or absence of others, may speak more to participants' positive attitudes toward whites than about their negativity toward blacks. In both the hiring (Dovidio & Gaertner, 2000) and university admissions (Hodson et al., 2002) studies, discrimination "against" blacks was actually expressed as giving the "benefit of the doubt" to whites with equally moderate or mixed qualifications as blacks. Similarly, Gaertner and McLaughlin (1983) found that whites differed in their spontaneous associations with whites and blacks, exhibiting stronger association of positive characteristics with whites than with blacks, but not demonstrating stronger negative associations with blacks than with whites, reflecting pro-white rather than an antiblack bias. Thus, rather than acting *against* blacks in an open and overt manner, which would be a more obvious indication of racism, aversive racists act *in favor of whites at the expense of blacks*, leaving blacks at a serious disadvantage.

Overall, then, contemporary racial bias such as aversive racism is often the result of pro-ingroup bias rather than anti-outgroup hatred. This pattern of findings is consistent with the assertion that "[t]he negative affect that aversive racists have for blacks is not hostility or hate. Instead, this negativity involves discomfort, uneasiness, disgust, and sometimes fear, which tend to motivate *avoidance* rather than intentionally destructive behaviors" ([italics added] Gaertner & Dovidio, 1986, p. 63). This element of aversive racism is key in distinguishing it from more traditional forms of racism, and makes it more difficult to recognize. Thus, while traditional racism is characterized by activities such as writing nasty racial epithets or openly refusing to hire blacks, aversive racism is characterized primarily by preferential treatment toward white over black individuals when such actions can be masked in situations where racist motivations are not directly apparent (Dovidio & Gaertner, 2000; Hodson et al., 2002). Rather than characterizing aggression against blacks by those openly admitting hatred of blacks (for example, burning crosses and lynching), aversive racism involves a relatively well-meaning but prejudice-denying type of person who is likely to distance himself or herself from blacks (for example, hiring ambiguously qualified whites over similarly qualified blacks), either as a result of direct discomfort with blacks or from the motivation to remove oneself from situations in which personal behaviors could be construed as racist in origin.

Combating Aversive Racism: Dilemmas and Recommendations

Given the rather subtle nature of aversive racism, it typically goes unrecognized, even by those harboring the bias. This aspect of aversive racism poses a significant challenge to prejudice intervention programs. Because aversive racists do not readily acknowledge personal prejudice, they may not see the benefits of intervention. Even worse, aversive racists may resist participation in such programs because, consciously, they may not acknowledge the *personal relevance* of the intervention ("I'm not racist; therefore I don't need this intervention") or, unconsciously, may be motivated to avoid situations that can expose their biases.

Further complicating the intervention issue, straightforward attempts to limit bias by asking people to suppress stereotypic thoughts can lead, at least temporarily, to an ironic, subsequent *increase* in the use of stereotypes. This "rebound effect" (Macrae, Bodenhausen, Milne, & Jetten, 1994) is particularly likely to occur among college students who are relatively high in prejudice (Hodson & Dovidio, 2001; Monteith, Spicer, & Tooman, 1998), those who are most likely to be aversive racists (Hodson et al., 2002). Thus, straightforward instructions to control or limit the expression of bias may result in temporary negative consequences for those prone to aversive racism.

Alternatively, it may be possible to capitalize on the good intentions of aversive racists and harness these intentions to create and sustain longer-term reductions in bias. With repeated practice with counteracting their automatic associations underlying stereotypes, for example, people are able to reduce stereotyping over time, even at an unconscious level (Kawakami, Dovidio, Moll, Hermsen, & Russin, 2000). Rather than asking participants to suppress stereotypes without necessarily activating personal goals or incentives to control prejudice (Hodson & Dovidio, 2001; Macrae et al., 1994; Monteith et al., 1998), inducements to avoid prejudice through the activation of personal egalitarian standards and guilt can successfully reduce prejudice, at least in some circumstances for some people. For instance, Monteith (1993) led participants to believe that they had evaluated a person in a prejudiced manner (experiments 1 and 2), and then examined the consequences of this violation from personal, nonprejudiced standards.

Monteith (1993) demonstrated that low-prejudice individuals, after believing that they had engaged in prejudicial behavior, experienced heightened levels of guilt and self-focus (experiment 1) and were less likely to engage in subsequent activities that could be construed as prejudicial, such as rating prejudicial jokes as funny (experiment 2). The successful inhibition of prejudice in these cases was possible for those low in prejudice (those with the motivation to be nonprejudiced). Given that aversive racists generally consider themselves low in prejudice, and are motivated to not be prejudiced, this research suggests that making the potential for prejudicial interpretations of behavior salient may encourage aversive racists to control or limit the expression of prejudice by working on internal guides and standards, consistent with the aversive racism framework. Nevertheless, we fear that aversive racists may steer clear of situations that encourage close examination of deviations from personal standards, so this strategy may still be met with some resistance.

To test the efficacy of employing discrepancies from personal standards in prejudice reduction, Dovidio, Kawakami, and Gaertner (2000) recently adopted a strategy in which white participants worked on a task that made them aware of discrepancies between what they *would* do and *should* do in an interracial context (Devine & Monteith, 1993). As expected, "would-should" discrepancies resulted in increased interracial guilt, especially for those low in prejudice. After a three-week interval, participants were tested again, and expressions of bias decreased for both low- and high-prejudice individuals, especially for the former. Thus, attempts can be made to build on the good intentions of aversive racists to address unconscious negative feelings and beliefs and to develop enhanced sensitivity to the potential of their bias.

Son Hing, Li, and Zanna (2002) directly tested the effectiveness of hypocrisy induction, via the supposed violation of personal prejudice standards, in an effort to reduce prejudice in aversive racists. In the first phase of the study, self-reported attitudes toward Asians were tapped. In the second phase, participants completed a series of measures, including an implicit (indirect) prejudice measure. In the third phase, participants wrote passages on the importance of treating minorities well on campus, which was allegedly to be forwarded to a public audience. After writing a pro-minority paper, participants in the hypocrisy condition (versus control) were asked to think of instances where they personally reacted negatively toward an Asian person. Finally, attitude and discrimination measures were collected. The results supported the prediction that inducing hypocrisy in aversive racists (here characterized as those disavowing prejudice on self-report scales but showing prejudice on the less-direct measures) would invoke more favorable attitudes toward the outgroup. In particular, aversive racists expressed high levels of guilt about their treatment of Asians and exhibited significantly higher levels of donations to an Asian group on campus. The authors conclude that "the hypocrisy induction procedure forced aversive racists to become aware of the negative aspects of their attitudes that they typically repress" (Son Hing et al., 2002, p. 77), and, presumably, bring these biases under control.

The strategies outlined thus far essentially render ambiguous or potentially intervention-resistant situations less ambiguous in the interest of harnessing the good intentions of the individual in question. This is in keeping with our first proposition, that ambiguous situations and contexts that allow for nonracist interpretations of thoughts and behavior more readily facilitate the expression of racial bias. The interventions aim to limit access to the contextually ambiguous areas toward which aversive racists gravitate in order to maintain nonprejudiced self-images.

Another approach is based on our second proposition, namely that aversive racism frequently involves pro-ingroup more than anti-outgroup bias. Thus, in conjunction with the strategies already suggested, interventions may also be aimed at capitalizing on ingroup-favoring tendencies, influencing who is considered part of the ingroup ("we"). According to the common ingroup identity model (Gaertner, Mann, Murrell, & Dovidio, 1989; Gaertner & Dovidio, 2000), inducing people to focus on common or shared social identities (for example, "university student"), often in conjunction with maintaining the original social identity (such as "psychology student," "engineering student," etc.), results in recategorization of social boundaries, such that individuals formerly categorized as outgroup members come to enjoy the benefits of being included in the ingroup.

The benefits of common ingroup categorization have been demonstrated across a variety of situations, including laboratory settings and field settings (Gaertner & Dovidio, 2000). A recent experiment examined the implications of shared common identities in a natural setting at a university football game (Nier et al., 2002, experiment 2). As white fans were about to enter the stadium before a highly competitive game, they were approached by either a white or black research assistant, who asked fans for a favor, namely to complete a short survey about food preferences. Key to the induction of a common ingroup identity, the experimenters manipulated whether the research assistants wore a hat identifying the assistants as supporters of either the University of Delaware or the West Chester State team. Because assistants only approached white fans wearing either Delaware or West Chester fan-based clothing, it was possible to examine the amount of helping that was offered to the black (versus white) research assistant as a function of whether or not the assistant was perceived as a member of the ingroup or outgroup in terms of fan support. It was predicted that prejudice against the black assistants would be reduced when the research assistants were supporters of the same (versus different) team as the respondent (that is, having a common identity). As expected, black interviewers were offered more help with their task when they were affiliated with the same team as the respondent (59 percent) versus when affiliated with a different team (36 percent). In contrast, the effect of same-team versus different-team support did not influence help offered to white assistants (44 percent versus 37 percent). This study clearly demonstrates the advantages of inducing a common group identity to promote interracial cooperation.

Hodson (2003) recently examined the benefits of common ingroup recategorization between white and black inmates in a prison setting in Britain. In this investigation, white prisoners reported the amount and type of contact (for example, "all inmates are treated equally") with black prisoners, cognitive intergroup representations (for example, "we are all part of one group," "we are two separate groups"), intergroup anxiety, and attitudes toward blacks. As expected, consistent with the mere exposure effect (Zajonc, 1968), the amount of contact with black inmates was directly related to favorable attitudes toward black inmates. Key to this chapter, favorable intergroup contact conditions in prison predicted stronger common group representations ("we are all part of one group"), which in turn predicted lower levels of intergroup anxiety, which then predicted more positive attitudes toward black inmates. Thus, interventions to improve race relations in prison could focus on creating more frequent or more positive intergroup contact or encouraging inmates to focus directly on shared group categories in prison (Gaertner & Dovidio, 2000).

Changes in the way people categorize themselves and others can also occur as a result of national and international events. After the terrorist attacks on the United States on September 11, 2001, Americans, both blacks (Wade, 2002) and whites (Saad, 2002) experienced an increase in the salience of a shared American identity and an associated increase in negative attitudes toward a common outgroup: immigrants (Saad, 2002). Moreover, we (Dovidio et al., 2004) have found experimentally that increasing the salience of terrorist threats to Americans as a whole rather than specifically to white Americans led whites to see black persons more as members of their own group and less as a member of a different group, and produced more positive feelings and attitudes to blacks and other racial and ethnic minority groups (Latinos and Asian Americans). Thus, extending ingroup boundaries to make them increasingly more inclusive may represent a practical method, with potential widespread impact, of combating both subtle and blatant forms of racism.

CONCLUSIONS

The face of racism has transformed from a more direct, overt form of traditional prejudice to a more indirect, covert, and subtle form

Toolbox for Change

For	Perceptions and biases	Strategies for change
Individuals	Basic cognitive processes	Emphasize *personal* relevance
	Unacknowledged negative emotion	of intervention programs
	Personal denial of prejudicial attitudes	Disambiguate the situation
	Behavioral "leaks" of prejudice in ambiguous situations	Recategorization (induce common ingroup identification)
	Interracial avoidance strategies	Accentuate personal standards
Community	Social norms	Recategorization (induce
	Cultural practices	common ingroup identification)
	Historical injustices and inequality	Promote *positive* interracial contact
	Interracial avoidance and segregation	Accentuate community standards
Practitioners/ educators	Aversive racism is subtle and difficult to recognize	Recategorization (induce common ingroup identification)
	May exhibit and thereby teach subtle racism	Improve interracial contact conditions
	Fail to recognize personal relevance of reduction strategies	Improve perceptions of interracial contact conditions
		Promote *positive* increased contact

characterized by ambivalence and pro-ingroup biases. However, this new form is no less dangerous or less detrimental than the traditional form to interracial relations and society as a whole. Rather, we argue that because it has become more subtle, it is all the more difficult to recognize and combat, and it may exert its negative influence with relative ease and impunity. After all, because aversive racism is not personally recognized by aversive racists, its negative consequences are typically manifested under conditions of ambiguity, when it is difficult to recognize and consequently difficult to remedy. Nonetheless, aversive racism among whites is very detrimental to blacks because it can result in decreased helping toward blacks in emergency situations (Gaertner &

Dovidio, 1977), increased capital sentencing of blacks (Johnson et al., 1995), and in decisions that limit the educational and career opportunities of blacks (Dovidio & Gaertner, 2000; Hodson et al., 2002). These biases perpetuate racial inequality for generations to come. Moreover, these aversive racism processes and biases are not limited to reactions toward blacks. Rather, we have witnessed aversive racism in attitudes toward Latinos (Dovidio, Gaertner, Anastasio, & Sanitioso, 1992) and women (Dovidio & Gaertner, 1983), as well.

In the course of this chapter, we have reviewed some strategies to combat aversive racism (for a summary, see Toolbox for Change). Some of these intervention strategies are grounded in harnessing the good intentions of the aversive racist, others in automatizing more favorable mental associations, and others are grounded in capitalizing on the pro-ingroup biases such individuals express. We contend that a combination of these strategies will be most effective at combating contemporary prejudice.

REFERENCES

Brewer, M. B. (1979). Ingroup bias in the minimal intergroup situation: A cognitive-motivational analysis. *Psychological Bulletin, 86,* 307–324.

Brigham, J. C. (1993). College students' racial attitudes. *Journal of Applied Social Psychology, 23,* 1933–1967.

Darley, J. M., & Latané, B. (1968). Bystander intervention in emergencies: Diffusion of responsibility. *Journal of Personality and Social Psychology, 8,* 377–383.

Devine, P., & Monteith, M. (1993). The role of discrepancy-associated affect in prejudice reduction. In D. Mackie & D. Hamilton (Eds.), *Affect, cognition and stereotyping: Interactive processes in group perception* (pp. 317–344). San Diego, CA: Academic Press.

Dovidio, J. F. (2001). On the nature of contemporary prejudice: The third wave. *Journal of Social Issues, 57,* 829–849.

Dovidio, J. F., & Gaertner, S. L. (1983). The effects of sex, status, and ability on helping behavior. *Journal of Applied Social Psychology, 13,* 191–205.

Dovidio, J. F., & Gaertner, S. L. (1998). On the nature of contemporary prejudice: The causes, consequences, and challenges of aversive racism. In J. Eberhardt & S. T. Fiske (Eds.), *Confronting racism: The problem and the response* (pp. 3–32). Newbury Park, CA: Sage Publications.

Dovidio, J. F., & Gaertner, S. L. (2000). Aversive racism and selection decisions: 1989 and 1999. *Psychological Science, 11,* 319–323.

Dovidio, J. F., & Gaertner, S. L. (in press). Aversive racism. To appear in M. P. Zanna (Ed.), *Advances in experimental social psychology.* San Diego, CA: Academic Press.

Dovidio, J. F., Gaertner, S. L., Anastasio, P. A., & Sanitioso, R. (1992). Cognitive and motivational bases of bias: The implications of aversive racism for attitudes toward Hispanics. In S. Knouse, P. Rosenfeld, & A. Culbertson (Eds.), *Hispanics in the workplace* (pp. 75–106). Newbury Park, CA: Sage Publications.

Dovidio, J. F., Kawakami, K., & Gaertner, S. L. (2000). Reducing contemporary prejudice: Combating explicit and implicit bias at the individual and intergroup level. In S. Oskamp (Ed.), *Reducing prejudice and discrimination* (pp. 137–163). Hillsdale, NJ: Erlbaum.

Dovidio, J. F., Smith, J. K., Donnella, A. G., & Gaertner, S. L. (1997). Racial attitudes and the death penalty. *Journal of Applied Social Psychology, 27,* 1468–1487.

Dovidio, J. F., ten Vergert, M., Stewart, T. L., Gaertner, S. L., Johnson, J. D., Esses, V. M., et al. (2004). *Perspective and prejudice: Antecedents and mediating mechanisms.* Manuscript submitted for publication. Colgate University, Hamilton, New York.

Fairchild, H. H., & Cowan, G. (1997). The O. J. Simpson trial: Challenges to science and society. *Journal of Social Issues, 53,* 583–591.

Fiske, S., & Taylor, S. E. (1991). *Social cognition* (2nd ed.). New York: McGraw-Hill.

Gaertner, S. L., & Dovidio, J. F. (1977). The subtlety of white racism, arousal, and helping behavior. *Journal of Personality and Social Psychology, 35,* 691–707.

Gaertner, S. L., & Dovidio, J. F. (1986). The aversive form of racism. In J. F. Dovidio & S. L. Gaertner (Eds.), *Prejudice, discrimination, and racism* (pp. 61–89). New York: Academic Press.

Gaertner, S. L., & Dovidio, J. F. (2000). *Reducing intergroup bias: The common ingroup identity model.* Philadelphia, PA: Psychology Press.

Gaertner, S. L., Dovidio, J. F., Banker, B., Rust, M., Nier, J., Mottola, G., et al. (1997). Does racism necessarily mean anti-blackness? Aversive racism and pro-whiteness. In M. Fine, L. Powell, L. Weis, & M. Wong (Eds.), *Off white* (pp. 167–178). London: Routledge.

Gaertner, S. L., Mann, J., Murrell, A., & Dovidio, J. F. (1989). Reduction of intergroup bias: The benefits of recategorization. *Journal of Personality and Social Psychology, 57,* 239–249.

Gaertner, S. L., & McLaughlin, J. P. (1983). Racial stereotypes: Associations and ascriptions of positive and negative characteristics. *Social Psychology Quarterly, 46,* 23–30.

Hamilton, D. L. (1981). *Cognitive processes in stereotyping and intergroup behavior.* Hillsdale, NJ: Erlbaum.

Hodson, G. (2003, September). *Interracial contact in prison: The pros for cons.* Talk presented at University of Kent, Canterbury, UK. EAESP/SPSSI Social Inclusion and Exclusion seminar series (Theme: The social psychological analysis of social inclusion and exclusion).

Hodson, G., & Dovidio, J. F. (2001). Racial prejudice as a moderator of stereotype rebound: A conceptual replication. *Representative Research in Social Psychology, 25,* 1–8.

Hodson, G., Dovidio, J. F., & Esses, V. M. (2003). Ingroup identification as a moderator of positive-negative asymmetry in social discrimination. *European Journal of Social Psychology, 33,* 215–233.

Hodson, G., Dovidio, J. F., & Gaertner, S. L. (2000). Projected racism: Individual differences in perceptions of intergroup attitudes. Unpublished manuscript.

Hodson, G., Dovidio, J. F., & Gaertner, S. L. (2002). Processes in racial discrimination: Differential weighting of conflicting information. *Personality and Social Psychology Bulletin, 28,* 460–471.

Johnson, J. D., Whitestone, E., Jackson, L. A., & Gatto, L. (1995). Justice is still not colorblind: Differential racial effects of exposure to inadmissible evidence. *Personality and Social Psychology Bulletin, 21,* 893–898.

Kawakami, K., Dovidio, J. F., Moll, J., Hermsen, S., & Russin, A. (2000). Just say no (to stereotyping): Effects of training in the negation of stereotypic associations on stereotype activation. *Journal of Personality and Social Psychology, 78,* 871–888.

Kovel, J. (1970). *White racism: A psychohistory.* New York: Pantheon.

Macrae, C., Bodenhausen, G., Milne, A., & Jetten, J. (1994). Out of mind but back in sight: Stereotypes on the rebound. *Journal of Personality and Social Psychology, 67,* 808–817.

McConahay, J. B. (1986). Modern racism, ambivalence, and the modern racism scale. In J. F. Dovidio & S. L. Gaertner (Eds.), *Prejudice, discrimination, and racism* (pp. 91–125). Orlando, FL: Academic Press.

Monteith, M. (1993). Self-regulation of prejudiced responses: Implications for progress in prejudice-reduction efforts. *Journal of Personality and Social Psychology, 65,* 469–485.

Monteith, M., Spicer, C., & Tooman, G. (1998). Consequences of stereotype suppression: Stereotypes on AND not on the rebound. *Journal of Experimental Social Psychology, 34,* 355–377.

Mullen, B., Brown, R., & Smith, C. (1992). Ingroup bias as a function of salience, relevance and status: An integration. *European Journal of Social Psychology, 22,* 103–122.

Mummendey, A., & Otten, S. (1998). Positive-negative asymmetry in social discrimination. In W. Stroebe & M. Hewstone (Eds.), *European review of social psychology* (Vol. 9, pp. 107–143). Chichester, UK: Wiley.

Nier, J. A., Gaertner, S. L., Dovidio, J. F., Banker, B. S., Ward, C. M., & Rust, M. C. (2002). Changing interracial evaluations and behavior: The effects of a common group identity. *Group Processes and Intergroup Relations, 4,* 299–316.

Perdue, C. W., Dovidio, J. F., Gurtman, M. B., & Tyler, R. B. (1990). "Us" and "them": Social categorization and the process of intergroup bias. *Journal of Personality and Social Psychology, 59*, 475–486.

Plant, E. A., & Devine, P. G. (1998). Internal and external motivation to respond without prejudice. *Journal of Personality and Social Psychology, 75*, 811–832.

Robinson, P. H., & Darley, J. M. (1995). *Justice, liability, and blame.* Boulder, CO: Westview Press.

Saad, L. (2002, September). Have Americans changed? Effects of September 11 have largely faded. *Gallup Poll News Service.* Retrieved September 11, 2002, from www.gallup.com/content/default.asp?ci=6790

Schuman, H., Steeh, C., Bobo, L., & Krysan, M. (1997). *Racial attitudes in America: Trends and interpretations.* Cambridge, MA: Harvard University Press.

Sears, D. O. (1988). Symbolic racism. In P. A. Katz & D. A. Taylor (Eds.), *Eliminating racism: Profiles in controversy* (pp. 53–84). New York: Plenum Press.

Son Hing, L. S., Li, W., & Zanna, M. P. (2002). Inducing hypocrisy to reduce prejudicial responses among aversive racists. *Journal of Experimental Social Psychology, 38*, 71–78.

Wade, B. H. (2002). How does racial identity affect historically black colleges and universities' perceptions of September 11, 2001? *Journal of Black Studies, 33*, 25–43.

Zajonc, R. B. (1968). Attitudinal effects of mere exposure. *Journal of Personality and Social Psychology, 9* [Monograph Suppl. No. 2, part 2].

CHAPTER 7

"What's Race Got to Do, Got to Do with It?" Denial of Racism on Predominantly White College Campuses

Carole Baroody Corcoran
Aisha Renée Thompson

This chapter is cowritten by two (outwardly) very different women who met as student and teacher. Three years later in 2004, we continue to feel a similar sense of urgency and share crucial concerns regarding the enrollment status of blacks and (for those who are enrolled) the noxious racial climate and reality of their lived experiences at predominantly white institutions of higher education.

The first author (CBC) is a Syrian-Irish American and tenured full professor with a PhD in psychology. Her formal academic journey began in a northern midwestern industrial city in 1958 when she attended kindergarten at the public school closest to the rental property where her family resided. Edison was a predominantly "Negro" grade school reflecting the neighborhood composition. At that time the term *minority* was not a descriptor applied to students. The second author (ART) is black, a student who just recently graduated from college with a bachelor of science degree in psychology. Her own path of formal education began in 1985, when she was enrolled in pre-kindergarten. Brown was an exclusive, predominantly white, private academy located about half an hour's drive from her home in an affluent suburb of northern Virginia outside of Washington, DC.

This chapter will explore how and why (1) the denial of racism, (2) the pressure to assimilate, and tokenism, and (3) placing the burden on people of color all serve to maintain and bolster the existing university power structure known as the status quo. These dynamics also support and contribute to a pattern of resistance that has substantially weakened or eliminated programs designed to create and foster an environment that encourages true diversity. A framework will be presented to illustrate the necessity of moving from an individually focused examination of the racial climate and curriculum to a sociocultural (macro-level) approach that includes an analysis of power at the institutional level.

Most whites (faculty, administrators, and students) are taught to see racism as individual acts of meanness perpetrated by members of a group, and never as an invisible system that confers dominance and privilege to certain groups but not others (McIntosh, 1988). If we move from examining individual prejudice to challenging institutional power, the majority group faces an uncomfortable dilemma. That is, the dominant group must acknowledge its complicity in such an imbalanced system. Seeing oneself as the custodian and beneficiary of institutional racism conflicts with good intentions and a self-image as a just and thoughtful person. Accordingly, in order to provide tools for breaking through denial and discomfort, two concepts will be introduced and explored: unacknowledged white-skin privilege (McIntosh, 1988) and aversive racism (Gaertner & Dovidio, 1986).

Students' voices and data on perceptions of the racial climate collected from one predominantly white campus in 1988, 1998, and 2003 are included and inform the positions espoused in this chapter. Specific examples and perceptions collected from the campus will serve as a case study to illustrate individual and institutional dynamics that generalize to other predominantly white institutions of higher education.

> There is a growing harmony between different racial groups, but the College focuses so much on diversity that it only increases racial tensions. (Asian American student)

Indeed, the changing nature of white racism has been reflected in a preference for avoiding dialogue for fear of creating "racial tensions." Thus, whites (and perhaps even some blacks within the white academy) may increasingly prefer and adopt a "color-blind" racial perspective. Reactive and proactive recommendations will be provided to counter indifference, resistance, and backlash to continued attempts to change the curriculum and climate at predominantly white institutions of higher education.

> I never realized how racism is still a part of society until I came to college. I always thought that racism was something that didn't exist

anymore among our generation, something obsolete like the 8-track or acid wash jeans or something. I always associated racism with "old people." It still blows my mind that young people of today could actually believe in such antiquated ideas . . . that they are superior to someone because of race. It has made me realize that there is still a lot for people to learn and that not everybody is as open minded . . . . (Black student)

Of course the notion of "diversity" encompasses much more than black/white race relations; and the ideas expressed in this chapter apply to the many other socially constructed categories (gender, sexual orientation, social class, and physical mobility) where "target" or low-status members suffer oppression, and "agent" or high-status members enjoy the benefits that accrue to the oppressors. For many reasons (acknowledged or not), the two "original sins" (genocide and slavery) at the root of the United States have received cursory, biased, or little attention in the still-predominantly white academy. Given our short history as a nation, for blacks, the legacy and impact of slavery and segregation remain fresh wounds still without remedy to date. Thus, black/white race relations persist as a painful yet critical indicator of any claims of progress with respect to "diversity."

WHITE FEMALE PROFESSOR, BLACK STUDENT, WHITE COLLEGE, 2003

. . . sometimes, I think, a great way to find out how things really are is to talk with white students on campus! I don't know if you're doing that already but if not, ask them and see what they say. I myself am intensely curious, and more than that, would really like to know what the racial climate here *really* is like. What I hear is from the brave and brazen—besides that, I can forget it. I'm black. Nobody's going to come up to me and tell me what they really think. (Black student)

In 2003, the professor (CBC) posed this question to her then-student coauthor (ART) as well as her peers who were also enrolled in an advanced research lab and seminar course. From these examples of students' written responses below, can the question be guessed?

1. Image: a bruised, beaten up bald eagle not all is well in USA
2. Like the black box they use in magic shows that appear to have nothing in them but there really is something hidden
3. Peanut butter and bananas I think they go well together but not everyone does

4. Like a roller coaster

5. Oil and water in a bottle. Two liquids which are close to each other in proximity, might slightly mix but there is still separation.

6. Tight ropewalker

7. Venn diagram [The student also drew three overlapping circles, but with almost no intersection common to the three.]

The question was, What metaphor or image would you choose to represent current U.S. race relations?

During that same course in 2003, the second author (ART) and her research partner conducted a seminar session devoted to their empirical research project. They had chosen to use the available research pool (white introductory psychology students) to examine implicit attitudes (prejudice) and automatic stereotyping of blacks (Wittenbrink, Judd, & Park, 2001). As a (presumably) lighter fun activity to end their seminar session, they decided to anonymously survey forty white students prior to class, in order to create a game for us to play that they dubbed *Racial Feud*. Based on the television game show *Family Feud*, seminar students were randomly assigned to two "families," and these two student teams competed for points and prizes by trying to match the top five answers (most popular) given by the whites surveyed.

Admittedly, the white students surveyed were a (nonrepresentative) convenience sample who were asked questions specifically aimed to elicit stereotypes of blacks. Still, student members on both competing "family" teams continued to "strike out" in their repeated attempts to match the top five survey responses given. Below are some of the questions and answers from the survey. Cover the answers before reading further if you want to test yourself and see how your "family" would do.

What is the number one widespread stereotype of black people?

1. Crime and violence

2. Rapper, gangster

3. Ignorant

4. Loud

5. Always late, cp (colored people) time

Stereotypically, where is the number one place black people work?

1. Low income/blue collar

2. They don't

3. Drug deals

4. Fast food

5. Housekeeping

What is the number one biggest advantage that black people have over white people?

1. Affirmative action

2. They can jump (athletics)

3. They can dance

4. None

5. Well endowed

Who is the most famous black person dead or alive?

1. Martin Luther King Jr.

2. Michael Jordan

3. Oprah Winfrey

4. Colin Powell

5. Rosa Parks/Malcolm X

What is the number one advantage whites have over blacks?

(Only a few people answered this question, but they all had the same response.)

1. Because they're white

Did you fare better than our class? I do not think any of us will forget that seminar class. After playing *Racial Feud*, we left class exhausted (we had laughed and screamed outrageous answers). But we were also stunned by the results of questions that are not typically asked of the dominant racial group. We were forced to confront existing negative perceptions of blacks. We realized that these pernicious stereotypes (easily avoided or ignored by whites) are a ubiquitous part of the subordinate groups' campus racial climate.

> Socially, Blacks are pressed into being very passive and always grinning, otherwise they are immediately typecast as being hostile and aggressive. (Black student)

> I know quite a few people who have no problem telling racist jokes in all white company and who use the N word at will. (White student)

WHITE COCHAIR, CURRICULUM TRANSFORMATION GRANT PROJECT, WHITE COLLEGE, 1988

In 1985, with two years of teaching and research experience and a PhD, I was hired by a predominantly white liberal arts college. I was young, untenured, and eager to tackle an outdated curriculum that lacked a single course in areas of my scholarly interest (for example, women's studies and African American studies). With a colleague (hired the following year), we organized a substantial number of like-minded students and faculty and set to work. By 1988, he and I had cowritten an ambitious grant proposal for substantial external funding to incorporate race, class, and gender studies into existing courses.

My collaborator, a white male (also young and untenured), was contacted by a top administrator, informed that our grant proposal had been funded, and invited to a luncheon to discuss plans for the awarded grant. When he called me and learned that I had not been notified, he insisted that I come along to the luncheon meeting. I was completely ignored at the event. My male coauthor of the grant went and pulled up a chair for me at a small table where I had no place setting. The men at the table were served and began eating. At that point, my male colleague protested on my behalf, and I was brought utensils and a plate of food. While I was feeling increasingly humiliated, my presence remained unacknowledged (not to mention my role as coauthor of the grant award being ignored). Despite the grant's budget that included allocations for two coordinators, my male coauthor was informed that the college had decided that the grant project could be headed by only one person. There was no mention of me or why my white male junior colleague would be the one to receive course reductions and administer our interdisciplinary race, class, and gender diversity project.

Breaking with tradition in the white male academy, I became cochair of our project only because my male co-author adamantly refused to have any role in it without me. Later upon hearing about my success-fully funded grant, my department chair told me that if he had known I was writing the grant he would have told me not to do it (precisely the reason I had not informed him). A loophole needed to be closed, and it was. From that point on I had an additional layer of institutional barriers to surmount: namely, at every turn I would require my depart-ment chair's signature of approval. Also, except for one colleague, my department was opposed to diversity initiatives or, at best, not supportive of race and gender scholarship. My personal feelings and academic interests were no longer just "individual" but had shifted to the realm of "institutional."

Our curriculum transformation project and the model we designed were a huge success, receiving national media attention and acclaim. We hosted major conferences on campus, and other institutions invited the coleaders to help them start similar programs. Noted scholars were brought to campus to speak and conduct faculty workshops. Each summer, intensive faculty institutes were held for faculty to read and discuss new race and gender scholarship across disciplines and in-corporate race and gender scholarship into a new or existing course. A resource library of books and videotapes was started. A newsletter sent to students, faculty, and staff facilitated new lines of communica-tion among these groups, which led to new friendships, alliances, and cosponsored activities. Roughly a third of our faculty chose to partic-ipate in transforming their courses; and as a team, we developed new courses, including interdisciplinary introductory courses in women's studies and ethnic studies.

With a supportive coalition of the faculty, we successfully passed an across-the-curriculum requirement that all students (before graduat-ing) enroll in the "race and gender intensive" courses being created. We developed criteria, proposal procedures, and oversight methods for race- and gender-intensive courses. Our work then served as a template for the addition of "global awareness" and "environmental awareness" across the curriculum requirements. Although it was not a part of our grant project, amazingly, the faculty successfully voted to include sexual orientation as a category in the college's discrimina-tion policy and institute a parental-leave, infant-care policy. The institution (and not just the curriculum) was visibly changing, and the faculty felt empowered.

Still, we would learn that not everyone was thrilled by our sweeping accomplishments. Soon we began to face individual and institutional resistance and backlash. No matter what the stated standards or criteria were, "race and gender" faculty and our initiatives began to face unprecedented outcomes: actions, inactions, or decisions that never applied to other colleagues or their projects. Internally, development grant awards that were recommended for funding by our standard faculty peer review committees were singled out only if they were "race and gender" projects and then inexplicably denied funding from the top administration. One egregious example of administrative fiat happened after a small group of us stayed over holiday break to cowrite a subsequent race and gender proposal at the behest of the dean of the faculty. We would later learn from outside sources that the college secretly turned down the substantial external grant awarded for proposal. These tactics prevented internal and external funding from supporting our successful initiatives and had a chilling effect on faculty, staff, and student morale as well as the campus racial climate.

In 1992, I (CBC) wrote the following to express my mounting concerns and alarm over events I felt were clear evidence of the institution's waning commitment to our various diversity initiatives:

> A model curriculum transformation program started in 1988 struggles for institutional funding at the end of its external grant period. A department's candidate search is called off after the hiring pool fails to contain a single minority candidate. A special faculty meeting is held to deal with animosities aroused over the debate surrounding the political nature of a proposed new course in Ethnic Studies. Three African American students receive a racially motivated death threat. All of these events occurred during 1992 at a typical predominantly white college campus. Why have so many well-intentioned programs and individuals failed to radically improve enrollment, the curriculum and campus climate with respect to race?

Like other young activists in the late 1960s and early 1970s, I (CBC) understood that there was a profound connection between social change on an individual and an institutional level. Our slogan back then, "the personal is political," was powerful, but so were its consequences, particularly when the dominant group recognized the potential for an actual power shift. Sentiments expressed by the student voice below became commonplace and increasingly represented administrative and faculty opinions as well:

> The only racism I've seen at this school is reverse racism. The students here are constantly bombarded with Multi Cultural Events. I am surprised that there are not more minorities here because recruitment is certainly heavy for minorities. I think [the college] should be concerned with a potential student's academics and less with their ethnicity. Get rid of the boxes to check off gender and race, then maybe minorities with lower GPA's won't be getting in here, when I was stuck on the waiting list! Isn't it true that admissions officers are almost always minority graduates? Hmm!? And why is it that prospective black high schoolers get their own special "recruitment weekend" here? And why when [the college] wants to promote campus unity, do they invite only new black students to school early for a special "bonding opportunity." Don't we all bond during orientation weekend? [The college] says they want unity, so why do they promote segregation? If there's any animosity coming from White students it's because they feel *some* of the black students got in because they are black, not because of their merits. If the "race box" was eliminated on the application, that would alleviate the problem. If you need it for data purposes, why not ask after a student is accepted? (White student)

In a sense, we became a victim of our own success. I felt that this growing "backlash" mentality was becoming a powerful rallying point for our ideological opponents and, increasingly, members of the dominant social group. In contrast to its old counterpart, "the personal is political," the new slogan could be captured as "the political is personal." It aptly described a dominant group phenomenon, namely, the realization that institutional change could affect one's (previously unchallenged) individual sense of entitlement:

> There was a speaker on campus speaking about Affirmative Action and how it should be abolished. After the session White students began to say that it's because of these Black students that I have all of this tuition to pay. The next morning there were KKK signs up on campus. (Black student)

BLACK CIVIL RIGHTS LEADER, MULTICULTURAL CENTER, WHITE COLLEGE, 2000

> Would it be considered racism on the faculty/administration's part to not recognize and honor minority faculty and professors more? For

example, James Farmer is one of the greatest resources in the Civil Rights Movements. He is in a picture at the MLK Museum in Atlanta, yet when track books come out or admissions catalogs, he is downplayed or not even highlighted! Students hear about him through word of mouth (no thanks to the administration). I wonder what percentages are minority vs. White faculty and staff? (Black student)

Civil rights leader James L. Farmer Jr. (1920–1999) organized the nation's first sit-in and founded the Congress of Racial Equality (CORE) in 1942. Farmer organized the Freedom Rides in 1961 to desegregate interstate bus travel in the South and dedicated his life to human rights activism, for which he was awarded the Presidential Medal of Freedom by President Bill Clinton the year before he died. Farmer relocated to be with his family and became a visiting professor of history and American studies at our predominantly white college. In 1988, our multicultural center was renamed in honor of James Farmer and with the word out on our various diversity initiatives, we started to attract more interest from black students and faculty.

However, both nationally and locally, the tide had seemed to shift. We realized that the obstacles and lack of support described above were not happening just to us. Rather, most institutions of higher education with diversity programs were experiencing increasing resistance and setbacks similar to those we faced. Gender- and race-conscious diversity programs came under attack along with their faculty and staff. We found ourselves being derided by conservatives who co-opted the term *politically correct* and distorted it to take on new meaning. Just as the term *liberation* had been easier to ridicule when opponents shortened it to *lib*, the term *PC* became two letters used to characterize inclusiveness efforts in higher education as "reverse racism" and segregation against whites.

The college spends too much time trying to be politically correct. Yes there is a definite problem with the number of minority students here; however [the college] should not sacrifice any of its academic reputation to attract any race or gender for diversification. Students do not need to be constantly reminded of their similarities and differences in order to maintain an open mind. (White student)

During this period, James Farmer's health declined. Still, he continued to teach his course on civil rights, which became the most popular course on campus. Students as well as local residents read his stirring autobiography and fought to gain one of those coveted 200 seats to hear "that booming baritone" relay firsthand accounts of the civil rights movement and those leaders who were no longer alive to tell their own stories. Meanwhile, the faculty and staff were unhappy about the way the college treated our hero. Why had James Farmer not been named a distinguished professor with commensurate pay, health insurance, and better support? By the time James Farmer died on July 9, 1999, the administration had met most of these demands.

The following summer, prior to the first anniversary of Farmer's death, faculty from our embattled race, class, and gender project happened upon the minutes from a student affairs retreat held in May 2000 after school ended. Incredibly, these minutes outlined a series of proposed changes for the James Farmer Multicultural Center that would be in place upon our return to school in the fall. For example, the center was centrally located and occupied premium space (next to Admissions). The center was relocated to the second floor of a very small house located off the beaten path at the edge of campus (we dubbed it "the back of the bus"). The budget and staff were being significantly reduced as well. Further, the classification of the center's administrator (who did not return) was changed, downgraded from vice president for multicultural affairs to dean to acting director. Protests ensued with our black students leading the fight to save the center as they knew it. These brave students graduated a year or two later, completely drained, disheartened, and bitter.

For the most part, white students remained unaware or vaguely aware of what had happened. Many have come to believe (incorrectly) that the changes were overturned and that the center was returned to its former status. Those concerned whites (who at our urging) wrote letters to protest the changes were answered with a letter from the president and a memo from the vice president of student affairs and the dean of students. The letter informed them of "our goal to expand multicultural programming," that "unfortunately, misinformation concerning the reorganization of the James Farmer Multicultural Center has been circulated," and that ". . . there will be an increase in staff, physical space and financial resources" for Multicultural Affairs. Using the guise of restructuring, there were no increases or expansion; indeed, the opposite took place.

In 2002, there was a controversy surrounding a hiring in Admissions and our public claims in support of affirmative action. I (CBC) wrote the following in an attempt to shift the debate and instigate a much-needed dialogue with respect to our level of commitment to diversity at the college:

> Along with many other faculty, staff and students, I have been involved in "diversity" efforts at the College since I arrived in 1985. I know I am not alone in my perception that we have "lost ground" particularly since our unsuccessful efforts to stop changes made by administrators in the year following James Farmer's death. These included drastic cuts in the very Center bearing his name. Our coalition also (again unsuccessfully) strongly opposed the elimination of the cabinet level position (Vice President for Multicultural Affairs) that had been created specifically to address "diversity" concerns and support for our students of color. As I now routinely teach classes with no or perhaps one "minority" student, similar to classes before our collective "diversity" efforts over the years, I can't help but wondering whether evidence of the fears we expressed in protest have come to pass. Alarmed at the composition of my classes I began requested statistics on African American students enrolled in Fall 2001, and was told that there were 197 African American students out of total enrollment of 4426 students, and 25 African American students in our first year class out of 851 students. . . . How are we doing with respect to student "diversity" since the contentious changes in the summer of 2000?

Dialogue did not take place; and the number of black students applying, accepted, and attending continued to fall. In the fall 2003 incoming class, twelve out of the 888 students identified as black, yet the institution claimed an overall minority percentage of 12 percent. In data provided for an article in our student newspaper, the decreasing numbers of black students were combined with the increasing number of Asian American students. Thus, the breakdown of the 12 percent total minority enrollment was 8 percent black and Asian American, 3 percent Hispanic, and 1 percent multiracial (Templeman, 2003).

In contrast to concern and alarm, most of our diversity-related programs have been quietly eliminated, and the few that remain have been cut back significantly. In a recent department meeting, the department chair reported on the provost's meeting with all the department heads. The discussion came after we had been named "the most homogeneous college in the U.S." according to the *Princeton Review*'s 2003 edition of "The Best 345 Colleges." The chair informed us that our rating was considered unfair and inaccurate because the administration had learned that other colleges also had equally dismal enrollments. Information brought not just a sense of relief but also a sense of vindication—as in being falsely accused of the problem. Instead of a catalyst for change or self-reflection, our top rating as "not diverse" received only one other mention.

Here is a quote from our student newspaper, the *Bullet*, at the time:

> College officials said they feel the ranking [of] the *Princeton Review* is not important to the College's overall ranking. "You have to remember that the *Princeton Review* is only one of many publications that ranks colleges and we are not recognized as the least diverse by the majority of them." (Templeman, 2003)

A student had this to say:

> When [the college] sees minority problems as not existing they will never have satisfied minorities graduating from this school. It is [the college's] problem to educate its community about race gender, diversity, etc. If change is to happen we must start from the top because the people at the top have the power. (Black student)

WHAT'S GOING ON? THE DENIAL OF RACISM: CUMULATIVE EFFECTS

> There was no question that Racial tension existed on this campus. You knew that you were the only minority in the class and you learned to accept this. People expected you to listen to a type of music, hangout with only minorities, and have limited academic success. They changed their speech when they talked to you as opposed to their white counterparts because in their mind consciously or not you didn't grow in the same neighborhood but in actuality you lived on the same block. (Black student)

The legacy of racism remains alive and well on predominantly white college campuses across the country today. During the 1980s, a period of national political conservatism, there was an alarming rise in racial incidents on college campuses (Farrell & Jones, 1988). These disturbing patterns of events were the impetus for many of the diversity initiatives now being maligned. In assessing the racial climate of a mostly white campus in 1988, a consultant pinpointed the denial of racism as the primary problem:

> The most obvious problem on which many others suspend is that of denial. Denial alone is enough to support racism in a community, it offers no support to those who experience day to day inequities and

empowers those who choose to disregard others rights and need for cultural identification. (Fries, 1988)

Almost two decades later, data from many institutions of higher education support the position that little has changed with respect to whites' (faculty, administrators, and students) denial of the existence of racism on predominantly white campuses, and that this denial creates an uncomfortable and at times hostile environment for students, faculty, and staff of color (Feagin, Vera, & Imani, 1996).

On one hand, whites' denial of the problem maintains the status quo and supports the current university power structure and the racial imbalances already in place. On the other hand, the denial of racism contributes to a pattern of institutional resistance that successfully undermines programs and other efforts to create a campus environment that is inclusive of people of color, one that reflects and appreciates diversity. If top administrators and the majority of faculty and students fail to recognize or claim that racism exists on campus, initiatives aimed at improving the climate and curriculum will not be taken seriously or treated as a priority worthy of attention and adequate funding. Further, if a college or university refuses to acknowledge the existence of racism, its institutional norms will undoubtedly convey an implicit yet powerful message of intolerance. Such a permissive atmosphere makes it more likely that blatant racism will be expressed through overt incidents.

In our ongoing assessment of the racial climate, both white and black students continued to report overt examples of racism, ranging from frequent references to blacks as "monkeys" and monkey noises being made, to examples of black male students (and a faculty member) receiving different treatment from police often because it was assumed they did not belong to the college. Dismissive comments like that of the student quoted below were frequently reported by white students when they were asked if they were aware of any racial incidents on campus:

[Racist incidents] Frequent racial jokes, students sticking within their ethnic/cultural group. Although it seems fairly obvious that [the college] is predominantly White, I feel that there is little tension between students of divergent races and backgrounds. (White student)

What happens at our predominantly white institutions when the denial of racism is allowed to freely flourish and contribute to an atmosphere of white resistance and intolerance? Three specific types of problems that white campuses face from the denial of racism are discussed below.

CONFUSING THE FAILURE TO NOTICE WITH THE FAILURE TO EXIST

> To ignore race and gender bolsters people's sense of themselves as not thinking in a prejudiced manner. (Eberhardt & Fiske, 1994, p. 216)

Whites, having never experienced oppression by virtue of their race, see themselves as racially unmarked, indeed as not having any racial identity. Whites' location at the top of the power structure allows them to experience themselves as racially neutral, that is, embodying the "norm" (Lorde, 1984). Because whites belong to the most powerful racial group and have access to and control over more resources, they have the privilege of not paying attention to race or to the perquisites that accompany their membership in an advantaged racial group. It is psychologically appealing for whites to adopt a "color-blind" stance, that is, claiming not to see race (and particularly their own racial superiority). Indeed, rather than being "color-blind," whites can be more accurately described as being "color evasive" (Frankenberg, 1993) when it comes to race, racism, and particularly the benefits of white racial status. That is, despite claims to the contrary, whites do see color. However, many whites avoid the recognition that color matters and thereby refuse to see their advantaged racial position in terms of power relations. In contrast, people of color have rarely if ever had the luxury of being unaware of their racial identity or of their membership in an oppressed group with a long history of legal discrimination, exclusion, and racism. People of color are socialized from an early age to understand and be prepared for the ever-present possibility of becoming a target of white racism. Further, there is evidence that whites and blacks define racism differently. Whites tend to think of racism as isolated individual acts of blatant bigotry, things that are relatively rare and exceptional. On the other hand, blacks view racism as a pervasive condition, a set of institutional practices that result in racial oppression that must be negotiated daily (Blauner & Lichtenberg, 1992). Clearly, because whites have traditionally been the source of (or at least, the passive beneficiaries of) racism and not its target, their awareness of institutional racism tends to be negligible.

[Racial incident] None really, just some segregation-eating wise. KKK signs being torn down, posters offending black students. Overall racial tension here is not bad. Everyone in my dorm is nice no matter their race or skin color or ethnicity. (White student)

It is not surprising then that at predominantly white institutions, the failure to notice racism is confused with its absence. That is, because whites fail to recognize the salience of their race and, more importantly, the practices of institutional racism, they mistakenly believe that racism does not exist. In fact, the failure to notice racism actually illustrates and substantiates the depth of white racism (Rothenberg, 1988). In addition, since definitions of "what's real" are constructed by the dominant group, if whites are unaware, by default, the subordinate group's experiences of racism will be denied.

Anything that I have witnessed is light-hearted that did not seem significant of anything except lingering stereotypes. But all of the people that make jokes do not have anything against minorities, and in fact are friends with minorities. (White student)

How do "minority" versus "majority" students experience their campus environment? When black students' responses to questions about the racial climate on a mostly white campus are contrasted with a comparable group of white students' perceptions, it becomes clear that students encounter, and must negotiate, a radically different educational and social environment as a function of their race. This is true as well for other marginalized categories, such as gender, class, sexual orientation, age, and physical ability. Black students and a comparable sample of whites at a predominantly white college completed a survey to assess the racial climate on campus in 1988, 1998, and 2003. The difference in the percentages of black versus white students who answered affirmatively to the following selected questions clearly illustrates gaps in the perceptions and experiences of the two groups that are both wide and persistent despite changes in patterns over time. [Further, the responses reported here represent only part of a more extensive data set. The more comprehensive analyses raise some provocative questions and possibilities regarding student trends in perceptions over time. These and other findings are beyond the scope of this chapter.]

In separate interviews conducted just prior to the 1988 survey, it was found that white students thought the racial climate was accepting of black students and that blacks got along well on campus. However, black students held a very different view of the climate on campus.

Black students felt they were under suspicion for their behavior, isolated, verbally abused, and they reported experiencing a denial of their
feelings by white students, faculty, and administration (Fries, 1988).
(See Feagin et al., 1996 for further discussion and documentation

Table 7.1
Racial climate in 1988, 1998, and 2003

	Percentage responding yes	
Racial climate results in 1988	Blacks	Whites
I feel I am a part of the college.	41%	78%
I feel that my ethnic/cultural heritage is adequately represented.	19%	78%
There is evidence of racism at the college.	70%	41%
I have been the only member of my race in a class.	98%	0%
I feel comfortable raising questions when I don't understand the material.	39%	50%
I often feel socially isolated.	43%	0%
I am seldom aware of my race on this campus.	22%	81%
I find it easy to make friends here.	54%	70%
I feel like dropping out or transferring.	15%	17%
Overall, I'm happy at the college.	50%	80%

	Percentage responding yes	
Racial climate results in 1998	Blacks	Whites
I feel I am a part of the college.	33%	74%
I feel that my ethnic/cultural heritage is adequately represented.	8%	83%
There is evidence of racism at the college.	89%	16%
I have been the only member of my race in a class.	83%	2%
I feel comfortable raising questions when I don't understand the material.	37%	69%
I often feel socially isolated.	43%	0%
I am seldom aware of my race on this campus.	22%	73%
I find it easy to make friends here.	31%	61%
I feel like dropping out or transferring.	37%	27%
Overall, I'm happy at the college.	15%	73%

continued

Table 7.1 (continued)

Racial climate results in 2003	Percentage responding yes	
	Blacks	Whites
I feel I am a part of the college.	67%	67%
I feel that my ethnic/cultural heritage is adequately represented.	8%	81%
There is evidence of racism at the college.	50%	24%
I have been the only member of my race in a class.	88%	5%
I feel comfortable raising questions when I don't understand the material.	50%	64%
I often feel socially isolated.	63%	26%
I am seldom aware of my race on this campus.	25%	40%
I find it easy to make friends here.	50%	83%
I feel like dropping out or transferring.	54%	28%
Overall, I'm happy at the college.	50%	72%

of these disparate perceptions at predominantly white colleges and universities.)

By 1998, the gap between whites' and blacks' perceptions of evidence of racism on campus increased dramatically (from a difference of 29 percentage points in 1988 to a difference of 73 percentage points in 1998). This huge chasm was primarily due to a dramatically much more positive view of the racial climate in white students' perceptions reported ten years later (46 percent of whites reported evidence of campus racism in 1988 compared to only 16 percent of whites in 1998). In contrast, black student reports of campus racism increased from 70 percent to 89 percent of students during that same time period. Thus, while almost half of the white students surveyed in 1988 saw evidence of racism, ten years later the vast majority of whites surveyed reported a campus lacking racism. Further, the vast majority of black students reported evidence of racism in 1988, and an even higher majority concurred ten years later.

Nationally, black enrollments reversed and declined during the 1980s. Interestingly, the number of black students on our campus hit a peak before the end of the 1980s, and the enrollments continued to decline from 1998 to the present. In 2003, the gap in whites' and blacks' perceptions of the racial climate narrowed substantially to a difference of only 24 percentage points. Here we see yet a different pattern of black versus white reports. With fewer black students on campus, only half of the blacks surveyed reported evidence of racism, while whites' reports of racism increased from 16 percent to 26 percent.

Clearly, these findings are open to numerous interpretations, and all should be made with caution. It is important to remember that many changes took place from 1988–2003; most notably, the college became much more selective. Accordingly, the economic background of students changed as well, with both black and white students coming from more privileged social class status and better (also more predominantly white) high schools. This socioeconomic class difference could make it easier for all students to adopt and maintain a more "color-blind" stance, a question that we are pursuing in the comprehensive data set. Overall, however, we did find qualitative and quantitative support for the notion that whites' failure to notice race easily translated into a denial of the existence of racism, and created a pernicious environment for black students on campus.

> As a black woman attending a campus that was predominantly white was a familiar experience. After all it had been the story of my life. If you grow up in an environment where you expect to be the minority you begin to think that it just happens that way and think nothing of it. Having been taught not to notice race you simply blend in anyway you can. You dress like them, you talk similarly, you listen to similar music and you just try to fit in and have fun. You grow up thinking that's the way it is and nobody tells you to question why you are always the minority you just are. They have brainwashed you not to see and to think of your circumstance as normal. But through it all no matter how well you assimilate you are always black you know it and they are not going to let you forget it. (Black student)

THE PRESSURE TO ASSIMILATE, AND TOKENISM

> Assimilation, in this paradigm, is assumed to be a one-way street along which new arrivals "give up" one identity and "take on" another one. Old identities are "melted down" into "new ones." (Wellman, 1993, p. 37)

Today's universities are often portrayed as having been taken over by leftists bent on enforcing political correctness and multiculturalism to the detriment of academic excellence. In reality, mostly white colleges and universities continue to be conservative institutions run almost solely by white, upper-class men. People of color and white women are brought into an institution governed by white male norms and are expected to "blend in" and, in short, to assimilate to the existing campus milieu. Students, faculty, and staff people of color are put under tremendous pressure to affirm and mirror the dominant group's values and culture and deny their own. Assimilation is assumed to be a one-way process whereby "minorities" adapt to the prevailing white norms; while white students, faculty, and administrators carry on with "business as usual." In fact, if whites do acknowledge any racial problem on campus, they claim that the problem is minority students' tendency to "keep to themselves" and not to "mix in" with whites. However, whites fail to consider that extracurricular activities at substantially white campuses represent white interests, traditions, and values that may make students of color feel excluded or, at the very least, not included. When students of color socialize with each other and create their own programs and activities (like whites do), they are accused by whites of self-segregating. Think of the daily experience of the lone black student attending white classes. Not surprisingly, survey research indicates that students of color (must) cross ethnic and racial lines much more frequently than whites do and that it is white students who are more prone to segregate themselves (Feagin et al., 1996). Indeed, the suggestion that minority students needed to mingle more with white students was one of the justifications given by our dean of students for moving the James Farmer Multicultural Center from its central location to the second floor in an obscure small house where (white) student affairs staff were located. The following quotes suggest this:

> What's up with those black girls, they are always sitting together in the cafeteria. They really shouldn't ostracize themselves with their clubs and other activities. It's so hard to get to know them because they already come in knowing each other and don't want to make friends. (White female student)

> I hear the White students complain about the lack of diversity at [the college] but they are not willing to take a stand. Everything involving diversity of students for the most part is left up to the minority organizations. It is very upsetting that I can go to another organization that's outside my comfort group but others cannot do the same. We have to leave our comfort groups and put ourselves in situations to associate with others, they don't. (Black student)

Assimilation is a first requirement of those who are chosen as tokens in the workplace of the dominant culture: "He's black but he's just like us" (Pharr, 1988, p. 62).

Tokenism and assimilation are ways of co-opting people of color. Tokenism often takes the form of hiring a few people of color to deflect concerns about diversity while leaving the existing power structure intact and unchanged. People hired as tokens tend to be those who appear to their employers as most likely to fit in with and not challenge the prevailing white male institutional norms and values. These tactics give the false impression that a person of color merely needs to work hard and that his or her efforts will be rewarded as meritorious in a color-blind, barrier-free environment. Tokenism and assimilation support the implication that if people of color fail to occupy positions of importance, it is because they lack the intelligence, motivation, or ability necessary to measure up to whites' standards of excellence and not because of practices that reflect institutional racism. According to Pharr (1988), the tokenized person is in a classic "no-win" position. Typically such a person is given a highly visible, attractive position, yet often has little autonomy and real power. Tokens may find themselves under pressure to remain separate from other members of their racial group while simultaneously acting as representatives for their entire race. Since a token is expected to be a "team player," identifying racism in the organization will be seen as disloyal and problematic. At the same time, tokens receive pressure from their racial group to make changes from within the system. However, this is untenable because tokens are isolated and lack the support system, power, and resources to enact such changes (Pharr, 1988). Even when tokens are intent on using their position to break down stereotypes of their racial group, stereotype disconfirmation often involves displaying an exaggerated version of the powerful in-group's attributes and behaviors (Fiske & Ruscher, 1993).

Thus, upon closer inspection, assimilation pressure and tokenism are hardly benign processes perpetrated by misguided but well-meaning individual whites who mistakenly view racial barriers in the academy as a problem of the past. Instead, these are institutional methods that function to keep people of color from organizing, forming coalitions, and gaining access to power and resources that could be used to disrupt the status quo and threaten the power structure of the white-dominated academy. Thus, assimilation and tokenism help to ensure that entrenched white male norms of self-interest maintain a stronghold on the academy and continue undisturbed.

The school used their minority students as tokens in a very obvious way. They chose those who resembled their model minority student and "postered" them (literally) on any form of campus recruiting information. The token minority students appeared on the brochures to attract people to come to the school of the like minded. They used minorities to send a message that they valued diversity. However they forget to mention that they only create this diverse and culturally stimulating environment one weekend out of the year . . . the perfect opportunity to invite all of the potential minority Freshman to come and visit. They have an opportunity to stay with a student of color and enjoy a weekend surrounded in events that may appeal to them . . . once they get here they'll simply learn to make do. (Black student)

PLACING THE BURDEN ON PEOPLE OF COLOR

I heard about some students Fall Semester raising the Confederate Flag out of their window. I wouldn't know, I am White! Everything is easygoing for us, except getting jobs. (White student's reaction to being asked about the racial climate on campus)

The denial of racism is also costly to people of color on a very practical level. The academy is a microcosm of power relations in our culture. At white institutions, there are few people of color in tenured teaching or administrative leadership positions. Since whites tend to think of themselves as racially unmarked, white faculty and administrators assume that race issues or problems are the peculiar concerns of people of color and therefore do not affect them. Thus, blacks who are in lower-ranking positions or are untenured are often expected to take on the added burden of single-handedly changing the curriculum and racial climate, usually without compensation, adequate support, or resources. This is true for black students as well. If there are racial tensions or actual incidents on campus, white students may be sympathetic, but they too assume that it is a problem that does not directly pertain to them. In contrast, faculty and students of color are left feeling the brunt of the situation, and these feelings may contribute further to a sense of isolation and alienation on a predominantly white campus.

I do know that one of my favorite professors decision to leave [the college] due to his treatment as the seen and not heard token black professor affected my judgment of [the college's] regard for minority professors which I think are vital for a well balanced liberal arts education. Only so much can be done to recruit minority students or professors, but once they are here, they should receive the attention necessary of their isolated state as the nonwhite minority. (White student)

In this case, whites' denial of their racial privilege and of the existence of racism has a deleterious effect on people of color in the academy, and it saps energy that might otherwise be invested in more personally productive activities. For example, it is commonplace for students of color to be put into the position of being asked to "speak for their race" both inside and outside the classroom (Feagin et al., 1996). Being the recipient of such unexpected and unwanted attention is not only stressful, but it also serves as a reminder of whites' lack of awareness and insensitivity. For example, the only black student in a history class reported that during a lecture on slavery, the professor stopped, singled her out, and asked how she felt about slavery. She responded by saying "I don't know. I wasn't around then," and subsequently dropped the course. As Feagin and his colleagues (1996) point out, it is the cumulative effects of many such incidents that create a racialized social structure on campus that people of color have little power to define or significantly change. Why should students, faculty, and staff of color (who are already in a disadvantaged position) have the additional burden of educating whites and managing problems caused by white racism, while their white counterparts can proceed unencumbered to pursue their academic goals?

> It does make me feel out of place because in most of my classes I'm the only black person; and people feel that any statement I make, even if it's only my personal opinion, is the basic view of blacks as a whole. (If they would just think about it they would realize how ignorant such a generalization is—just put the shoe on the other foot.) (Black student)

All people have a racial identity that determines their location in a racialized hierarchy of power relations. Thus, it is critical for whites to realize that the racial climate at white colleges and universities is the collective responsibility of all members of the academy. Without this recognition, the campus climate at these colleges and universities will remain a noxious one for people of color and particularly for blacks.

MOVING FROM THE INDIVIDUAL TO THE INSTITUTIONAL: AN UNCOMFORTABLE DILEMMA

> They tell me not to segregate myself but little do they realize they have done that for me. They claim that they have tried to give me a support system so that I feel comfortable in this environment but what they

have failed to do is create a system where I need no additional support. It is going to take a lot more than hiring one minority professor, creating a club for people of color and having one hip-hop dance party to make me feel comfortable in this environment. (Black student)

Neither whites nor people of color seem to understand that there is a clash here between a social group perspective, learned by people of color through the social experience of racism, and an individualized perspective, learned by whites through their racial socialization (Scheurich, 1993, p. 6).

Just like other hierarchical institutions, the academy prefers to focus on individual strategies and solutions to racism. Such methods serve to deflect attention from larger institutional issues, such as scrutinizing who holds the power and how that power is used (McIntosh, 1988). For example, when racial incidents do occur on campuses, the most common response from top administrators is to label such events "isolated incidents." Similarly, if institutions of higher education do take any action to combat racism on campus, they tend to hire consultants (often conservatives from the corporate world) to conduct one-time-only "sensitivity training" workshops. The underlying premise of these workshops is that if people would learn to be more aware and sensitive to each other, then racial problems would disappear. Again, this reflects the dominant group's definition of racism.

> Ultimately though any change that is going to take place will have to be in the hearts and minds of anyone who is racist. (White student)

Although it is important for members of an academy to be sensitive and respectful of others, such a strategy does nothing to address institutional racism or remedy the current power imbalances in the structure of higher education.

As Scheurich (1993) cogently points out, whites are heavily invested in the idea of individualism, whereas people of color (since they are constantly aware of their membership in an oppressed group) are much less likely to be seduced by the notion that success is purely the function of individualized choices and efforts. In describing the effects of the disproportionate distribution of resources to middle and upper-class whites and how their values become codified as standards of excellence, he states,

> One of the main ways this happens is that the ways of the dominant group become universalized as measures of merit, hiring criteria, grading

standards, predictors of success, correct grammar, appropriate behavior, and so forth, all of which are said to be distributed as differences in individual effort, ability, or intelligence. Membership in a social group and the group-related inequitable distribution of resources and power thus disappear under the guise of individualism. (p. 7)

Similarly, Eberhardt and Fiske (1994) critique the myth that merit-based standards of selection operate in the absence of affirmative action. They note that merit is always mediated by power and that powerful groups are able to view their achievements as merit-based, while less-powerful group members' achievements are perceived as due to (often from whites' perspective, unfairly applied) group-based benefits. Thus whites are unable to recognize their group-based advantages, yet at the same time they ascribe such motives to the successes or advancements of people of color. Interestingly, the former speaker of the U.S. House of Representatives, Newt Gingrich, invoked the preeminence of individualism in his speech aimed at counteracting President Clinton's call for a national dialogue on racism:

We need to treat individuals as individuals, and we need to address discrete problems for the problems they are and not presume them to be part of an intractable racial issue. . . . We will not be successful in moving our society forward if we submerge individuals into groups. (Yang, 1997)

The fact remains, however, that once well-meaning whites realize that racism still exists (despite the fact that it may be unintentional) and that our institutions are rigged to ensure that the current power structure stays in place, they face an uncomfortable dilemma. This realization forces these whites to acknowledge their complicity in a system that is unbalanced and to understand that they themselves are beneficiaries of such a system. This knowledge is disquieting and conflicts with white people's self-images as just and fair people. Such a shift in awareness from individual prejudice as problematic to the focusing on institutional racism allows whites to see how they have benefited from a system that oppresses others. This flies in the face of such whites' strong convictions that their own rewards and stature are the result of a meritocracy, that is, a system that rewards all individuals equally and only based on the merits of their work. Once white people recognize whose interests are served by the denial of racism and indifference toward people of color, they also realize that whites must bear the responsibility for dismantling such an unfair system. No wonder denial is so comfortable for well-meaning whites! (Particularly since breaking through that denial will undoubtedly result in threatening cherished beliefs and questioning the dominant group's as well as their own positive self-image.)

TWO USEFUL CONCEPTS: UNACKNOWLEDGED WHITE-SKIN PRIVILEGE AND AVERSIVE RACISM

In this section, we will explore two concepts that help illuminate the tendency for whites to deny racism; consequently, they are useful in breaking through that denial.

White-Skin Privilege

It seems being culturally aware is the new trend; that when it comes to appreciating other cultures on campus, many students in this predominantly white school don't know how to act. In the classroom and out of the classroom are two different things. (White student)

As a white person, I realized I had been taught about racism as something that puts others at a disadvantage, but had been taught not to see one of its corollary aspects, white privilege, which puts me at an advantage. (McIntosh, 1988, p. 71)

McIntosh describes unacknowledged white-skin privilege as an "invisible weightless knapsack of special provisions" that whites cash in daily, while remaining oblivious to their unearned advantages. She compiled a personal list of forty-six ways in which she regularly experienced white privileges that her black colleagues did not share. As she notes, some of these entitlements help her to feel welcome and comfortable, instead of feeling like an outsider, while others allow her to escape fear, hostility, danger, and violence. Still others allow her to ignore or disparage anything outside of the white dominant culture with impunity. Below are some examples from her own list:

• I did not have to educate our children to be aware of systemic racism for their own physical protection.
• If a traffic cop pulls me over or if the IRS audits my tax return, I can be sure I haven't been singled out because of my race.
• I can arrange my activities so that I will never have to experience feelings of rejection owing to my race.

- I can be reasonably sure that if I ask to talk to "the person in charge," I will be facing a person of my own race.
- I can easily find academic courses and institutions that give attention only to people of my race.
- I can choose blemish cover or bandages in "flesh" color and have them more or less match my skin.
- I am never asked to speak for all the people of my racial group.
- I can turn on the television or open the front page of the paper and see people of my race widely and positively represented.
- I can remain oblivious to the language and customs of persons of color who constitute the world's majority without feeling in my culture any penalty for such oblivion.

Can you come up with some of your own examples?

Several layers of denial protect and prevent an awareness of these privileges. McIntosh maintains that whites are explicitly taught not to recognize these racially marked benefits. Indeed, while whites may understand the concept of "minorities" as "disadvantaged"; as the majority group, whites have not been taught to think of themselves as over-advantaged. Because of the hierarchical nature of power, for a group to be disadvantaged, another group must be over-advantaged. Plus, whites are taught to see racism as individual acts of meanness directed at a group and not an invisible system that confers dominance and privilege to certain groups but not others (McIntosh, 1988). As long as whites remain unaware of white privilege, they are not forced to acknowledge whose interests are served by such a system, and this system of white privilege remains unchallenged and unchanged. Thus, whites experience a comfortable denial of the personal benefits they derive from their white-skin privilege, as well as the existence of an organized racial system that translates into unearned entitlements for whites and institutional racism for people of color.

McIntosh discusses how the concept of unacknowledged white-skin privilege helped her to understand why whites were rightly seen as oppressive by people of color, even when whites did not view themselves that way. Becoming aware of the multifaceted nature of white privilege can serve as a real eye-opener for well-intentioned whites who are sympathetic to the plight of people color. The realization that doors open and opportunities are bestowed merely because of one's white skin color is profound for many whites. Of course, other attributes such as gender, class, and sexual orientation may mitigate these advantages. Nevertheless, the notion of white-skin privilege seriously calls into question the belief in meritocracy, that is, the idea that rewards are distributed solely by merit and that other factors such as race are not influential. Further, as McIntosh points out, even if whites do not accept or agree with racism, they still stand to benefit from white privilege.

Aversive Racism

Prejudiced thinking and discrimination still exist, but the contemporary forms are subtler, more indirect, and less overtly negative than are more traditional forms. Furthermore, the contemporary form of prejudice is expressed in ways that protect and perpetuate a nonprejudiced, nondiscriminating self-image (Gaertner & Dovidio, 1986, p. 279).

> We know how to sound aware and diverse, but not how to show it with our actions. (White student)

Although more blatant and overt forms of racism have declined nationally, social scientists have documented a rise in a newer, more subtle, and indirect type of racism. In social psychology, Gaertner and Dovidio (1986) use the term *aversive racism* to describe the subtle bias and discrimination expressed by whites who are sympathetic toward people of color and consider themselves nonprejudiced. They characterize aversive racism as the result of two conflicting influences. On one hand, aversive racists espouse strong egalitarian values and support democratic norms of fairness and equality. On the other hand, these whites have been socialized in a racist culture where it is impossible for even the most well-meaning whites to avoid developing negative beliefs about people of color. These negative messages are pervasive and operate on both an individual psychological level (for example, our cognitive predisposition toward stereotyping and categorizing into in-group versus out-group) and on a sociological level (such as negative media portrayals and social stratification systems). The existence of these inevitable racial biases along with deeply held democratic beliefs about justice and racial equality leads to feelings of conflict and ambivalence. According to Gaertner and Dovidio (1986),

> Because of the importance of the egalitarian value system to aversive racists' self-concept, these negative feelings and associated beliefs are

typically excluded from awareness. When a situation or event threatens to make the negative portion of their attitude salient, aversive racists are motivated to repudiate or dissociate these feelings from their self-image, and they vigorously try to avoid acting wrongly on the basis of these feelings. In these situations, aversive racists may overreact and amplify their positive behavior in ways that would reaffirm their egalitarian convictions and their apparently nonracist attitudes. In other situations, however, the underlying negative portions of their attitudes are expressed in subtle rationalizable ways. (p. 271)

Therefore, rather than expressing hostility and hatred toward people of color, aversive racists experience feelings such as fear, discomfort, and anxiety. In keeping with whites' denial of racism, these unpleasant emotions often result in them avoiding people of color. In addition, research shows that aversive racists will search for nonracial factors to justify their negative attitudes or behaviors toward people of color. For example, Gaertner and Dovidio (1986) note that, for years, children were bussed to schools for a variety of reasons without public outcry. However, it was only when bussing became a way to achieve desegregation that there was strong opposition, supposedly not to the mixing of the races but to bussing itself (a nonracial factor). Similarly, in the 1992 example incident described earlier, when a special faculty meeting was held to discuss the approval of an ethnic studies course, opponents of the course objected to it based on (so-called) nonracial factors, such as the qualifications of the instructor (even though the instructor was a person of color); of course, no other class or instructor had ever been scrutinized by the entire faculty in such a way. In this way, whites may display discriminatory behavior toward people of color but still maintain an image of themselves as nonracist.

An incident of racial insensitivity or what made me realize other peoples view, was . . . when we all wrote essays about affirmative action and had to talk about our views briefly in class. Of course *everybody* who wasn't of color was against it, and I'm not kidding. I'm personally divided on the subject, but when I heard why some people were against the practice, I realized how out for themselves many people are. The Whites in my class felt as if their positions in life were greatly threatened. One boy said how he was extremely upset that he didn't get Duke [University] due to Affirmative Action, because colleges are very strange about how they admit people. (Black student)

Sam Gaertner and John Dovidio review research that demonstrates this type of discrimination by whites. Liberal whites' objections to affirmative action policies ignore the subtext of threatening white privilege and instead focus on presumably nonracial factors such as perceived procedural unfairness (see Dovidio & Gaertner, 1996, for a comprehensive discussion of how unintentional racial biases impact affirmative action). Finally, research has demonstrated that although aversive racists are usually vigilant about avoiding behaviors that could be construed as anti-racist, their unintentional biases may instead be manifested in pro-white behaviors. In social psychology, this is known as showing favoritism toward the in-group as opposed to derogating the out-group (Dovidio & Gaertner, 1996).

> There are a few whites that try to be friendly to minorities but often they come across very fake and are never as friendly when they are surrounded by their peers. They're friendlier alone when less whites are around to see them being nice. (Black student)

An understanding of aversive racism is useful in breaking through the majority group's denial of white racism. In a way, it can let well-meaning white people "off the hook," since such an understanding acknowledges that it is virtually impossible to grow up white in a racist culture without internalizing some degree of racist ideology. Realizing this inevitability, then, does not preclude whites from being good and just people. After all, it is the tension between these two contradictory impulses that is the source of aversive racism. Gaertner and Dovidio correctly point out that traditional methods of changing blatant and overt forms of racism are ineffective for aversive racists because given their nonprejudiced self-view, aversive racists believe such messages are irrelevant to them. However, work by social psychologists indicates that an awareness of the discrepancy between automatically activated negative stereotypes and endorsed nonprejudiced beliefs can motivate well-intentioned whites to consciously overcome the effects of their prejudice on their behavior.

After white students study the research on aversive racism in my (CBC) courses, most say that previously they refused to label themselves as racists but now can see that they are in fact aversive racists. Hopefully, learning to recognize the source of interracial discomfort and tension along with awareness itself can counteract aversive racism and short-circuit the process that normally results in expressions of biased behavior toward blacks accompanied by whites' lack of awareness.

> I don't really pay attention to racial issues on campus. All I know is that the school is mainly White, which I find really eerie. I grew up

in the military so I'm used to social isolation and diverse cultures. I'm used to being around different people and I consider myself pretty tolerant but I wouldn't go so far as to say I'm not racist. I'm uncomfortable talking with black people but not with other groups and I don't know why. But I am aware of this problem only I don't know how to fix it. (White female student)

Like McIntosh's concept of white privilege, aversive racism has implications that go beyond unintentional personal prejudice to institutional racism. One of the most important findings in the aversive racism research literature is that when normative standards are strong, discrimination is least likely to occur. In contrast, when normative guidelines are weak or absent, discrimination is more likely to occur. According to Gaertner and Dovidio (1986),

In terms of interracial behavior, the presence or absence of norms governing appropriate behavior is a critical factor mediating the expression of prejudice. When norms are clear, bias is unlikely to occur; when norms are ambiguous or conflicting, discrimination is often exhibited. (p. 279)

Thus, the denial of white racism by individuals and institutions of higher education provides an environment where proper normative guidelines will be absent and discriminatory behavior toward people of color will continue to be expressed.

Culturally different students get along better when they are not forced together by programs [at the college]. I find it disturbing that minority students are given so many special programs here. I believe this fosters a resentment within the student body and a reinforcement of stereotypes already prevalent in society. (White student)

COLOR VERSUS POWER, BLIND VERSUS EVASIVE, SHOULD NOT VERSUS DOES NOT

I don't know of anyone in a position of authority on this campus who is my own race. (Black student)

Based on more than two decades of research findings, the American Psychological Association (APA, 1997) developed a pamphlet to debunk the notion of color blindness. Presently, aspects of color-blind attitudes have become an empirical question of interest, and in our research we have used the recently developed Color-Blind Racial Attitudes Scale (Neville, 2000). Neville provides a succinct summary of the crux of the problem with the color blindness concept when it is deconstructed:

> Simply, colorblind racial attitudes refers to the belief that race should not and does not matter. The first part of this concept seems admirable; a reasonable person probably would not publicly argue that social and economic resources should be disproportionately available to specific racial groups. However, scholars have argued that the latter half of this perspective is problematic, citing that the continuance of racism makes it impossible to ignore the importance of race in people's experiences; thus race does matter. . . . (p. 4)

In short, perhaps we can all agree that (ideally) race should not matter. However, that race does not matter is an absurdity, a baldfaced lie with all evidence supporting the contrary (see, for example, Helms, 1992; and Jones, 1997; among many others). Color blindness is a white fantasy that only the dominant group can pretend to believe by the continual processes of denying racism and evading the reality of power.

At our own institution, during what we now call "the good old days" of diversity, one department was able to hire two black faculty members consecutively. Both were rising scholars and very popular teachers. The first chose to leave because of the racial climate, and then the second one was hired and followed suit. Such departures are in large part due to the inability to thrive in an illusory color-blind white environment. After all, remember the *Racial Feud* responses? If our black faculty (or students) seek a reflection of themselves on a predominantly white campus, they will find others of their race plentiful in the predominantly black housekeeping, dining hall, or maintenance staff. Out of close to 200 full-time tenure-track faculty positions at our college, one can count all four blacks without using one full hand. If you are at a predominantly white campus, count and calculate percentages for how many blacks occupy your prime faculty positions. As is the case with our student homogeneity, we are the norm and not the exception. My (CBC) white students are always surprised by what they find after completing an assignment I give at the beginning of the semester. I simply ask students to take the institution's organizational flowchart and code those positions by race and gender. Although the results are completely obvious, most white students are trained to see only individuals and thus express shock when they are required to look at race, gender, and power on an institutional level.

From the framework presented in this chapter, the Clinton administration's 1997 commission on race relations represented an anti–color-blind perspective. If nothing else, its existence acknowledged the effects of the denial of racism and stated the need for white awareness and engaging in what Johnnella Butler terms "difficult dialogues" (Butler, 1991). As coauthors who differ in race and hence white privilege, we ask, "difficult for whom?"

At the time, George Curry, editor in chief of (the now-defunct) *Emerge* magazine, when asked his view of President Clinton's new race relations commission and what issue it should address, said,

> The new presidential commission should focus on what Rev. Joseph Lowery of the Southern Christian Leadership Conference leadership Conference calls the 51st state—the state of denial. This country is in denial about both the history and the extent of racism in the United States. [The recent Gallup poll on race relations showed that whites "perceive that their neighbors are prejudiced, but that they personally are much less so."] Until we can admit that racism has permeated every aspect of American life, from the writing of the Constitution to our perceptions of one another, we will not begin to make any real progress in this area. ("What Should," 1997)

When the first author (CBC) was the age of the second author, another common slogan was some version of "If you're not part of the solution, you're part of the problem." In 2004, it is still true that until the dominant group recognizes and chooses to see their power, we will be perpetuating the status quo by taking no action at all. When well-meaning whites choose to do their own "race work" motivated by their own good and self-interest, the trends described in this chapter will not be reversed.

> I am White, but I am used to going to school with Blacks. At [the college] it seems everyone is White and at times it is unsettling. An all White America is a false America. It is sad, but most colleges are divided along racial lines. It's not anyone's fault really. That's just the way it is. (White student)

As Peggy McIntosh (1988) pointed out, the dominant group needs to consider this question: having privilege, what (if anything) are we willing to do to lessen it? In order for white male and female educators to teach our students that for racism, the "personal" (individual) is indeed "political" (institutional), we must assume responsibility for the racial climate. Are we willing to move first from avoidance or denial to awareness? Will we take the next step, namely discomfort, and proceed further to decision? In this uncharted territory we must also be able to acknowledge that for racism, the political (institutional) indeed becomes personal (individual), and we must be willing to give up our own entitlement in order to redistribute power, thereby enacting real institutional change. Clearly, for any change to happen, racial tensions now festering barely below the surface must finally be confronted by the predominantly white male academy. There will be no overnight pill for the dominant group to merely swallow and wake up refreshed with racism magically banished from their system. Instead, the dominant group *necessarily on their own* must be willing to withstand and process our nation's unpleasant and inevitably painful racism, past and present, before the healing can even begin. At that point, should we reach it, "difficult dialogues" will for whites have become "*necessary* dialogues." Only then can the opportunity that can bring about a decrease in the manifestations of racism finally exist.

CONCLUDING COLORS: BLACK, RED, WHITE, AND BLUE

> No one bothered to tell me that racism still existed. The same demon thoughts that raised their heads fifty years ago have not died but now wear a mask so that I can't see them as easily. . . . But I have become unplugged from the lies that they beg me to believe. . . . They want nothing more than for you to think that racism does not exist. Everyday a little pain and heartache just to remind you that the things that they get without thinking twice you may never have. But this is done very subtly so that even a minority is unaware of the status quo. You mustn't think that your Blackness plays a role in your disadvantage but rather a personal or individual flaw. So you assume the burden and responsibility. Any time that you dare state the obvious about the discrepancies in power you have just played the race card. (Black student)

As teacher and student, the two authors have come full circle. We have been able to shift and take on each other's roles but not each other's skin. In the end, we remain two (outwardly) very different women who share a common cause and strong concerns. Black and white, black and Syrian-Irish American, our very different paths did intersect at a point in higher education at a predominantly white institution. We like to think of it as a sort of confluence where there is much urgent work that needs to be done. Armed with our data sets and others, we have many critical questions that are imperative to ask and answer about blacks at all levels within the white academy. Of course, the majority of blacks remain excluded from the white academy in (growing) disproportionate numbers. Unlike those who can, by avoiding looking, claim not to see; once we look, we cannot avoid looking, and we claim to see disturbing evidence in our nation's collective heap of denial and racism.

Unfortunately, we feel that our president, George W. Bush, and his current administration are absolutely heading in the wrong direction with their hardly veiled anti-affirmative action stance. We view this as the culmination of the persistent denial of racism and its tangible results—namely, an effective dismantling of institutional programs aimed at social change that parallel and mirror the very process and consequences we have described in our analysis of predominantly white higher education. Thus, we see folly inherent in their position regarding the most recent legal challenges to affirmative action. The Bush administration adopts a strategy designed to masquerade as innocuously color-blind what is in fact color-evasive and deliberately power-blind. Instead of strong leadership and the clear normative standards that social psychology demonstrates are imperative on a national level to decrease subtle and overt racism, we are faced with more than a void. Rather, President Bush serves as a pied piper who (mis)leads the growing chorus of anti-diversity voices that we have examined on white campuses.

It has not escaped our attention (or sense of irony) that this particular president embodies and represents many of the concepts discussed in this chapter. We pose a few questions:

- Does George W. Bush exemplify the outcome of a fair selection system, a meritocracy where the best and brightest are the most deserving?
- Did George W. Bush receive (color-blind) admission to Yale University on the basis of his academic record and the merits of his hard-earned achievements?
- Could anyone (regardless of race and gender) with stronger credentials able to pull themselves up by their (cowboy) bootstraps take the seat awarded to George W. Bush at one of the most elite white universities in the land?
- Or did the president benefit from a system that privileged his family's tremendous wealth and accompanying sense of entitlement?
- Did Yale University lower its standards to let George W. Bush in because of his race, class, or gender status to the detriment of a nonwhite

poor male or female with higher scores, better grades, and more accomplishments?

From our own answers, we seem to have not reverse racism but, instead, an affirmative action program for rich white males already firmly in place. As a recent critique (Shaw, 2003) points out,

> The president's opposition to the University of Michigan's diversity efforts is woefully misguided. His mischaracterization of the selection process encourages white students who are not admitted to the school of their choice to blame affirmative action. Perhaps it is easier to attack the minuscule number of minority students accepted than to accept rejection. . . . ("Race Still Matters," 2003)

We must bother to look and then carefully scrutinize the current numbers and actual enrollments of blacks at white colleges and universities without aggregating data for specific minority groups. Do these numbers tell a different story, of growing gaps among the percentages of Asian American, white, black, and Latino high school seniors who go on to attend four-year colleges, a story that suggests a reversal of the gains made by blacks in the decades prior to the 1980s? For example, with (again) aggregate data drawn from the 2000 Census, Greene and Forster ("College Diversity," 2004) wrote an editorial arguing against affirmative action. Although we disagree with their position on affirmative action, we do find the numbers they present to be instructive. They state that of the 1.2 million black and Latino eighteen-year-olds in the United States, 631,000 graduate from high school with regular diplomas. Greene and Forster maintain that, of those graduates, only 287,000 take the courses necessary to enroll in a four-year college. After subtracting 69,000 unable to pass a twelfth-grade reading test, they arrive at two numbers: 218,000 for "college-ready minorities" and 244,000 "minorities" admitted to college that year.

In closing, we would like to end with the words of Theodore M. Shaw, associate director-counsel of the NAACP Legal Defense and Educational Fund, who represented black and Latino student interveners in the University of Michigan affirmative action case involving undergraduate admissions. He is someone we suspect may have gained entrance to the academy at least in part because of the color of his skin.

> Our nation's progress in reversing the effects of our long, dark night of slavery and legalized separation—begun merely a generation ago—did not emerge serendipitously. Deliberate efforts to redress racial inequality

have netted tangible results. Despite progress, entrenched racial inequality from cradle to grave remains a feature of the American landscape. Colorblindness is not reality. Let us see race, and then act justly. ("Race Still Matters," 2003)

Toolbox for Change

Promoting social change: Everyone can do something to combat prejudice

Actively contributing to oppression	• Verbally or physically harassing target group members • Telling oppressive or offensive jokes • Perpetuating stereotypes • Avoiding the target group • Considering discrimination to be a problem of the past
Inactively contributing to oppression by denying or ignoring	• Accepting the status quo • Believing we live in a color-blind society • Refusing to acknowledge one's own privilege • Ignoring acts of discrimination • Pitying the targets of oppression • Believing that you have experienced and fully understand the oppression of the target group
Recognizing oppression	• Recognize one's own privilege • Do not believe a problem does not exist simply because it is not blatantly visible. • Avoid blaming others or yourself for the social constructs of society. • Take ownership of your conscious or unconscious prejudices. • Know that the past is not your fault but the present and the future are your responsibility.
Educating self and others	• Interrupt jokes or stories that perpetuate prejudice. • Interact and learn from people of the target group. • Help others understand their own privileges. • Teach others to appreciate and value diversity. • Raise a child to be knowledgeable of oppression and how to be an ally.

continued

Toolbox for Change (continued)

Supporting and encouraging	• Listen and validate the concerns and experiences of the target group. • Become active in your school or community to promote diversity. • Work to support other allies. • Elect politicians who actively support endeavors to increase social justice. • Do not expect external rewards but let the intrinsic motivation of doing the right thing be your encouragement.
Initiating and preventing	• Challenge the norm. • Start a program/organization that increases appreciation for diversity in your school or community. • Speak for change: let lawmakers, policymakers, and those with power know the importance of combating oppression. • Fight policies and laws that have the potential to support oppression. • Expose areas in your school, organization, job, or community that do not appreciate diversity (for example, if your school does not have minority faculty, complain to the administration). • Do not grow weary of doing well.

ACKNOWLEDGMENTS

In addition to Aisha Renée Thompson, I would like to gratefully acknowledge the contributions of so many of my undergraduate students who have worked over the past fifteen years—discussing, collecting, and presenting data on the racial climate as student projects over the years in two of my research courses—particularly Kevin Paine, John Kelly, Colleen Inson, Marsie Turner, Tiffany Hanback, Stacie Evans, Trevor Bopp, and most recently, "Laura" and slacker Sean.—(CBC)

REFERENCES

Blauner, B. & Lichtenberg, J. (1992, June 8). Blacks and whites define word "racism" differently. *The Washington Post.*

Butler, J. E. (1991). The difficult dialogue of curriculum transformation: Ethnic studies and women's studies. In J. E. Butler & J. C. Walter (Eds.), *Transforming the curriculum: Ethnic studies and women's studies* (pp. 1–19). Albany, NY: State University of New York Press.

Curry, G. (1997, June 15). What should the president's initiative focus on? Outlook. *The Washington Post.*

Dovidio, J. F. & Gaertner, S. L. (1996). Affirmative action, unintentional racial biases, and intergroup relations. *Journal of Social Issues, 52,* 51–75.

Eberhardt, J. L., & Fiske, S. T. (1994). Affirmative action in theory and practice: Issues of power, ambiguity, and gender versus race. *Basic and Applied Social Psychology, 15*(1&2), 201–220.

Farrell, W. C., & Jones, C. K. (1988) Recent racial incidents in higher education: A preliminary perspective. *The Urban Review, 20,* 211–226.

Feagin, J. R., Vera, H., & Imani, N. (1996). *The agony of education: Black students at white colleges and universities.* New York: Routlege.

Fiske, S. T., & Ruscher, J. B. (1993). Negative independence and prejudice: Whence the affect? In D. M. Mackie & D. L. Hamilton (Eds.), *Affect, cognition and stereotyping: Interactive processes in group perception* (pp. 239–268). San Diego, CA: Academic.

Frankenberg. R. (1993). *White women, race matters: The social construction of whiteness.* Minneapolis, MN: University of Minnesota Press.

Fries, S. (1988). Racial assessment report of Mary Washington College. Unpublished manuscript, University of Maryland–College Park.

Gaertner S. L., & Dovidio, J. F. (1986). The aversive form of racism. In J. F. Dovidio and S. L. Gaertner (Eds.), *Prejudice, discrimination and racism.* Orlando, FL: Academic.

Greene, J. P., & Forster, G. (2004, January 7). College diversity: Fix the pipeline first. *The Washington Post.*

Helms, J. (1992). *A race is a nice thing to have: A guide to being a white person or understanding the white person in your life.* Topeka, KS: Content Communications.

Jones, J. M. (1997). *Prejudice and racism* (2nd ed.), New York: McGraw-Hill.

Lorde, A. (1984). *Sister outsider.* New York: Crossing Press.

McIntosh, P. (1988). White privilege and male privilege: A personal account of coming to see correspondences through work in women's studies. Working Paper #189. Wellesley College Center for Research on Women, Wellesley, Massachusetts.

Neville, J. (2000). The COBRA Scale. *Journal of Counseling Psychology, 47*(1), 59–70.

Pharr, S. (1988). *Homophobia as a weapon of sexism.* Little Rock, AR: Chardon.

Rothenberg, P. (1988). Integrating the study of race, gender, and class: Some preliminary observations. *Feminist Teacher, 3*(3), 37–42.

Scheurich, J. J. (1993). Toward a white discourse on racism. *Educational Researcher, 22*(8), 5–10.

Shaw, T. (2003, March 1). Race still matters. *The Washington Post.*

Templeman, C. (2003, January 23). MWC named most homogeneous college in U.S. *The Bullet, 76*(12). Retrieved from http://www.unh.edu/residential-life/diversity/index.html

Wellman, D. T. (1993). *Portraits of racism* (2nd ed.). Cambridge: Cambridge University Press.

Wittenbrink, B., Judd, C. M., & Park, B. (2001). Spontaneous prejudice in context: Variability in automatically activated attitudes. *Journal of Personality and Social Psychology, 81*, 815–827.

Yang, J. (1997, June 19). Newt Gingrich: Reward individuals. *The Washington Post.*

CHAPTER 8

Combating Racism through the Kuumba Learning Model Technique: Elementary Students' Perspectives

Karen B. McLean Donaldson

Racism in United States Schools: Nightmares of Getting Shot

One student exclaimed that, "In classroom 58, students and the teacher all got on the floor behind her desk to protect themselves from the stray bullets. The teacher called the principal, and the principal called the cops." Another student chimed in with, "and, the cops blocked the whole area off with yellow tape, just like they always do when there is a murder." All of the students said they have nightmares of getting shot, or of family members getting killed. The students commented that if it were a white school, the students would be better protected, especially after people were killed. A student stated that, "Some of the kids didn't come to Kuumba today because they are too scared to be at the after school program without protection."

(Affinity Kuumba session, January 2004)

The three Kuumba (Swahili word meaning "creativity") exploratory projects presented in this chapter will highlight varied forms of racism that impact our schools and the lives of the students who attend them. Elementary student voices from different backgrounds and geographical areas help to demonstrate early experiences of youth regarding racism, their social consciousness, and cries for help. Racial oppression and discrimination must begin to be acknowledged, understood, and addressed at elementary levels, because these levels are where it starts. This age group is most vulnerable to the cruel realities of racism that often psychologically damage them for life. Primary school anti-racist curricula can give strategies for survival, achievement, and social activism that can carry on throughout one's educational experience and into adulthood.

The introductory scenario began with the Kuumba leadership workshop held at an inner-city elementary afterschool program. The program was scheduled to have the long-awaited Africa-to-America cultural art workshop on this day. However, the fourth and fifth graders were too preoccupied and anxious, and asked to do an affinity session to talk about the traumatic event from the previous day. They opened by addressing their concerns using a racism analogy about white communities getting more services and attention than black communities. They began to ask questions about why they had to feel scared and hopeless while whites did not. One child remarked, "You always see blacks on television fighting, but whites don't have to fight over the scraps, so they don't kill each other. They have better houses, jobs, and schools. They get all the money and we can't even feed our families." These young students clearly had an opinion of race-based poverty and its correlation to the violence within their school community.

Racism as trauma is evidenced here, as the students shared that they could not concentrate on school work because they were worried that someone in school or at home could be shot like the man and woman who were shot down in front of one of their classrooms the previous day. Without any prompting, the elementary students shared their sentiments, such as, "It probably was gang-bangers who killed those people yesterday. There is a lot of that going around here." Another responded, "My cousin and I had to crawl under a car last week when gang-bangers were shooting on our block from their car." In response to recalling incidents, another student said, "Not too long ago a boy from our school was pushed in front of a truck by two other boys. He was killed, and we saw the blood on the street where he was killed." The students were asked what they would say to people who might say that these incidents could not possibly be true. One answered, "Come over here and see for yourself and you'll see we're not lying." Another remarked, "You don't have to believe me. Wait until you see it on the news." One student responded, very irritated, "Why would I want to tell a fable like that to anyone?" Another student concluded,

"Everybody is so busy hatin' when we should be educatin'. All people should have equal chances; that would help stop the violence."

We followed by discussing safety, addressing their fears, and conceptualizing creative social action strategies that could help change the condition of their community. The students suggested having a neighborhood performance highlighting school concerns about violence and human rights. One boy said, "Black people need to come together to solve their own problems." They thought that people would listen more to an antiviolence social justice production by children than by adults. Seeking to bring youth biases to the global forefront, students also wanted to get involved with similar international youth projects, such as a leadership afterschool program in South Africa that performed against AIDS, violence, and other youth injustices. Racism is "real-life" for many students; therefore their social awareness is often more developed than we realize. In addition, many students around the globe desire education that is cross-cultural and equitable. A growing body of literature, attendance of international education conferences, and direct experience with international cross-cultural projects indicates this youth international interest.

This chapter features youth perspectives on combating racism using a creativity and anti-racist education method called the Kuumba learning model. It examines the relationship of cultural literacy to student success, and it gives recommendations for cross-cultural teaching and learning practices. Furthermore, it addresses racial prejudice and discrimination in P-12 school systems.

RESEARCHERS REVEAL TARGETS OF RACISM

A number of researchers and educators reveal that racism is a major problem within our nation's schools (Pine & Hilliard, 1990; Murray & Clark, 1990; Sleeter, 1992; Donaldson, 2001; Nieto, 2003; Kailin, 2002). Through these researchers, we have learned that students of color are generally targets of racism.

There are many ways in which racism is manifested in schools today. Some common factors include biased curricula, standardized testing, tracking, ability grouping, disproportionate detention and suspension rates, inequality in the amount of instruction time, lowered teacher expectations, and racial epithets or other forms of violence that are often minimized by teachers and administrators (Murray & Clark, 1990; Donaldson, 1996; Nieto, 2002). An anti-racist education school district study in the Northeast reported that 88 percent of 2,000

secondary students of varied ethnic heritages directly or indirectly
experienced racism in their schools. A follow-up anti-racist curriculum
study in that school district documented three major ways in which
racism affected students' learning, attitudes, and behavior: (1) by belit-
tling their self-esteem, causing diminished interest in school; (2) by
heightening students' perceived need to overachieve academically,
causing undue stress and educational resentment; and (3) by making
them feel guilty and embarrassed at seeing other students victimized
(generally reported by white students) (Donaldson, 1996).

It is difficult to accept that young children experience racism in
school. However, they experience all of the common racist factors
mentioned above, as well as blatant racist acts. For example, some nationally reported and consecutive racial violence incidents in elementary
schools included the following: (1) A teacher in North Charleston, South
Carolina, wrote with an indelible marker, "Where are my glasses?" on
the face of a five-year-old girl. A similar case was being investigated
in South Carolina's Aiken County, where a teacher wrote on a boy's
face because he was late for class (*South Carolina News Summary*,
1997, October 23; Associated Press, 1997, January 8). (2) A teacher
in Cambridge, Massachusetts, taped her third grade student's mouth
(*Cambridge Chronicle*, 1997, March 27; *Boston Globe*, 1997, March 20).
(3) Another kindergartener was placed in the restroom as a "time-out"
for his disruptive behavior and was made to eat his lunch there (*The
Des Moines Register*, 1997, February 22). All of these children were
children of color, who are generally the targets of such racist acts
(Donaldson, 1996, 2001).

In 1954, the Supreme Court ruled unanimously in the case of *Brown v.
Board of Education of Topeka, Kansas* to outlaw school segregation.
The ruling declared that segregated schools were "inherently unequal."
Yet in 2004, fifty years later, the growth of segregation and equitable
access in our schools are issues facing communities across the country.
Schools with a majority of students of color coupled with low socioeconomic status are generally less well funded than those with middle-
and upper-economic status. Demographics indicate that approximately
46 million students (89 percent of all United States students) attend
public schools, and it is estimated that 39 percent of those are students
of color. However, the U.S. Department of Education's 1996 *Condition of Education* documents that 88 percent of U.S. teachers are white
(Gordon, 1998). This imbalance often results in a clash of cultures in
which middle-class white teachers have difficulty relating to students of
different backgrounds and cultures (Cushner, McClelland, & Safford,

1992). Many teachers leave college unprepared to effectively teach in diverse environments or to address the ills of racism that plague our educational institutions (Donaldson & Tartakov, 1997).

Students have often commented that teachers are the greater threats of racism in schools because of their lack of multicultural perspective and teaching. Furthermore, teachers are seen as the adults who are around students most within the school environment and have the authority over them. A student once asked, "If a teacher is being racist or ignorant, who is going to believe a teacher over me?" Frequently students have stated that it is hard to give respect to a teacher who does not relate to the real world of students (Donaldson, 1996). In general, many educators lack awareness of prejudice and discrimination in schools and how racism negatively impacts student success (Donaldson, 2001).

Students perceive racism in schools as all-inclusive. For instance, multicultural and anti-racist education generally does not permeate school curriculum. Students often remark that they do not see their cultures or other cultures in the curriculum. Furthermore, numerous students from the Kuumba exploratory projects have said that schoolmates, teachers, administrators and staff, counselors, parents, and communities knowingly or unknowingly participate in racist behavior. For example, one child came into the program asking to learn how to "help people understand that Chinese people could see just as normal as anyone else, and that he has a real family although he is Chinese and his parents are white" (KMES post prejudice on the playground performance discussion/observation notes, 1997). The Kuumba model teaches about stereotypes and works with the student to create positive avenues to address ignorance and bigotry.

KUUMBA LEARNING MODEL CURRICULUM FRAMEWORK

Discovering the Creativity, Cross-Cultural, and Anti-Racist Methods of the Kuumba Model

"I like the teacher that talked about where she came from, and how long she has been in the United States." "I learned a lot about Cesar Chavez that I didn't know." One student said, "The whole school should have Kuumba in their classes" (Kuumba intern reflection notes, 2003).

The Kuumba learning model curriculum, both written and unwritten—that is, materials, methods, policies and procedures, teachers, resource personnel, and the student body—reflects cross-cultural considerations and approaches (Donaldson & Tartakov, 1997). The Kuumba curriculum is shaped to accurately reflect the cultural diversity within the United States and to teach students that by responding to these realities within the nation and the world, students can develop decision-making and social action skills (Banks, 1997). The Kuumba curriculum was first developed and implemented by Drs. Karen B. McLean Donaldson and Carlie Collins Tartakov, combining over fifty years of teaching experience (including grade school and college) in combination with the principles of multicultural and global education. Included in that have been the input and involvement of the community, parents, and students. Some of the initial curriculum pillars that helped to construct the framework included the Integration, Interdisciplinary, and Effective Curriculum Models of James A. Banks (1997) and the Multicultural Characteristics Model of Sonia Nieto (1992). In addition, directors and staff used the Racial Identity Model of Beverly Tatum (1997), and the Affinity Group Model of Phyllis C. Brown (1995).

The goal of the exploration projects was to study the impact of a multicultural curriculum on young children. In wanting to show some evidence of what the developers think to be true—that children do learn better and develop higher self-esteem when exposed to a multicultural educational setting—the attention is on the development of the curriculum.

Before highlighting samples of infusing Kuumba concepts into basic subject areas and presenting the voices of students within each project, it is important to briefly define the three core pedagogical components of the Kuumba model.

Creativity

Creativity results from originality of thought or expression and is productive or generative. Kuumba is a philosophy of creative intelligence that is practiced within many cultures. Interdisciplinary creative and cultural arts are multisensory strategies that address the sundry learning styles and intelligences of all students (Gardner, 1983). Sternberg and Grigorenko state that creative ability is a part of successful multiple intelligence and is used when a person creates, invents, or discovers (2000). When students have the opportunity to learn through multiple intelligence, then cognitive, affective, and social enhancement will often appear (Campbell, Campbell, & Dickinson,

1996). The arts are an integral aspect of multiple intelligence and learning styles. They are a way of life for many cultures, and they address a variety of issues in unique ways. Many students comment on how the creative arts media make learning any subject more interesting, fun, and open.

The Cross-Cultural

"Cross-cultural" involves the ability to use the standards of perceiving, evaluating, believing, and doing that are associated with one or more cultures beyond one's native culture. It is the ability to interpret and evaluate intercultural encounters with a high degree of accuracy and to show cultural empathy (Bennett, 1997). In addition, a twenty-first-century paradigm shift of combining multicultural and global education disciplines has been on the horizon for various scholars, and the term *cross-cultural* has been proposed for this new transformative paradigm (Donaldson & Seepe, in press).

Anti-Racist Education

Anti-racist education is critical pedagogy that seeks to take a stand against racial injustice and oppression (Donaldson & Verma, 1997). It is recognized as a leading characteristic of multicultural education (Nieto, 2003). Anti-racist education at an elementary level often includes lessons in appreciating the contributions and experiences of all ethnic racial groups and in becoming aware of racial prejudice and discrimination (Donaldson & Verma, 1997).

This foundational combination of creativity, cross-cultural, and anti-racist education uniquely fills a void for students desiring to have "real-life" concepts within education. Students have made comments such as, "Kuumba activities have taught me to be less shy and more open"; "to become more worldly"; "to follow my dreams, and don't let anyone limit me or my ideas"; "I am a creative genius, and I like that"; "It has helped us to examine how we think about ourselves, and other cultures that we live with here on this earth"; and "to not be afraid to take a stand against social injustice."

KUUMBA AS AN ACADEMIC DISCIPLINE

The basic theories and practice are adaptable at all educational levels. Students learn about cross-cultures, social justice, peace and global education, cultural identity development and socialization, oppression, and democratic citizenship. They learn these concepts through an array of creative strategies and multiple intelligences that often include the arts as an integral medium for learning. The overarching concept encompasses an interdisciplinary and holistic academic approach that fuses anti-racist, cross-cultural, and creativity components into one technique. The Kuumba model is transformative knowledge that is integrated into all subject areas and/or is taught as a cross-cultural studies discipline.

Students bring in homework from multiple disciplines and, with the academic mentors (cross-discipline college students), complete home assignments with multicultural concepts of understanding integrated into the learning process. Some examples of Kuumba inclusion in basic subjects are as follows.

Motivating Science and Technology Inquiry

Research suggests that many students in our nation's elementary schools have an inadequate grounding in science and technology and are therefore unable to use the necessary skills and understanding they will need in the next century (Tartakov, 1995). In spite of recent improvements and achievements, scores are low in science and technology compared to many global nations. In addition, white females, children of color, and people who are physically challenged fall below other groups (Tartakov, 1995). With this in mind, the model attempts to address factors that enhance learning in science and technology. Such factors include teaching and learning styles, stereotyping, the self-fulfilling prophecy, and ethnicity and learning.

This unit is geared toward motivating scientific inquiry through exploring our environment through culture: recognizing differences and likenesses through observations and recording skills, understanding how science and technology fit into our lives, and becoming aware of contributions that diverse cultures have made to science and technology. The rationale for stressing science and technology is that they are on the cutting edge of productivity in the new millennium, and many do not believe or understand that anti-racist multicultural education concepts can be infused into these subject areas.

For example, one of the first lessons emphasized the science of skin color by having students mix color paints to match their complexions. Race has a function, and though we may look different on the outside (our genetic inheritance), for good reasons we are more alike in significant ways. Issues of adaptation are discussed.

Student Empowerment through Affinity Exchange

All the Kuumba learning model exploratory projects have been multiaged and grade-level cohort groups; students learn to explore relevant issues and to be architects in their own learning. This group activity is based on "multicultural affinity"(blended) exchanges, which were the final stage of the cultural affinity group model cofounded by Phyllis Brown, the Fort River Elementary School, and the University of Massachusetts (1994–1995). Traditionally, from Brown's paradigm, students are placed into same-race support groups and eventually moved into "blended" group discussions. As our students make up small multicultural sample groups, the approach is to have blended group class discussions from the beginning to the end of the project-a micro (pluralistic) society working out issues of prejudice and awareness collectively.

The students set goals and programs that help them take control of their own lives. For instance, if they identified for themselves a social need, they could consider getting involved in some kind of social action project, such as raising money or providing some other needed resource, such as letters to senators. This part of the curriculum is meant to assist in developing citizen action skills. Citizen and social action skills are often featured in the multicultural education integration work of James A. Banks. Kuumba affinity curriculum often includes entrepreneurial rites of passage and leadership studies, as well as community professional lectures and activities series. These combinations encourage reinforcement in basic subject areas, collective work and responsibility, and social action efforts. The students often conduct fund raising, such as bake sales, for cross-cultural education (hands-on) field trips.

Thus, the decision to adopt a Kuumba learning model was related in part to the awareness that children are more successful when they are able to identify and embrace who they are and where they come from, across a wide spectrum of specific cultural characteristics. Additionally, bridging the awareness that children live in a diverse society with multiple cultures could only enhance their appreciation and understanding of the world they live in. The Kuumba model allows and provides for live experiences of interactions and communications; thereby solidifying children's sense of self-confidence in their place in society.

PROJECT ONE: KMES (KUUMBA MULTICULTURAL EXPERIMENTAL SCHOOL)

The First Kuumba Exploratory Project: Curriculum and Student Response in a Rural Suburban Social Context

The Kuumba Multicultural Experimental School (KMES) Research Project began as an official pilot study in August 1997. The study took place in a small midwestern city, where the population as of 1995 was 48,691.

KMES was established on a large state university (Iowa State University) campus with an enrollment of 25,000 undergraduate and 8,000 graduate students. It was housed on campus at a cultural center for blacks. The structure itself was a house that provided a homey and relaxed environment for the program. The participants had access to computer laboratories, gymnasiums, and large meeting rooms in the residence halls, the College of Education, the kitchen, and the basement. On Wednesdays, an early release day for the schools, twenty program participants were released fifteen minutes earlier than their classmates to attend KMES classes from two until five o'clock in the afternoon. The program followed the K–12 academic calendar.

In the ethnic makeup of the Ames community, except for schools in and around the state university campus, students of color were so few that their presence or impact on the school sites was miniscule. During the 1997–1998 academic year, there were no teachers of color at the elementary level.

Although the participants came from various schools throughout the city, seven out of the twenty came from one school. They ranged in ages from five to twelve years old and were enrolled in kindergarten through the sixth grade. The students' cultural and ethnic backgrounds included black, Asian, Latino, and white groups. Many of the families described themselves as of mixed heritage, such as African-black American, black-Cape Verdean–Native American, and Mexican-white American. Religious backgrounds included Muslim, Jewish, and Christian.

The theme of the pilot study was that all inhabitants of the world were part of the human family. This acknowledgment lends itself to the development of strong intercultural relationships. The KMES research project sought to create an anti-racist education curriculum and implementation prototype and add to the research of the local school district, state, and beyond.

The notion of the Kuumba multicultural school stemmed from the need to create an educational alternative for the multicultural community in a small midwestern town by fostering the concept of diversity through the arts.

One of the youngest, a five-year-old boy, helped to raise questions of what kinds of content students are truly capable of processing, and whether the notion of the multiculturalism experiences as defined above is applicable for elementary students.

In the lesson plan "Africa to America," students participated in a re-creation of Africans being forced to come to America. Students were asked to hold hands and form a line, linking them together, recreating the experiences of being chained. One of the researchers became aware that a five-year-old white boy was not holding hands and instead was obviously apart from the link. The researcher's initial perceptions ranged from thinking that the process was overwhelming for him to thinking that he was being uncooperative. However, when she asked him why he was not part of the link, he whispered ". . . I am stopping what is happening." He shared with his teacher/researcher that he would not allow the Africans to be forced. By breaking the link/chain, this five-year-old was attempting to re-create history and take responsibility for his legacy as a white student. The perceptions that students would be responsive, could process, and could feel the experiences of others was impressive regarding recognition of how powerful the experience of teaching multiculturalism was.

How best to balance the different developmental needs of children? Students quickly grasped being a welcome part of the process. While students initially struggled with integrating multicultural concepts into everyday realities—for example, kids did not want to naturally share and more naturally wanted to exclude differences—day by day, participant interactions improved. They seemed to naturally "get" that they had unique identities, that they were capable and were behaviorally problem-solvers. They understood the social issues and the parameters around becoming change agents. They made up their own rules in terms of discipline and were aware and considerate of each others' needs. Perhaps the children were not consciously aware of the shift, but they began to treat each other more justly than when they first came into the project.

Findings from Project One

The KMES research (pilot) project explored the impact of an anti-racist–multicultural curriculum on the learning and development of elementary school-aged children. It examined the relationship of cultural literacy to student success, gave implications for curriculum practice, and added to the needed literature on the effectiveness of multicultural teaching. The hope here was to demonstrate to regular classroom teachers that anti-racist multicultural teaching does make a difference for all students. Working constructs guided project inquiry, such as what the students were saying about the curriculum, growth in understanding anti-racist multiculturalism, student reaction to curriculum implementation, student learning and behavioral development, student sensitivity toward peers and others, and students' ability to understand class assignments.

Some of the major findings were as follows:

1. Students were able to grasp the contents of the anti-racist multicultural curricula within the context of the various subject areas.

2. Students enhanced their respect for other cultures and learned to better appreciate differences (both domestic and global).

3. Students were better able to contextualize the lessons when they included hands-on empathy and/or experiential lessons; experienced the lessons more holistically (global village concept; parents, teachers, friends, community; the whole village to raise and teach the child); and when other teaching techniques included cooperative learning and discovery, student-centered assignments, student process folio assessment, and multicultural concepts that included examining social justice issues.

4. Students became more equipped to handle biased or prejudice situations at their (public) regular schools, and were quicker to step in to articulate the importance of sensitivity to others. Coming into the project, many students were quite reserved. They said they did not or were too afraid to meet new people. They often exhibited selfish behavior and fought over seating or made negative comments about other children in class. Yet, by the end of the school year, these same students were reminding each other to "treat your neighbor as you want to be treated" and/or "don't be prejudiced," and so on.

Assessment tools were used to determine the learning styles and multicultural awareness of K-6 students and to apply those discoveries to revising culturally biased standardized tests and curricula. Once those assessments were culturally adapted, they were retested to examine whether students had more success with the cultural inclusive versions, and to see how the KMES students (with cultural intervention) fared on the adapted tests. For example, the Iowa Test Basic Skills was modified for use in the KMES research project. By tailoring the test to the specific needs and learning styles of the students, we hoped to eliminate much of the variance in test scores attributable to systematic error (bias). Likewise, a battery of tests and research procedures were adopted to determine the learning styles, aptitudes, and progress of each KMES student. The test battery for the first-year pilot study consisted of the following:

1. Student Attitude Assessment (SAA)/Project Multicultural Education (MCE): Assessing Children's Awareness About Diversity (designed by Clark County School District Compensatory Education Division, Las Vegas, NV)
2. Multiethnic Identity Measure
3. TIMI (Teele Inventory for Multiple Intelligence)

A yearly progress research report was started and used as a guide to continue ongoing data collection and analyses. The evaluation summaries included common themes and concerns "falling out" from the data. Recommendations were made from these common responses. In addition, external evaluators were called in on an ongoing basis to critique the design and success of the project. Furthermore, some of the (public school) teachers of the KMES participants relayed to the project that they observed changes in the participating students, and that the program had a positive impact on their learning. Increased self-esteem, problem-solving, and other academic enhancement were noted by some of the students' regular (public school) teachers and by parents.

The KMES research project was an exciting project during its infant stages; growth of the students was visible. Furthermore, coping skills to address racism and prejudice (especially for the students of color while in mainstream classrooms) became evident through the affinity class discussions. The project directly reached hundreds of people, such as KMES students, teachers, academic mentors, parents, researchers, planners, and college classrooms. A variety of articles were written on the project, and the state board of education awarded the project the Educational Equity Recognition Award in October 1999.

PROJECT TWO: KLC (KUUMBA LEARNING CENTER) EXTENDED DAY PROGRAM

After taking a new faculty/administrator appointment in the Graduate School of Education (GSOE) at Alliant International University in California, Donaldson continued the educational explorations of the Kuumba learning model. The GSOE Partners for Success Program was able to contract the Kuumba center to administer a pilot extended day program for grades 5–9. GSOE faculty, graduate students, guest professionals, and the GSOE Cross Cultural Studies Institute administered the project. The findings from this small sample pilot were similar to those of the Iowa State University pilot study: students gained cultural openness, greater enthusiasm about education, empathy for social injustice, and confidence in using creative styles of learning. This second pilot allowed the Kuumba learning model to advance its theory and practice and to sophisticate its research agenda.

During the eight-week period, April 9 through June 6, 2002; the Kuumba Learning Center Extended Day Program was piloted at Alliant International University, at the San Francisco Bay area campus, under the direction of Dr. Karen B. McLean Donaldson, systemwide director of the Cross Cultural Studies Institute and professor in the Graduate School of Education. This Alliant program was based in large part on the original Kuumba Multicultural Experimental School Research Project, implemented in 1997 by Drs. Donaldson and Tartakov.

Center facilitators (instructors and assistants) included faculty members, graduate students, and local school district teachers who were also graduate students. The professional principles guiding all graduate work at the GSOE also shaped practice carried out through the Kuumba center. However, a special emphasis was placed on the principle that all graduates would demonstrate and apply cross-cultural competencies. In fact, several of the Kuumba center key learning experiences resulted from work in the graduate course Cross Cultural Curriculum Theory and Development, offered during the spring term. Community mentors included parents, and also professionals in medicine, social services, community organizing, and the airline industry, who served as presenters and role models for the students.

In contrast to the midwestern setting, the San Francisco Bay area is made of large, multicultural, multilingual urban cities and towns. The majority of public school students are enrolled in schools where the student body represents anywhere between four and forty-four different cultural and/or language groups. In 1999–2000 (most current data available), district enrollment for the Alameda Unified School District was 10,802.

The largest ethnic group in the Alameda schools is white American; in the Oakland schools, the largest group is black. The twenty-three students enrolled in the Kuumba center included eleven blacks, one Latino, one Asian American, five Arab Americans, five mixed-heritage students, and no Native Americans. There were eight elementary students, nine middle school students, and six high school students.

TAILORING THE PROGRAM: RESHAPING CURRICULUM AND INSTRUCTION

Much like the original KMES research project, the Kuumba Learning Center sought to enhance student learning and achievement through the use of various cross-cultural teaching and learning styles, educational testing techniques and measurements, and by offering tutorial assistance in basic subject areas. The program focus expanded beyond cultural awareness to include practices and behaviors that taught democracy through programs that affirmed the rich knowledge and cultural bases that diverse students and their families brought to schools and communities.

Facilitators combined multicultural and global education practices to create a diversity paradigm that promoted world citizenship. Because students came from elementary, middle, and high school settings, the instruction and pedagogy were adjusted to accommodate this large range of developmental levels. The overarching themes reflected in each segment of the curriculum were social justice and universal membership in the human family.

Although the material conditions and demographics in the San Francisco Bay area setting are distinctly different from those of the midwestern city where the KMES project first started, the need for the program in the Bay area was as great if not greater. Moreover, a rich multicultural, multilingual setting like the Bay area is ideal for programs aimed at developing strong intercultural relationships by fostering diversity through the arts.

APPLYING THE KUUMBA LEARNING MODEL WITHIN URBAN AND MULTICULTURAL DEMOGRAPHICS IN THE SAN FRANCISCO BAY AREA

KLC Curriculum Strands and Program Segments

One of the main goals for the Kuumba Learning Center curriculum is the development of cross-cultural competence. For many students, the sessions are the first periods of formal instruction on these concepts.

A cross-cultural education model was adopted for the program, in part because of our awareness that children are more successful when they are able to identify and describe themselves across a wide spectrum of cultural characteristics and to embrace the complexity of that reality. It was also adopted because expanding student awareness of the multiple cultures that exist in our diverse society enhances their appreciation and understanding of the world. This education model provides multicultural interactions and communication that can build the self-confidence students need to develop cross-cultural competence.

Homework and Grade-Level Activities Strengthened

This segment included small group sessions organized by grade levels. These sessions highlighted the affinity rites of passage that most of the students were experiencing at this point in their development. The participants were especially interested in discussing their issues, problems, and ideas for resolving them. As the students shared concerns and insights, it became clear that peer sharing at these age levels was a powerful instructional tool.

As the program progressed, some of the older students expressed the need for more time to work on homework assignments. Consequently, students could elect to spend as much as two hours working on homework assignments at each session. During these sessions, tutorial assistance was available in the basic subject areas as needed.

Turning on Learning: Language and Mathematics

The third segment included core courses in mathematics and language issues, and entrepreneurial explorations. These sessions featured student-centered activities that emphasized cross-cultural teaching and learning styles and focused on mathematics or language and sometimes the interconnections between these areas.

The curriculum and instruction for the experiences in language included the development of a knowledge base about the critical importance and roles that language plays in culture and, consequently, in cross-cultural studies. Language allows us to express and communicate our needs, emotions, values, ideas, and so on. Language, along with the arts, both performing and visual, is the most-often used/recognized representation of culture.

The students spent time exploring their own linguistic repertoire and added to it through introductory lessons in American Sign Language. Discussions on rites of passage and their own adolescent experiences led to an art activity during which the students made a mask of life, with plaster bandages that were fitted to their faces, removed, allowed to dry, and then painted to represent who they were at this point in their development. Students selected empowerment descriptors such as *strong*, *brilliant*, *intelligent*, and *warrior* to describe their masks. These words were expressed in a sign language interpretive dance that the students performed for family and friends. The masks were worn in the beginning of the dance and removed with pride to show their true faces. The students used poetry to describe the symbolism of hiding behind a false face. One student said, "it is like hiding the fact that you like learning, so your friends won't think you're some kind of nerd. We wear masks a lot to pretend that we are so cool."

Role-playing and other dramatic exercises were incorporated into many aspects of instruction to help make literacy development active and student-centered. Students from the elementary school contingent produced and presented "Three Mexican Folktales" as part of the Kuumba Learning Center closing celebration.

All grade level students engaged in social justice theater and dance exercises stemming from the work of Augusto Boal (1985), and the students used multimedia that included video production, photography, and newsletter/communication in-house publication.

In the mathematics strand, mathematics was introduced as the language of analysis. It was discussed as a tool for understanding the world and things around us. Lessons focused on learning how to state predictions and estimations, and understanding a census and tabulations. Students explored the idea that data could be disputed.

There were other activities not done due to time constraints, but in a longer session, recommendations for the program included exploring composition through still photography and the creation of photo essays, and providing opportunities for the participants and staff to explore the complexities and evolution of cross-cultural development in the cultural groups that make up the United States and some parts of the world. For example, learning about the African influences in Latin America could help the participants to create respectful and effective alliances with their peers both in the program and in their school settings.

The success of the Kuumba Learning Center is especially impressive because the changes needed on three dimensions of the program were especially challenging. First, the program was expanded to include a greater range of developmental levels among the students, elementary to high school age; second, the rich cultural and linguistic diversity of the San Francisco Bay area setting is inherently more complex and personal for most, if not all, of the participants; and third, the time frame was reduced to eight short weeks, and the physical space available was limited to three classrooms at the university.

PROJECT TWO: FINDINGS SIMILAR
TO THE KMES PROJECT

Several instruments were developed to evaluate the Kuumba Learning Center (KLC) program and its impact on student participants. Those instruments included a post-student evaluation survey; parent open-ended two-narrative questions; and focus group interviews with students, parents, faculty, and internship graduate students. In addition, grade school and graduate students kept program journal notebooks for reflection, observation, and class notes. Overall sentiments revealed that students enhanced their self-confidence, motivation for learning, math and creative skills, homework and testing assignments, social consciousness, and respect for others. Some examples from exit focus group interviews with student participants included, "KLC helped me to understand algebra and get a better perspective on it," "It taught me so many more things about education, and how to understand my regular classroom teachers better," "I made new friendships from different cultures other than my own," "It taught me about being an entrepreneur and managing a budget, and setting goals for establishing a youth business," and "It taught me about real injustices such as the gentrification policies that evict Oakland residents from their houses for no just cause." These findings were similar to the Iowa KMES findings in 1997, such as bridging cultural and social injustice awareness, academic achievement, and creative social action strategies.

Measurement instruments and techniques will continue to be piloted among culturally diverse students enrolled in extended-day programs similar to the Kuumba Learning Center experience. The knowledge gained will be used to continue work on instruments and techniques that reflect the validity and reliability standards required by communities of color most affected by the use of such measures, educators, and psychometricians.

PROJECT THREE: FOX (PSEUDONYM) ELEMENTARY SCHOOL AND THE KUUMBA LEARNING MODEL PILOT RESEARCH PROJECT

An Inner-City School Project

Enrollment for Oakland Unified School District during 1999–2000 was 55,051.

As is evident from the two tables, the larger school district, Oakland Unified, is approximately five times the size of Alameda Unified. During the academic year 2002–2003, the Graduate School of Education (GSOE) Cross Cultural Studies Institute agreed to test the Kuumba learning model in one of the GSOE Partnership Schools. The Fox Elementary School located in Oakland, California, became the KLM pilot school. The kindergarten–grade 5 inner city school has an enrollment of over 1,000 students and has been listed as one of the lowest-performance schools within the Oakland Unified School District.

The KLM/Fox Research Pilot Project (2002–2003) focused on fourth and fifth grade students (360 students divided into six fourth-grade and six fifth-grade classrooms for a total of twelve classrooms). Three fourth- and three fifth-grade treatment classrooms were selected by the school principal based upon teachers expressing an interest in the program, and/or behavior and academic performance being lacking. The other six classrooms served as the control group for the pilot.

The pilot sought to test (using quantitative and qualitative methods) the academic and cultural effectiveness of the Kuumba learning model: to enhance student cultural appreciation and academic performance and to measure the outcome of the learning model's curriculum integration and intervention. The education intervention consisted of eight weeks of specialized instruction given to students regarding reading, mathematics, and cross-cultural studies. Each week, each treatment classroom received one hour of KLM instruction. The Kuumba "human family unit" was infused into regular classroom reading and mathematics curriculum.

At the end of the pilot study, the Fox Kuumba students were asked to write on a poster board the things that they had learned in Kuumba as it related to combating prejudice and discrimination. Some of those responses were as follows:

Helping others; learning and teaching together; we are one.

Being a good team.

Sometimes we learn things new.

It takes teamwork to do something.

Looking at your future, working as a team, do your work, and hanging on!

War is not the solution.

Don't be prejudiced. Please do not start wars.

Don't judge.

It is not prejudice, it is life.

Why war when it brings worse results? Why hurt when you can help? Why be alone when we can be a team.

Help the community like us.

Education is important for many things in life.

You can be everything if you believe.

Why can't we just get together and be blood brothers and sisters? Stand together.

Feed the hungry. Don't kill.

Education is the key to ending prejudice.

The design of the KLM/Fox pilot study was typical of the KLM conceptual framework. In addition, the GSOE Cross Cultural Studies Institute faculty and graduate students participated in both KLM instruction and research. Furthermore, the PACE (Psychology of Ability, Competency, and Expertise) at Yale University became the external evaluators for the pilot project. The treatment (Fox) teachers observed and participated in KLM sessions, teacher meetings, and interviews. KLM/Fox proposed a full-scale study to begin in 2003–2004, in which Fox teachers would receive professional development and guidance to teach and integrate the KLM curriculum.

Experimental Design

Data were obtained from more than 400 students. However, due to missing information (lack of names on forms, and lack of completing all tests, etc.) at this time, complete pretest and posttest information is available for only 302 children. This number can be improved when more work on the identification of nonmatched test forms occurs.

Treatment Group

There were seventy-eight girls and sixty-nine boys in the treatment group ($n = 147$). Their mean age was 9.99 years, SD = .74; and 74 percent (108) self-identified as black and 16 percent (23) as Latino. The remaining thirteen children included five multiracial, two Asian, two white, and four Pacific Island students. Nearly half (43 percent) of the sample were Protestant, 16 percent were Catholic, and 31 percent did not indicate a religious preference. Most of the children lived with both parents (44 percent, $n = 65$) or their mother (38 percent, $n = 55$). The living situations for the rest were equally divided between fathers and grandparents. Only 11 percent of the sample were receiving special education services, and 73 percent participated in the school's free lunch program. Regular church attendance was high with 50 percent of the sample indicating weekly participation in religious services, and family size was large (average of three brothers and/or sisters).

Control Group

There were seventy-two girls and eighty-three boys in the control group ($n = 155$). Their mean age was 10.06 years, SD = .83. In contrast to the treatment sample, only 14 percent (or twenty-three) self-identified as black and 57 percent (eighty-nine) as Latino. The remaining fourteen children included four multiracial, four Asian, four white, and two Pacific Islander students. The majority of these children were Catholic (53 percent), 16 percent were Protestant, and 22 percent did not indicate a religious preference. Nearly all of these participants lived with both parents (81 percent, $n = 126$) or their mother (17 percent, $n = 26$). The living situations for the rest were equally divided between fathers and grandparents. Nearly 30 percent of the sample were receiving special education services, and 80 percent participated in the school's free lunch program. Regular church attendance was also high, with 50 percent of the sample indicating weekly participation in worship, and family size was large (average of three brothers and/or sisters).

Between-Group Differences on Demographic Variables

A significant difference between the treatment and control groups was found on the ethnicity variable, $\chi^2(3, 301) = 109$, $p < .00001$. This was also the case with respect to religious preference, $\chi^2(2, 302) = 86$, $p < .00001$, and the person(s) with whom the child lived, $\chi^2(3, 300) = 62$, $p < .001$. Since these factors are highly correlated (that is, Latinos were usually Catholic and lived with both parents), only ethnicity needed to be used as an independent variable (or as a covariate) in future analyses. This difference can be explained by the recruitment process: the control group comprised three bilingual classrooms, whereas the treatment group contained none.

New Instruments Used in Project Three—Pretest Measures

Sternberg Triarchic Abilities Test (STAT)

Based on the seminal work of Robert Sternberg, the STAT was developed to assess three areas of cognitive functioning: analytical, practical, and creative. An abbreviated form of the instrument was used in the present study, with eight items on each scale. A total score (twenty-four items) was also obtained. This instrument has been used in a number of cross-cultural situations (Sternberg, Castejon, Prieto, Hautamaeki, & Grigorenko, 2001) with promising results. The test is not, however, without its critics (Brody, 2003).

Cross Cultural Studies Institute (CCSI) Cultural Openness Scale

A major goal of the Kuumba learning model is to increase the interest and receptivity of children to cross-cultural issues. Because assessment instruments suitable for use with inner-city elementary school children are lacking, GSOE CCSI faculty and graduate students developed a questionnaire to assess this construct. Following a literature review, fifteen items were generated with face validity (for example, "I like to try new things," "I enjoy meeting all kinds of people") answered using a five-point Likert scale. In many respects, the trait being assessed was similar to the openness factor of the Big Five model of personality that has been widely used in cross-cultural research (McCrae & John, 1992).

CCSI Self-Concept Scale

It was hoped that participation in the Kuumba Learning Project model would increase the self-efficacy of children. As before, the GSOE CCSI faculty and graduate students developed a questionnaire tailoring questions to be culturally appropriate for majority children of color living in an urban setting.

CCSI School Involvement Scale

The original twenty-five-item scale included questions about participation in and liking school activities (such as, "I am involved in school activities," "I show good school spirit"). Reliability for the twenty-five-item scale was $\alpha = .55$, and after revising the scale and removing one item, a twenty-four-item version was created that showed impressive reliability, $\alpha = .83$, and was used as a posttest outcome measure. On the final scale, one item was revised from a Likert-scale answering modality to a yes/no answer.

POSTTEST ANALYSES REVEAL COMMON FINDINGS

Overall Liking Ratings of the Kuumba Learning Model Project by Fox Students

This survey was administered only to students in the control group. The ratings of the fifty-two Cox elementary school students completing the Liking Questionnaire were very high, $M = 4.34$, SD $= .52$ (five-point scale). In general, the Kuumba project interventions were seen as interesting and informative. This is an important result, for it establishes an essential condition for effective learning (Durlak, 1998). Only fifty-two students completed the questionnaire because it was administered at a time when many classes were on field trips. The survey data are, however, consistent with qualitative data from student focus groups.

In conclusion, the model shows promise, is well liked by students, and recommends that it be implemented over a longer period of time (preferably the entire school year), and from the start of the academic term. The researchers also recommend that additional performance measures be added to complement those scales and assessments used during the 2002–2003 intervention.

SUMMARY OF THE KUUMBA EXPLORATORY PROJECTS AND WHAT YOUTH ARE SAYING

The purpose of this chapter was to exhibit evidence that education that is cross-cultural makes observable differences for elementary school children's attitudes and behavior. If teachers, other school personnel, and all stakeholders understand these positive changes and their

Toolbox for Change

For	Images/perceptions	Strategies for change
Individuals	"Racism is not as bad as it used to be."	Social action can help keep anti-bias legislation intact and progressing, that is, it can examine the current state of affairs regarding disappearing national and local policies that protect underrepresented groups as it relates to prejudice and discrimination.
		Vote for and support anti-bias policies.
	"I'm not a racist."	Become aware, understanding how groups suffer and are oppressed.
		Self-examination of racial prejudice and discrimination through diversity outreach and reading exploration.
		Adopt the view that if you are not part of the solution, you are part of the problem.
		Seek to understand what racism is, what its ill effects are, and stages of cultural identity development.
	"One person cannot make a difference."	Each one teach at least ten others.
		Take a stand against racial injustice.
		Identify allies.
		Speak out against prejudice and discrimination, such as racist jokes and other racist behavior that are often ignored.
	"Racism will always exist."	Only if we let it.
		Be optimistic, start with racism and prejudice-reduction within families, communities, and other affiliations.

Community	"Economic issues are more important than paying attention to prejudice and discrimination in schools."	Understand that racism is a system of power and privilege based on one's race. Racism economically oppresses and penalizes some groups and gives privilege to others based upon race. Therefore, racism is a leading characteristic of socioeconomic oppression.
	"We pay our taxes. Let the schools take the responsibility to address prejudice and discrimination."	It is the responsibility of the community: it takes a whole village to raise a child.
		Community leaders and organizations must put pressure on local and national governments to enforce equity throughout all public schools within their towns, cities, and states.
		Organize community education summits to address prejudice and discrimination.
		Support anti-racist education seminars, etc.
		Establish community volunteer programs within public schools.
		Role-model diversities.
Practitioners	"Racism no longer exists and ended with the civil rights movement of the 1960s."	Create racism-free environments.
		Re-education Racism in schools and efforts to reduce it should concern the total schools' environments.
	"Students embellish on racist experiences."	Do not dismiss student concerns regarding racist acts. Fully investigate situations and be proactive.
	"Race issues should be taught at home."	Students are most affected by racism in schools.
		It is recommended that students have a major role in helping to develop anti-racist curricula, and that educators understand the adverse effects of racism in schools on their students.

continued

Toolbox for Change (continued)

For	Images/perceptions	Strategies for change

	"Preparation is provided minimally in these areas."	For the most part, there is no national consensus on the importance and implementation of anti-racist creativity curricula offered in schools. Teachers and administrators can help in numerous ways:
		Follow up on students' concerns in the classroom and general setting;
		Provide anti-racist creativity professional development for educators, school counselors, and administrators;
		Design racism and prejudice units at all grade levels;
		Encourage student-peer teaching;
		Create multimedia curricula on anti-racist student performance, process, and discourse;
		   Enhance school policy directly to address racism in schools;
		Encourage administration leadership to support anti-racist policies; Put administration at the forefront of the movement;
		   Actively support anti-bias efforts;
		Colleges, that is, education and psychology programs, must bolster recruitment strategies for students of color.

implications, perhaps they will become greater supporters. This chapter also adds to anti-racist multicultural education research. Frequently, multicultural education scholarship is accused of not being grounded in empirical research. Opponents of multicultural education scholarship view the discipline as unable to prove that transforming the curriculum to become multicultural has a positive effect on student achievement. The ongoing efforts of the Kuumba learning model strive to add significantly to this growing body of research, and we encourage more implementation projects of this nature to get underway. The more research available, the better we are able to make our case to move beyond a reform movement into the worldwide practice of education that is cross-cultural, anti-racist, and creative.

Students have wide variations in how they assess Kuumba's ability to enhance their learning. Some comments include the following:

Finding friends to work with.
Helping to get a better understanding of my subjects.
Understanding regular schoolteachers better.
Increases my self-confidence.
I can be better than I think I am.
Education can be fun.
We can make a better world.
There are all different kinds of cultures.
The arts make it easy to communicate tough issues.
We are all very special.
How to be brave in a mean world.
I learn that I can reach my goal.
Even when we are different, we should love each other.
We must protect our world and nature.
You can be different and still fit in.
Never act like you can't help anyone.
Even if we're different, we can love each other.
I am in a room of other color people and I don't mind at all.
Get an education and you will get respect as you get it.
Never do drugs or fight.
Learning and teaching together.
We are one.
Enjoy what you are.
War is not the solution.

Prejudice is wrong.

You can be a hero.

The youth who participated in these projects mostly concur that this style of education helps to address real-life situations and makes education enjoyable. It gives them tools to combat prejudice and discrimination. The students expressed the need for everyone to join in to make education successful, and they want adults to know that they as young people have a lot of ideas to offer in making the world racism-free.

REFERENCES

Banks, J. (1997). *Teaching strategies for ethnic studies.* Boston: Allyn & Bacon.

Bennett, C. L. (1997). *Comprehensive multicultural education: Theory and practice* (4th ed.). Boston: Allyn & Bacon.

Boal, A. (1985). *Theatre of the oppressed.* New York: Theatre Communication Group.

Brody, N. (2003). What Sternberg should have concluded. *Intelligence, 31*, 339–342.

Brown, P. (1995). *Cultural identity groups overview and framework.* Unpublished document, Fort River School, Amherst, MA.

Campbell, L., Campbell, B., & Dickinson, D. (1996). *Teaching and learning through multiple intelligences.* Boston: Allyn and Bacon.

Cushner, K., McClelland, A., & Safford, P. (1992). *Human diversity in education: An integrative approach.* New York: McGraw-Hill.

Donaldson, K. (1996). *Through students' eyes: Combating racism in United States schools.* Westport, CT: Greenwood Publishing Group.

Donaldson, K. (2001). *Shattering the denial: Protocols for the classroom and beyond.* Westport, CT: Greenwood Publishing Group.

Donaldson, K., & Seepe, S. P. (In press). And the walls came tumblin' down: Cross cultural transformation. *Journal for Cross Cultural Transformation in Education, 1.*

Donaldson, K., & Tartakov, C. (1997). Multicultural education: An answer to racism. *The Des Moines Register.*

Donaldson, K., & Verma, G. (1997). Antiracist education definition. In C. Grant & G. Ladson-Billings (Eds.), *Dictionary of multicultural education.* Phoenix, AZ: Oryx Press.

Durlak, J. A. (1998). Why program implementation is important. *Journal of Prevention and Intervention in the Community, 17*, 5–18.

Gardner, H. (1983). *Frames of mind: The theory in practice.* New York: Basic Books.

Gordon, R. [principal researcher] (1998). *Education and race: A journalist's handbook.* Oakland, CA: Applied Research Center.

Kailin, J. (2002). *Antiracist education: From theory to practice*. New York: Rowman & Littlefield Publishers, Inc.

McCrae, R. R., & John, O. P. (1992). An introduction to the five-factor model and its applications. *Journal of Personality, 60*, 175–215.

Murray, C. B. C., & Clark, R. M. (1990). Targets of racism. *American School Board Journal, 17*(6), 22–24.

Nieto, S. (1992). *Affirming diversity: The sociopolitical context of multicultural education* (2nd ed.). New York: Longman Publishers.

Nieto, S. (2002). *Affirming diversity: The sociopolitical context of multicultural education* (4th ed.). New York: Longman Publishers.

Nieto, S. (2003). *What keeps teachers going?* New York: Teachers College Press.

Pine, G. J., & Hilliard, A. G. (1990, April). Rx for racism: Imperatives for America's schools. *Phi Delta Kappan*, 593–600.

Sleeter, C. E. (1992). *Keepers of the American dream: Multicultural and staff development*. Philadelphia: Farmer Press.

Sternberg, R., Castejon, J. L., Prieto, M. D., Hautamaeki, J., & Grigorenko, E. L. (2001). Confirmatory factor analysis of the Sternberg triarchic abilities test in three international samples: An empirical test of the triarchic theory of intelligence. *European Journal of Psychological Assessment, 17*, 1–16.

Sternberg, R., & Grigorenko, E. (2000). *Teaching for successful intelligence: To increase student learning and achievement*. Essex, England: Pearson Education Publishers.

Tartakov, C. (1995). *Ethnicity awareness intervention: Effects on attitudes and behaviors of science educators*. Ames: Iowa State University.

Tatum, B. (1997). *"Why are all the Black kids sitting together in the cafeteria?" and other conversations about race*. New York: Basic Books.

CHAPTER 9

Coping with Racism: A Spirit-Based Psychological Perspective

Carla D. Hunter
Ma'at E. Lewis-Coles

Numerous theories such as negrescence, racial identity, internalized racism, and stereotype threat, to name a few, attempt to capture the impact of racism on black consciousness, identity, feelings, and behaviors, and the stress that results from being reminded of one's disempowered status in an oppressive society. Some of these theories also highlight how blacks can negotiate and develop a positive identity despite the multiple manifestations of racism that are encountered. In addition, blacks' coping styles, such as the use of prayer, talking to friends, and/or keeping problems to themselves (Chiang, Hunter, & Yeh, in press) may also serve to buffer daily acts of discrimination and the experience of racism. Despite this, racism and the stress associated with racism continually affect blacks' self-esteem, emotional and physical well-being (Anderson, 1989; Fernando, 1984; Jones, Harrell, Morris-Prather, Thomas, & Omowale, 1996), and mental health (Klonoff, Landrine, & Ullman, 1999; Lewis, 2003).

Many in the field of African psychology (Kambon, 1992; Myers, 1993; Nobles, 1986; Utsey, Bolden, & Brown, 2001) believe that what is needed is a psychology of liberation for people of African descent. A psychology of liberation stresses the development of an African worldview, offers beliefs that empower descendants to reconnect with their heritage, and ultimately reengages their spirits in order to achieve adaptive mental health (Obasi, 2002; Parham & Parham,

2002). Historically, blacks are known to be religiously and spiritually involved people (Taylor, Chatters, Jayakody, & Levin, 1996). Religion and spirituality are common among blacks and known to be important components of psychological health for some (Constantine, Lewis, Conner, & Sanchez, 2000; Ellison, 1993; Lukoff, Turner, & Lu, 1992; Mattis, 2000).

Newlin, Knafl, and Melkus (2002) provide a description of spirituality for people of African descent based on current research. The researchers surveyed the literature and developed an analysis of the concept of "African American spirituality" that suggests cultural attributes specific to blacks including guidance, coping, and peace; and for blacks and whites involving global attributes such as transcendence, hope, strength, purpose in life, and interconnectedness with others or God/higher power. Moreover, for some blacks a particular religion may represent the practical expression of their spirituality (such as religious beliefs, thoughts, sentiments, and rituals [Jagers & Smith, 1996]). Despite the importance of black spirituality, very little of the psychological literature has explored the impact of racism on the spirit of blacks. Rather, the impact of racism has been deduced from the physical and emotional ailments seen in blacks, without integrating the concept of spirit. We believe that a discussion of racism and the spirit is needed in the psychology field. Furthermore, we also support using one's spirit to cope with racism. Thus, the purpose of this chapter is to (a) describe the impact of racism, (b) discuss the manifestation of racism on the spirit of persons of African descent, (c) describe a method for how to engage the spirit, and (d) provide an example of the practical application for dealing with racism.

BEARING THE BRUNT OF RACISM

Racism is an ideology or worldview in which individuals are categorized into racial groups according to observable physical traits. Harrell (2000) provides a comprehensive definition of racism that includes four central points: (a) a "system of dominance, power, and privilege that is based on racial group designations"; (b) "historical oppression based upon the dominant group's perception that other racial groups are inferior, deviant, or undesirable"; (c) "members of the dominant group create or accept their societal privilege by maintaining structures, ideology, values, and behavior"; and (d) exclusion of minority group members from "power, esteem, status and/or equal access to societal resources" (p. 43). As such, systematic racial inequalities and unfair practices based on skin color leave many blacks feeling powerless, helpless, and devalued.

Jones (1997) further discussed the multiple manifestations of racial beliefs in his description of a three-part organizational system of racism. Jones states that racism can be manifested in at least three ways: (a) individual racism, (b) institutional racism, and (c) cultural racism. Jones's model helps us understand that racism can be experienced at the individual level. Individual forms of racism are behaviors and negative communications about an individual based upon his or her race. Thus, individual racism occurs at the personal level. Institutional racism is reflected in the institutional and systematic policies and practices that impact blacks and maintain powerlessness and inadequate access to needed resources. Cultural racism forms out of the belief that the dominant group's cultural heritage, beliefs, and practices are superior. Cultural racism results in the devaluing of black cultural values. Essed (1990) provides an additional dimension—collective racism—to describe the concept of everyday racism, which is considered cumulative and endured by blacks throughout the day in work settings, public places, en route to and from home, on television, and in other popular media outlets.

If racism is a worldview, then discrimination is the collection of behaviors and attitudes that are consistent with a racist worldview. Discrimination is behavior perpetrated against individuals in the "inferior" group by those who belong to the majority group. For example, if in your worldview you believe black men to be violent and intellectually inferior, you may commit discriminatory acts that include turning black men down for loans, ignoring black male consumers (Sue, 2003), and at the extreme, commit acts of police brutality. In fact, racism and the resulting discrimination have been associated with poor physical and psychological health among blacks.

Chronic encounters with racism and/or perceiving acts of discrimination lead some blacks to have a number of different responses that can tax the body's physical defenses. Similarly, the stress of racism affects some blacks' emotions, thoughts, and behaviors and results in symptoms of psychological distress (for example, anxiety, sadness, somatization, depression, negative self-cognitions, and interpersonal sensitivity) (Lewis, 2003). Studies have shown that racism and discrimination affect blacks' physical and emotional well-being (Anderson, 1989; Fernando, 1984; Jones et al., 1996). Furthermore, racism and discrimination have been correlated with hypertension, cigarette smoking (Anderson, 1989; Jones et al., 1996; Krieger, 1990; Landrine &

Klonoff, 1996), substance abuse, eating problems, psychosomatiza-
tion, and depression (Comas-Diaz & Greene, 1994; Fernando, 1984;
Neuspiel, 1996; Thompson, 1992). At times, blacks experience what
Utsey, Ponterotto, Reynolds, and Cancelli (2000) termed *racism-
related stress*, which is one of six racism-related reactions. Additional
racism-related reactions described by Utsey and colleagues (2001)
include race-related trauma, race-related fatigue, anticipatory racism
reaction, race-related frustration, and race-related confusion. What is
lacking in our understanding of the impact of racism is a discussion
of the relationship between racism and spirit. As stated previously,
an important component of black mental health and culture is spirit,
and as such we cannot continue to understand adaptive black mental
health without integrating the role of spirit.

DRAWING UPON THE BLACK SPIRIT

In discussing the relationship between racism and the spirit, it is
helpful to further articulate what is meant by "spirit" and explain
its key concepts as defined by leading scholars of African philosophy
and African psychology (Ashby, 2002b; Grills, 2002; Kambon, 1992;
Myers, 1993; Parham, White, & Adjamu, 1999). In particular, the
essential features of spirit have been described by Myers (1993) as
"that permeating essence we come to know in an extrasensory fashion
(that is, via energy/conscious/God)" and the essence of the self that
is "consciously infused with Creative Life Force or Higher Power";
and by Grills (2002) as "that incorporeal, animating principle and
energy that reflects the essence and sustenance of all matter." Ashby
(2002a) states that spirit is all-pervasive and transcendental, beyond
time and space, encompassing our soul, mind, and body. Considering these definitions, we define spirit as the unseen divine energy
that functions interchangeably with an individual's soul, mind, and
physical body.

Spirit functions such that first it gives rise to the individual soul.
The soul is otherwise considered the unconscious mind (the part of
the mind outside a person's awareness). The soul or unconscious
mind then gives rise to the conscious mind (senses, thoughts, and
feelings). The mind in turn sustains the functions of the physical body,
such as the nervous system, brain, and ultimately behaviors. Thus, spirit,
known by many names, is the energy force behind the functions of
the soul, mind, and body. The energy from spirit, also known as life
force energy or *sekhem* in ancient Egyptian culture, comes into the

body by means of the breath and subtle energy channels (Ashby, 2000).

According to ancient Egyptian philosophy, the breath is transferred to seven main centers that correspond to the central nervous system. From the nervous system, the energy is distributed to the endocrine system (the system that regulates all body functions) and then various organs, muscles, and tissues. From this description, we can see the holistic interconnection of the body, mind, soul, and spirit. When the flow of energy in the body is able to move through the individual freely, one is able to experience guidance, coping, and peace. In essence, one is connected to his or her spirit. When the flowing of energy in the body among the soul, mind, and ultimately the physical body becomes disrupted, one is unable to access guidance, coping, and peace from one's spirit.

The experience of racism directly disrupts African descendants' spirits and manifests in their thoughts, emotions, and behaviors. Depletion of energy from one's spirit may occur when mental attention is drawn to perceiving or experiencing racism. The disruption to one's energy flow leads to confusion, poor coping, and agitated or dull states of mind. For example, a black woman working as a waitress at a fast food restaurant chain receives insults daily from coworkers who question her about wearing her hair in natural kinky styles. She frequently overhears white co-workers commenting that her hair is so curly, and black coworkers suggesting she "straighten her hair" with a chemical process. The woman may begin to unconsciously internalize some of these culturally racist remarks, which confuse her and distract her awareness of her spiritual essence. She may begin to think self-doubting thoughts about her appearance (such as "my hair *is* too kinky"). Once this occurs, she may begin to emotionally respond with feelings of embarrassment or anger. Behaviorally, the woman may experience labored breathing from the angry feelings, or she may verbally lash out at her coworkers and engage in passive-aggressive responses. These responses further deplete her energy. By the end of the day, she is tired and mired down in others' perceptions of her. Her conscious experience is overstimulated and becomes disconnected from her spirit. Over time, recurrent experiences of this nature disconnect the intimate connection between the mind and spirit and therefore spirit and the physical body. The mind and the physical body begin to function without the validating nature of the spirit. For blacks, a disconnection from spirit is particularly damaging because connection to spirit is part of African culture and enables blacks to foster adaptive mental health. What we advocate are practices for reengaging the spirit in the context of living in a racist and oppressive society. In the next section, we will turn to discuss a method rooted in an African worldview that empowers blacks to re-connect with their heritage and adaptively deal with racism.

BREATHING THROUGH EXPERIENCES OF RACISM

We put forth a description of a breath control or a proper breathing method to explain how to engage the spirit as a source of guidance, coping, and peace. Although widely accepted and adapted in main-stream culture, the proper breathing technique is also rooted in the spiritual practices of ancient Egyptian culture (Ashby, 2002b). Ashby (2002a) explains that the ability to control one's breath allows a person to control energy from his or her spirit. Controlling the spirit's energy flow into the body provides the ability to control the mind and senses. Therefore, proper breathing can be an effective way to restore and accumulate the energy from the spirit in the body when it is disrupted by experiences of racism. According to Ashby (2002b), many people in the modern world do not know how to breathe properly. They have learned to breathe by pushing out the chest in a "macho" fashion. This form of breathing does not allow for a significant amount of oxygen to be taken in, and vital energy is reduced and becomes stagnant in the subtle energy channels of the body, resulting in dullness and agitation or physical problems. "The stagnation of the flow of energy through the body has the effect of grounding one's consciousness to the physical realities rather than allowing the mind and body to operate with lightness and subtlety" (Ashby, 2002b, p. 195).

Belly breathing or abdominal breathing is used to perform proper breathing. It is the natural breathing pattern when one lies on one's back. The steps are to breathe in through the nose and push the stomach out; breathe out through the nose or mouth and pull the stomach in. This form of breathing can be practiced at all times, not just in the context of perceiving racism. In fact, we recommend that proper breathing be practiced throughout the day and not only when experiencing racism. It allows the energy of the spirit in the air to be rhythmically supplied to the body and the nervous system.

Here is a technique that can be done any time during the day for five minutes or at a moment when there is the need to gain clarity on how to effectively cope with racism and restore a sense of peace: close your eyes and allow your abdomen to expand as you breathe in through your nose. Visualize that you are taking in life force energy along with the air in each breath. See the energy remaining in your body as you expel the air slowly out of your nose or mouth. Visualize that all the nutrients of the air are being used in the body and that impurities are being carried away as you breathe out. You can just simply focus on the rising and falling of the abdomen with the breath. If your mind begins to get distracted, just return your attention to the rhythm of your breathing.

To illustrate the breathing method, consider that a black male who has learned the proper breathing technique and practices breathing daily will cope in an adaptive way with experiences of racism. For example, suppose he is racially profiled and subsequently stopped by police as he is driving home from work. He may evaluate the situation as a disruption to his peace of mind. This evaluation may be lead to confused thinking, for example, "Did I do something wrong?" and will cause him to feel angry and possibly behave in a confrontational manner toward the officer. While these feelings are a natural stress response to an experience with racism, the black male may also use the breathing techniques discussed here to adaptively cope and offset further psychological distress. Alternatively, he can achieve psychological resolution from the experience faster than someone who may not be equipped with the technique. If he has been practicing proper breathing, he might implement a proper breathing technique to manage his anxiety, fear, and anger. In allowing himself to breathe in, he will take in the life-force energy and will use his spirit to receive guidance on how to cope with the incidence of racial profiling and restore peace of mind. He will also slow down the anxiety and any other arousal that is occurring. In addition, he will minimize negative thoughts, harmful emotions, and potentially destructive behaviors. He may even go further and recognize that he is not at fault and that it is in fact the system that is oppressive and racist.

USING THE SPIRIT

The following case is an example of a recent consulting case of one of the authors who worked with an individual. The case material illustrates how the experience of racism can disrupt a client's ability to obtain guidance from her spirit, interfere with coping, and lead to disrupted peace of mind, such as in feelings of negative self-worth.

Nya's Experience: Race-Based Housing Discrimination

Nya (pseudonym used to protect the anonymity of the individual) is a thirty-four-year old middle-income, Baptist, single, black woman who currently works as a project director for a large research institution in a moderately sized city in the northeast United States. Nya has no significant psychiatric history. She was referred by her lawyer for a psychological interview to determine the impact of learning that she had been a victim of race-based stereotyping and discrimination. At the time of the referral, Nya was in the midst of preparing for a settlement hearing over a housing discrimination case. Her attorney, a white female, hoped to develop a greater understanding of the psychological impact of the racial discrimination incident on the client in order to substantiate claims for psychological damages in the settlement. The psychological consultant conducted a clinical interview with Nya via the telephone, and verbally administered a racism-related stress inventory, a culture-specific coping scale, and a symptoms checklist. The client requested to talk with the consultant on two additional occasions within the next two weeks to obtain guidance before the settlement hearing.

According to Nya, she was promoted to a supervisory position, approximately two years ago, which required her to relocate. She was excited about starting this new chapter in her life even though it required a move to the company's headquarters, which was approximately a one-hour drive from her home. Nya, described by her friends as a "go getter," decided that she would find an apartment closer to her new office. As she perused her local newspaper she came across an advertisement for a "beautiful, spacious, one-bedroom in a quaint family-oriented community." The address of the town house was close to her new office, and she decided to call the phone number provided in the ad. She contacted the landlords by phone to inquire about the advertised vacancy. She was provided with the address of the housing complex, told that the apartment was available, and an appointment was scheduled to view the apartment. Nya reported that she had a "good feeling" because an opportunity to live in the complex would shorten her commute to work from one hour to fifteen minutes.

Nya reported that when she arrived at the apartment complex for her scheduled appointment, the owner seemed surprised by her appearance and did not introduce herself to Nya. Rather, she asked the then-tenant to show Nya the apartment. After viewing the apartment, Nya expressed an interest in renting and asked about the next step that she should follow. The owner of the housing complex informed Nya that she (the owner) would have to consult with her co-owner and would contact her.

Nya did not hear from the owner for several days. Not easily discouraged, she then telephoned the owners of the apartment complex to again express her interest in the apartment. The co-owner told her that they were taking applications, they required three written references, and all applicants were being screened. Nya provided her name and address to the co-owner in order to receive an application by mail, but a couple days later she still had not received an application packet. Approximately one week later, Nya stopped by the apartment complex and spoke with the then-tenant, who confided that she showed the apartment that Nya was interested in to a Caucasian couple one day after Nya initially viewed the apartment. When Nya mentioned that she was being asked to provide an application and letters of reference, the then-tenant seemed surprised. The then-tenant, who was also white, told Nya that she (the tenant) did not have to submit written references and that the couple to whom the apartment was rented were not asked to submit an application or provide written letters of reference. Through tears, Nya shared with the psychological consultant that the then-tenant informed her that when Nya had walked away on the day she viewed the apartment, the owner commented, "We need to screen potential tenants more carefully. We have rented to *them* [blacks] before and it has always been a disaster." Later that day, one of the owners of the complex left Nya a message advising her that the apartment was rented, but if another vacancy became available he would call her. Immediately after this incident, Nya sought the support of her friends and family. She was advised by family and friends to seek legal counsel for housing discrimination and obtained the services of a local agency that provided legal support services to victims of discrimination.

Nya's Reaction to the Incident

During the initial consultation interview, Nya stated that upon learning of the racially stereotypical sentiments made by the owner, she felt "angry." In addition, learning of the race-based discrimination was devastating because the owner had not inquired any information about her except that her job location was near the apartment. Therefore, Nya was angry about how negative and unfavorable conclusions about renting to her could be drawn. She also stated that for several months following the incident, she suffered restless sleep patterns, difficulty concentrating on tasks, fatigue, reduced self-esteem, feelings of general mistrust, depressive symptoms, anger, worry, and withdrawal from her usual social activities. She sought out social support from family members whom she indicated were angered by news of the incident. She also had to inform her boss and coworkers of the situation because it was impacting her ability to concentrate and perform tasks effectively. Nya states that her self-esteem was particularly affected because prior to the incident she was not regularly concerned that such an event could happen to her. She reports repeatedly asking herself, "Why me? How could this happen to me?" She said that the incident "has changed my perspective of the world.... I feel like I had elevated myself beyond this. My parents raised us to believe we could do anything, go anywhere, live anywhere. I never saw anything as blatant racism before."

As court proceedings and litigation for the discrimination case filed by Nya have continued for over two years, she continues to suffer psychological distress. At the time of our interviews, she reported suffering restless sleep, lack of concentration at work, improved although still-reduced self-esteem, decreased trust of others in general, anger, and worry. She states that every time she has to relive or rehash the incident she gets angry. Now she questions whether other persons are judging her. She acknowledges, "I've moved forward, but it was always in my mind." During my second meeting with Nya, I inquired about how the discrimination and the case were taking a toll on her feelings about herself, her outlook, her thoughts, and her behaviors. She explained feeling confused about whether or not there was a reason for this to happen to her. The consultant provided reinforcement that she might be striving to find spiritual meaning in her experience. She went on to reflect that she believed the whole ordeal in some way was "bigger" than her. She pondered that there must be a spiritual purpose to everything happening to her, but that she was not ready to figure out the lesson because she was just too confused and angry. In the final conversation, Nya did not want to return to discussing the spiritual significance of her experience because she could not make sense of it. Rather, she chose to focus on her mixed feelings about more concrete issues of the settlement, like the amount of a settlement, whether or not to go to trial, and whether she should seek an apology from the defendant. Shortly after the monetary settlement of the case, Nya sent the consultant a message of thanks. The consultant replied, informing the client of the opportunity to share her story in this case study. Nya replied with the following sentiments:

> Wow! That sounds exciting. . . . Personally, I would be very interested in being part of the case study section knowing that what I went through could help others or at least put it into perspective for them . . . remember when we spoke, I felt like this whole ordeal was in some part "bigger" than me. Like there was more that I needed to do about this and maybe this is the answer. Maybe this opportunity is what was being given to me but at the time I didn't understand it. I kept thinking part of it was not to settle, but instead take the case to court, but for some reason that still didn't feel like the "thing to do." It kept nagging at me and I couldn't make sense of it. So, maybe this is the "thing" I was trying to figure out, the "something" that was bigger than me in a sense. It wasn't simply just knowing they discriminated against me but understanding there was more to it and there was a message I needed to give on a bigger platform than just the "courtroom."

REFLECTIONS ON USING THE SPIRIT

Nya's experiences suggest several ways that psychologists and counselors may intervene to address disruption to one's spirit. During the initial psychological consultation with Nya, she was made aware of the lasting impact that racism-related stress might have on the client's presenting symptoms, specifically her interpersonal sensitivity, depressive symptoms, and changing affective states. To assist the legal team and to help Nya cope with the racial incident, the consultant assessed her level of stress, behavioral and affective symptoms, and style of coping with the aid of clinical assessment tools. Consistent with the client's self report, the results suggested that she had not perceived substantial racism-related stress over her lifetime. The results supported her report of employing collective and spirit-centered forms of coping and experience of substantial psychological distress immediately following the event and to a lesser extent two years later. During the second meeting with Nya, the consultant used the assessment conclusions to explore how Nya's current and previous experiences with racism have taken a toll on her feelings about herself, her outlook, her thoughts, and her behaviors.

The client introduced the possibility of a spiritual purpose to the event. When the consultant directly explored spirit, the client said that she did attend church and at times she felt good when she thought about her relationship to God. Relying on an understanding of spirit, the consultant validated this experience and also emphasized to Nya that according to some psychological perspectives, spirit also represented her interconnection to something greater than herself and that engaging her spirit might aid in her ability to cope with the discriminatory event. If Nya were open to exploring the spirit-based aspect of her experience further, the consultant could share that from an African-centered perspective, racism-related stress creates blockages in the flow of energy and, as a result, this blockage disrupts the soul-mind-body-spirit connection. A disruption of the spirit leads her to experience confusion that impacts her ability to cope, her behaviors (lack of motivation toward normal activities), and thoughts (internalizing stereotypical perceptions). Nya could learn to use breathing as an important part of coping because breathing allows the energy to flow once again and facilitates the connective relationship to her spirit. This appears to be a plausible approach for Nya, as she is motivated to use spirituality to cope with her experience. For example, she may spend each morning engaging in breathing exercises that help reconnect her to her spirit. She can also participate in events at the community level that remind her that she is not alone in her experiences. Nonetheless, it is evident in the sentiments of her above message to the consultant that through the clinical interview, Nya was able to understand her experience in the context of learning about her spirit.

The toolbox at the end of the chapter provides a synopsis of suggestions for combating prejudice and discrimination based on engaging the spirit. These suggestions can be used by individuals, communities, practitioners, and educators.

CONCLUSION

Racism and discrimination affect the lives of blacks daily and are experienced in the individual, cultural, institutional, and collective realms. The impact of racism on blacks' physical and psychological health is well documented in the field of psychology. Racism-related stress has been correlated with depression, hypertension, negative self-cognitions, and internalized negative racial beliefs that may cause violence against self and others. Yet, as much as we know about the impact of racism on the mental health of blacks, we know very little about how racism impacts the spirit. This is ironic, given the importance and centrality of spirituality. In this chapter, we attempt to bridge this gap by offering a conceptualization of the impact of racism on blacks' spirit and its resulting psychological manifestations. We hope to alert readers,

Toolbox for Change

For	Perceptions based on racism	Strategies for change
Individuals	*Individual racism* Negative thoughts and feelings based upon race. Personal insults directed at self and others due to prejudice, stereotypes, and discrimination. *Everyday racism* Daily experiences or racism throughout the day, at work, in public places, en route to and from home, on television, and in other media outlets.	Use breath control exercises daily to foster engagement of spiritual guidance. Employ breath control techniques during specific incidents of discrimination, stereotypical treatment, or prejudice. Practice breath control throughout the day to help maintain peace of mind in the midst of everyday racist occurrences.
Community	*Cultural racism* Beliefs that the dominant group's cultural heritage and practices are superior.	Develop community rituals that affirm cultural heritage, beliefs, and practices, such as breath control based on African culture.
Practitioners/ educators	*Institutional racism* Systematic policies and practices that promote inadequate access to resources. Policies and programs that restrict choices, rights, mobility, and access for the nondominant racial groups.	Institute psychoeducational programs outside traditional psychology that empower blacks to reconnect with the spirit-based practices of their heritage. Develop training programs about black spirituality and the African origins of spiritual practices such as breath control. Teach awareness of one's assumptions and biases regarding the role of spirit.

whether they are practitioners, individuals, or members of the community, to the role of spirit in their lives and in their work with blacks. We also offer practical suggestions for coping with racism that will enable the reader to reconnect with the spirit. In this way, recognizing the role of spirit in one's life may serve as a resource to deal with experiences of racism and discrimination.

As a final note, we agree with leaders in the field who support using culturally congruent frameworks when working with people of African descent. As such, it is no longer appropriate when working with blacks to utilize theories that do not validate all facets of African cultural values. We hope that the ideas presented in this chapter continue the tradition of a psychology of liberation toward healing and optimizing the functioning of persons of African descent.

REFERENCES

Anderson, N. B. (1989). Racial differences in stress-induced cardiovascular reactivity and hypertension: Current status and substantive issues. *Psychological Bulletin, 105,* 89–105.

Ashby, M. (2000). *The Egyptian book of the dead: The book of coming forth by day.* Miami, FL: Sema Institute of Yoga.

Ashby, M. (2002a). *Kemetic diet: Ancient African wisdom for health of mind, body and spirit.* Miami, FL: Sema Institute of Yoga.

Ashby, M. (2002b). *The African origins of civilization, religion, yoga mysticism and ethics philosophy.* Miami, FL: Sema Institute of Yoga.

Chiang, L., Hunter, C. D., & Yeh, C. J. (in press). Coping attitudes, sources, and practices among black and Latino college students. *Adolescence.*

Comas-Diaz, L, & Greene, B. (1994). *Women of color: Integrating ethnic and gender identities in psychotherapy.* New York: The Guilford Press.

Constantine, M. G., Lewis, E. L., Conner, L. C., & Sanchez, D. (2000). Addressing spiritual and religious issues in counseling African Americans: Implications for counselor training and practice. *Counseling and Values, 45,* 28–39.

Ellison, C. G. (1993). Religious involvement and self-perception among black Americans. *Social Forces, 71,* 1027–1055.

Essed, P. (1990). *Everyday racism: Reports from women of two cultures.* Claremont, CA: Hunter House.

Fernando, S. (1984). Racism as a cause of depression. *International Journal of Social Psychiatry, 30,* 41–49.

Grills, C. (2002). African-centered psychology: Basic principles. In P. Pedersen (Series ed.) & T. A. Parham (Vol. ed.), *Multicultural aspects of counseling series: Vol. 18. Counseling persons of African descent:*

Raising the bar of practitioner competence (pp. 25–37). Thousand Oaks, CA: Sage Publications.

Harrell, S. P. (2000). A multidimensional conceptualization of racism-related stress: Implications for the well-being of people of color. *American Journal of Orthopsychiatry, 70*, 42–57.

Jagers, R. J., & Smith, P. (1996). Further examination of the Spirituality Scale. *Journal of Black Psychology, 22*, 429–442.

Jones, D. R., Harrell, J. P., Morris-Prather, C. E., Thomas, J., & Omowale, N. (1996). Affective and physiological responses to racism: The roles of Afrocentrism and mode of presentation. *Ethnicity and Disease, 6*, 109–122.

Jones, J. M. (1997). *Prejudice and racism* (2nd ed.). New York: McGraw-Hill.

Kambon, K. K. K. (1992). *The African personality in America: An African-centered framework*. Tallahassee, FL: Nubian Nation Publications.

Klonoff, E. A., Landrine, H., & Ullman, J. B. (1999). Racial discrimination and psychiatric symptoms among blacks. *Cultural Diversity and Ethnic Minority Psychology, 5*, 329–339.

Krieger, N. (1990). Racial and gender discrimination: Risk factors for high blood pressure. *Social Science and Medicine, 30*, 1273–1281.

Landrine, H., & Klonoff, E. A. (1996). The schedule of racist events: A measure of racial discrimination and a study of its negative physical and mental consequences. *Journal of Black Psychology, 22*, 144–168.

Lewis, M. E. L. (2003). *Perceptions of racism-related stress, culture specific coping and psychological distress among African Americans*. Unpublished doctoral dissertation, Teachers College, Columbia University, New York.

Lukoff, D., Turner, R., & Lu, F. (1992). Transpersonal psychology research review: Psychoreligious dimensions of healing. *Journal of Transpersonal Psychology, 24*, 41–60.

Mattis, J. (2000). African American women's definitions of spirituality and religiosity. *Journal of Black Psychology, 26*, 101–122.

Myers, J. L. (1993). *Understanding an Afrocentric world view: Introduction to an optimal psychology* (2nd ed.). Dubuque, IA: Kendall/Hunt Publishing Company.

Neuspiel, D. R. (1996). Racism and perinatal addiction. *Ethnicity and Disease, 6*, 47–55.

Newlin, K., Knafl, K., & Melkus, G. D. (2002). African American spirituality: A concept analysis. *Advances in Nursing Science, 25*, 57–70.

Nobles, W. W. (1986). *African psychology: Towards its reclamation, reascension and revitalization*. Oakland, CA: Black Family Institute.

Obasi, E. M. (2002). Reconceptualizing the notion of self from the African deep structure. In P. Pedersen (Series ed.) & T. A. Parham (Vol. ed.), *Multicultural aspects of counseling series: Vol. 18. Counseling persons of African descent: Raising the bar of practitioner competence* (pp. 52–74). Thousand Oaks, CA: Sage Publications.

Parham, T. A., & Parham, W. D. (2002). Understanding African American mental health: The necessity of new conceptual paradigms. In P. Pedersen (Series ed.) & T. A. Parham (Vol. ed.), *Multicultural aspects of counseling series: Vol. 18. Counseling persons of African descent: Raising the bar of practitioner competence* (pp. 25–37). Thousand Oaks, CA: Sage Publications.

Parham, T. A., White, J. L., & Ajamu, A. (1999). *The psychology of blacks: An African-centered perspective.* Upper Saddle River, NJ: Prentice-Hall.

Sue, D. W. (2003). *Overcoming our racism: The journey to liberation.* San Francisco: Jossey-Bass.

Taylor, R. J., Chatters, L. M., Jayakody, R., & Levin, J. S. (1996). Black and white differences in religious participation: A multisample comparison. *Journal for the Scientific Study of Religion, 35,* 403–410.

Thompson, B. W. (1992). A way outa no way: Eating problems among African American, Latina, and white women. *Gender and Society, 6,* 546–561.

Utsey, S. O., Bolden, M. A., & Brown, A. L. (2001). Visions of revolution from the spirit of Frantz Fanon: A psychology of liberation for counseling African Americans confronting societal racism and oppression. In J. G. Ponterotto, J. M. Casas, L. A. Suzuki, & C. M. Alexander (Eds.), *Handbook of Multicultural Counseling* (2nd ed., pp. 311–336). Thousand Oaks, CA: Sage Publications.

Utsey, S. O., Ponterotto, J. G., Reynolds, A. L., & Cancelli, A. A. (2000). Racial discrimination, coping, life satisfaction, and self-esteem among African Americans. *Journal of Counseling and Development, 78,* 72–80.

CHAPTER 10

Combating Racism: The Role of Psychologists and the United Nations

Thema Bryant-Davis
Corann Okorodudu
Bertha Garrett Holliday

COMBATING RACISM: THE ROLE OF THE AMERICAN PSYCHOLOGICAL ASSOCIATION AND THE UNITED NATIONS

Most societal traumas are traumas that may arise from racism, sexism, and classism, or the profound influence of social, economic, and political oppression. Racism is a potentially traumatizing and terrorizing form of victimization that affects ethnic minority children and adults. As sources of trauma, racist incidents may result in long-term continuous psychological effects such as posttraumatic stress disorder. Additionally, racist incidents are also constant sources of stress in the everyday lives of ethnic minorities in the United States as well as targeted group members internationally.

Racism has negative legal, social, economic, political, and educational consequences; and to eradicate racism, an interdisciplinary approach is needed. Not only do policymakers, economists, and educators play a role in addressing racism, but psychologists are also key contributors to eradicating racism. This chapter will first define racism, then explore the ways psychologists of the American Psychological Association (APA) have worked to address it through APA policies and through interventions at the United Nations.

Along with economic, social, and political consequences, racism has been found to have psychological consequences, including increased psychiatric and physiological symptomatology. For example, some critical characteristics of traumatic events are that they are threatening to life or life quality, cause severe harm or injury, and are marked by intense fear, helplessness, or horror. While it is obvious that racially motivated physical assaults threaten the lives of target group members, nonphysical forms of racism impair the quality of life of target group members through housing discrimination, employment discrimination, and unequal education. Within the United States, targets of racism include members of ethnic minority groups such as blacks, Asians, Latinos, and Native Americans. Globally, targets of racism include people of African descent, Asian descent, Arab descent, the Dalits of India, Roma gypsies, and other indigenous peoples.

Definition of Racism

Racism is defined as beliefs, attitudes, institutional arrangements, and behaviors that tend to denigrate individuals or groups because of these persons' phenotypic characteristics or ethnic group affiliations. Racism assumes many forms. Individual racism is closest to race prejudice and occurs when a negative action, such as verbal abuse, physical assault, or discrimination, is taken against a target group member or members by an individual aligned with the dominant and more powerful and privileged group. Institutional racism manifests when doctrines of racial superiority pervade the political, economic, educational, criminal justice, media, and health care systems of a nation or state. Cultural racism involves doctrines of racial superiority related to values, beliefs, and cultural forms. The promulgation of institutional and cultural racism may be covert or overt and may be directed at an individual or a group of people. Additionally, individuals or institutions may perpetrate these forms of racism.

THE AMERICAN PSYCHOLOGICAL ASSOCIATION'S RESOLUTION AGAINST RACISM

In 2001, the American Psychological Association prepared to send a delegation to the United Nations World Conference against Racism, Racial Discrimination, Xenophobia, and Related Intolerance (WCAR). As part of these preparations, the American Psychological Association approved its first resolution against racism. While the Association has prior resolutions against discrimination and poverty, this is the first resolution against racism. Resolutions serve to summarize existing psychological literature in a particular area and to advocate specific policy and procedural recommendations based on the literature. During the previous twenty-five years, the American Psychological Association showed its support for the fight against racism within the discipline of psychology and the Association by establishing the APA Office of Ethnic Minority Affairs, the APA Committee on Ethnic Minority Affairs, and the Society for the Psychological Study of Ethnic Minority Issues (APA's Division 45), supporting the biannual National Multicultural Conference and Summit (which is organized collaboratively by several APA divisions) that addresses racism and intolerance, adopting UN human rights instruments, supporting efforts by the United Nations to defend human rights, adopting resolutions against discrimination and in favor of increased resource access for ethnic minorities, and dedication of the 1999 Annual Convention to Racial and Other Diversity Issues in Psychology.

An initial draft of the APA resolution against racism was prepared by two of the American Psychological Association (APA) representatives to the United Nations: Dr. Thema Bryant-Davis and Dr. Corann Okorodudu, who serve as the APA's main representative to the United Nations. The APA Committee on International Relations (CIRP), in consultation with the APA Committee on Ethnic Minority Affairs (CEMA), modified the resolution's text, and an *ad hoc* group of representatives from the APA UN delegation, CIRP, and CEMA drafted a justification statement that cited the psychological literature in support of the resolution's claims. The revised resolution and its accompanying justification statement were forwarded to the APA Board of Directors, who approved the resolution as an emergency action on June 10, 2001. The following are key components of the resolution, including its articulation of racism's negative consequences and the ways that the American Psychological Association can actively work to eradicate it. The statements to follow are based on psychological research findings, which are cited in the bibliography at the end of the chapter instead of within the body of the text itself.

Overview

Through empirical research, psychologists have determined that racism continues to be a pervasive problem in the United States and internationally. Racism creates barriers to survival, security, development, and social participation. These barriers are manifested in such forms as police brutality, institutional blocks to employment, poverty, and political marginalization.

Effects of Racism on Targeted Groups

Perceived racist incidents may result in negative psychological, social, and physiological effects on targeted groups. Racism is a chronic stressor that often contributes to psycho-physiological diseases such as hypertension and diabetes. It also can contribute to depression, alcohol consumption, low self-esteem, internalized racism, chronic health problems, and psychological distress. The effects of racist incidents may also strengthen connectedness among members of targeted groups, reinforce spirituality and personal strengths, and build resilience.

In addition, psychologists have determined that racism has negative cognitive, behavioral, affective, and relational effects on children and adults. Possible cognitive responses include intrusive thoughts about racial incidents, and self-defeating thoughts. Behavioral effects may include increased conduct disorders, avoidance behaviors, high-risk behaviors, and substance dependence. Affective responses include depression and anxiety, and relational effects include isolation and distrust of others. The impact of racism begins as early as preschool and continues throughout life. It creates barriers to healthy development for those who are targeted by it.

Racism and Children

Racism negatively affects ethnic minority children academically and socially. It also has negative effects on their self-esteem and self-efficacy (their belief in their capabilities). This is a result of the racist incidents that they experience, witness, and hear about within their communities. It also is the result of media portrayals of ethnic minorities in film, television, and print. Ethnic minority children are stigmatized as being less intelligent and less capable, and these stigmatizing messages are sometimes internalized.

Gender and Racism

There are unique ways that racism interacts with gender and sexism, therefore creating some differing experiences for ethnic minority girls and boys and women and men. Girls and women are more likely to be brutalized by sexual violence and trafficking than their male counterparts are, and the associated legal cases of ethnic minority females are taken less seriously by criminal justice systems than the cases of their white female counterparts. In some countries, ethnic minority girls and women have fewer political, social, and legal rights than ethnic minority males. In terms of ethnic minority boys and men, they are more likely to be viewed as threats and therefore responded to with physical violence than are ethnic minority females. Throughout history, racist systems such as slavery and colonialism have aimed at the destruction of ethnic minority male-female relationships and to a larger degree the destruction of ethnic minority families. The consequences of these actions can still be seen today.

Racism and Poverty

Racism creates and maintains poverty for ethnic minorities. One of the core issues of racism is the denial of resources. Whether ethnic minorities are labeled lazy, savage, ignorant, or immoral, the existence of poverty is rationalized as being the fault of target group members. This allows for the economic, political, legal, and educational resources to stay in the hands of a few, while denying the rights to resource access of many. When people are denied jobs and housing and even the right to vote, they are pushed further into the depths of lack. Economic lack and racism are linked; together and separately they create psychological distress and physical health consequences. For those ethnic minorities who seek help, they sometimes discover institutionalized racism within physical and mental health care agencies, creating more distress and distrust.

Roots of Racism

Racial discrimination is the result of learned attitudes and behaviors. Children learn racist ideas from parents, religious institutions, governments, schools, and the media. People are taught stereotypes and stigmatized views of members of other races. These messages may be subtle or overt. A subtle example is a child noticing that whenever an ethnic minority man walks past, her mother grabs her hand and pulls her closer but never does this when a white man walks past. An overt example may be when a boy hears his father and uncles telling racist jokes about a particular group of people. Other messages may include ministers who preach against interracial marriage, schools that leave out the contribution of ethnic minorities in the history books, and media images of ethnic minorities as criminals or clowns. All of these messages serve to teach one group that they are intellectually,

socially, and morally superior to other races. These attitudes and behaviors continue to be taught and reinforced throughout the lives of
dominant group members.

Effects of Racism on Dominant Group Members

Although racism may benefit some dominant group members economically and politically, it has negative consequences for cognitive and
affective development. In terms of cognitions or thoughts, dominant
group members may build their lives on distorted thoughts and ideas
about themselves and others. This creates a very fragile sense of self.
For example, they may truly believe that there is no injustice and that
people who work hard benefit and those who do not, suffer. If people
hold this belief for most of their lives and then discover that injustice
does exist, or if they have the experience of working hard and yet not
getting ahead, they will experience distress, confusion, and anxiety.
At this point, they will have to expand their worldviews to understand
that injustice, including racism, does exist; or they will simply reason
that they are not advancing because of reverse discrimination. What-
ever the conclusion, distress will be involved.

Along with distress, racist beliefs create fear in dominant group
members. For example, when they are in the presence of ethnic minorities or anticipating the presence of ethnic minorities, they experience
anxiety and fear, especially when there are large numbers of ethnic
minorities. The fear sometimes manifests itself in aggression and hostility, which are also negative consequences for the ethnic minority
person as well as the dominant group member. Recently psychologists
even found that a dominant group member who holds racist beliefs can
suffer from poor concentration or academic performance when sharing
the room with an ethnic minority person. With the growing number
of ethnic minorities, there is sure to be an increase in distress, fear,
aggression, and irrational thinking among dominant group members
who hold racist ideas.

Call to Action

In recognition of all of the above, the American Psychological Association resolves to struggle against racism. Because it is important
to heal oneself before trying to heal others, the APA resolution calls
for the eradication of all forms of racism within the field of psychology,
including in scientific research and clinical practice. The American

Psychological Association denounces racism in all its forms and recognizes its negative psychological, social, education, and economic effects on children and adults. This includes covert and overt racism and individual acts of racial discrimination, as well as institutionalized racism. Psychologists are challenged to recognize their role in promoting social justice and human welfare nationally and internationally.

The American Psychological Association agreed to send a delegation to the United Nations' World Conference against Racism, Racial Discrimination, Xenophobia, and Related Intolerance. The APA also agreed to seek out diverse racial representation at all levels of its governance. All psychologists are called upon to discontinue all practices in research, practice, training, and education that promote or are based on racist ideology. Psychology researchers are especially challenged to conduct studies on effective tools for the alleviation of racial and ethnic injustice.

Psychologists are encouraged to speak out against racism and to take steps to stop racist activities. Psychologists are in a unique position to intervene in the perpetuation of racist attitudes and behaviors in counseling centers, schools, corporations, research institutes, and government agencies. Consistent with the mandates of the APA resolution, a delegation of six psychologists from the American Psychological Association went to Durban, South Africa, to attend the WCAR in the summer of 2001 to offer a psychological perspective of the causes, consequences, and solutions to racism and racist attitudes and behaviors.

WORLD CONFERENCE AGAINST RACISM, RACIAL DISCRIMINATION, XENOPHOBIA, AND RELATED INTOLERANCE

The American Psychological Association included two of the APA's representatives to the United Nations: Dr. Corann Okorodudu, the main representative to the United Nations, and Dr. Thema Bryant-Davis. In addition, the delegation included Dr. James Jackson from the APA Committee on International Relations in Psychology; Dr. Bertha G. Holliday, director of the APA Office of Ethnic Minority Affairs; Dr. Anderson J. Franklin from the Society for the Psychological Study of Ethnic Minority Issues; and Dr. William Parham from the APA Committee on Ethnic Minority Affairs.

To prepare for the WCAR in South Africa, pre-conference meetings were held in Geneva, Switzerland, and Washington, DC, which were attended by members of the APA WCAR delegation. At these conferences, the APA delegates distributed an advocacy statement that they created in consultation with the Health/Mental Health NGO caucus of the WCAR, which provided suggested language consistent with the major tenets of the APA resolution. The delegation also developed an APA declaration for the WCAR, whose content elaborated upon that of the APA resolution and whose structure mirrored that of the draft WCAR declaration, which was the centerpiece of WCAR deliberations. The APA lobbying statement and declaration noted the prevalence of racism and its mental health effects, among other effects. It also recognized the importance of interdisciplinary research to understand varied historic and contemporary forms of racism. Specific victims of racism were acknowledged in the APA declaration, including victims of trafficking, women and girls, migrants and refugees, racial minorities in multiethnic states, indigenous peoples, Africans and African descendants, racism victims with physical and mental disabilities, and persons who are victims of both racism and homophobia. The APA declaration acknowledged the need for an improved quality of life for all of these persons. In terms of remedies, the APA declaration called for institutions, governments, the United Nations, the World Health Organization, and physical and mental health care agencies to take active steps to eliminate racist practices and policies. The APA declaration also called for the development of prevention strategies, an international monitoring body to report on international actions taken against racism, and an institute to conduct international research and policy promotion aimed at the eradication of racism. Prior to the WCAR, the APA declaration was forwarded to every APA division and state psychological association, and to organized psychological association in other nations.

In Durban, South Africa, the delegation advocated for a psychological perspective of racism at both the Non-Governmental Organizations (NGO) conference and the United Nations' (governmental) WCAR conference. Over one hundred countries were represented, and the APA delegates were able to promote their perspectives and positions through dissemination of the APA resolution and declaration, interpersonal contacts, a two-hour panel discussion for NGO delegates, and an "intervention" (a position paper) that was read at a WCAR plenary session.

Outcomes

United Nations conferences outcomes are based on consensus. At the WCAR, all of the countries' participating nations and their government representatives worked to create a document on which all could agree. If a section did not have consensus, it was deleted. Nongovernmental organizations, such as the American Psychological Association, advocate for the inclusion of their particular concerns. As a result of the advocacy of the American Psychological Association delegation, mental health was acknowledged in three separate sections of the outcome document from the World Conference.

First, the various nations recognized that research studies and data collection on the impact and consequences of racism must include an analysis of mental and physical health care. It is important that along with education, employment, housing, and landownership, the significance of mental health be acknowledged.

Second, the conference's outcome document urged all states (nations) to recognize the right of every person to attain the highest standard of mental and physical health. This is a huge step. Mental health is recognized as an important human right. Beyond written laws and policies, each person has a right to attain the highest level of mental health. Since racial discrimination negatively affects mental health, it is clear that to protect the mental health of its citizens, a state has to work to eliminate racism.

Finally, the World Health Organization and other international agencies are called upon to recognize the impact of racism on mental health and to produce projects, research and otherwise, to ensure equitable health care for victims of racism. Given the number of persons who have been negatively affected mentally and physically by inequitable health care, this statement is incredibly important.

PSYCHOLOGISTS' ACTIVITY AFTER THE WORLD CONFERENCE

After the World Conference against Racism, Racial Discrimination, Xenophobia, and Related Intolerance, the APA delegation began educating other psychologists about the WCAR, its consensual processes, and related actions of the United Nations and others. Dissemination of such information occurred through briefings and reports to APA governance groups, articles in various psychology magazines and newsletters, presentations at the annual convention of the American Psychological Association and the Multicultural Summit and Conference (which is organized by several APA divisions), and at other organizational and university conferences and events. The delegation also sought to continue to educate nongovernmental agencies as

well as governmental representatives about the psychological consequences of and remedies for racism by disseminating the APA resolution and declaration at meetings within the United Nations and
to other nongovernmental agencies committed to working against
racism. In addition, the two delegates who are representatives to
the United Nations have advocated psychological perspectives and
interventions related for UN programs centered on racism and indigenous peoples' issues. APA UN representatives are members of the
Non-Governmental Agency Committee for Human Rights Subcom-
mittee for the Elimination of Racism. As a part of this group, they
planned and implemented the 2003 International Day for the Elimination of Racism program at the United Nations. This program
included morning and afternoon components and provided education to governmental and nongovernmental representatives about
anti-racist actions. In addition, one of the APA UN representatives,
Dr. Thema Bryant-Davis, spoke at the 2003 Permanent Forum of
Indigenous Issues on indigenous children and the mental health
consequences of racism and discrimination. Attempts to educate
the general public about the role of psychology in addressing the
consequences and causes of racism include the publishing of this
chapter.

Future Directions

Psychologists will continue to play an important role in combating
racism through their research, practice, training, education, and public
service. By sharing important research on the causes and consequences
of racism, as well as the effectiveness of various remedies, psychologists can help reduce the prevalence of racism around the globe. Psychologists have to continue to advocate for the mental health of those
targeted by racism. This advocacy must be within the mental health
arena, on the local government level, and at the United Nations.
Psychologists recognize the need to combat racist attitudes and practices, as well as internalized racism within themselves and within others.
Those of us who work in industries and organizations have to work
and speak against racism in hiring and promotion. We also have to
continue to speak against racism in the criminal justice system, education system, and political system. Only by continuing to speak and
work to combat racism within the field of psychology, in our local
communities, throughout our nation, and internationally, can we hope
to make a difference.

SUGGESTED READINGS

American Psychological Association. (2001). *Declaration for the UN World Conference against Racism, Racial Discrimination, Xenophobia, and Related Intolerance.* www.apa.org/pi/oema/racismdeclaration.pdf

American Psychological Association. (2001). *Intervention of the American Psychological Association Delegation to the World Conference against Racism (WCAR).* www.apa.org/pi/oema/wcarplenary.html

American Psychological Association, Public Interest Directorate, Office of Ethnic Minority Affairs. (1999). *Racism and psychology: Why we dislike, stereotype and hate other groups and what to do about it.* Washington, DC: Author.

Anderson, N. (1989). Racial differences in stress-induced cardiovascular reactivity and hypertension: Current status and substantive issues. *Psychological Bulletin, 105,* 89–105.

Armstead, C., Lawler, K., Gorden, G., Cross, J., & Gibbons, J. (1989). Relationship of racial stressors to blood pressure responses and anger expression in black college students. *Health Psychology, 8,* 541–556.

Bentancourt, H., & Lopez, S. R. (1993). The study of culture, ethnicity, and race in American psychology. *American Psychology, 48,* 629–637.

Bernard, N., Holliday, B. G., Crump, S. L., & Sanchez, N. (1998). *Psychology and racism: Annotated bibliography.* Washington, DC: American Psychological Association, Office of Ethnic Minority Affairs.

Carter, J. (1994). Racism's impact on mental health. *Journal of the National Medical Association, 86,* 543–547.

Carter, R., & Helms, J. (2002, September 28). *Racial discrimination and harassment: Race-based traumatic stress.* Paper presented at the American College of Forensic Examiners Conference, Orlando, FL.

Clark, R., Anderson, N., Clark, V., & Williams, D. (1999). Racism as a stressor for African Americans: A biopsychosocial model. *American Psychologist, 54,* 805–816.

Comas-Diaz, L. (2000). An ethnopolitical approach to working with people of color. *American Psychologist, 55,* 1319–1325.

Corner, J. P. (1991) White racism: Its root, form, and function. In R. L. Jones (Ed.), *Black psychology* (pp. 591–596). Berkeley, CA: Cobb & Henry.

Cross, W. E., Jr. (1990). *Shades of black.* Philadelphia, PA: Temple University Press.

Daniel, J. H. (2000). The courage to hear: African American women's memories of racial trauma. In L. Jackson & B. Greene (Eds.), *Psychotherapy with African American women: Innovations in psychodynamic perspective and practice* (pp. 126–144). New York: Guilford Press.

Gaines, S. O., & Reed, E. S. (1995). Prejudice: From Allport to DuBois. *American Psychologist, 50,* 96–103.

Galster, G. (1990). Racial steering in urban housing markets: A review of the audit evidence. *Social Science Research, 18,* 105–129.

Ginorio, A., Guitierrez, L., Cauce, A. M., & Acosta, M. (1995). Psychological issues for Latinas. In H. Ladrine (Ed.), *Bringing cultural diversity to feminist psychology*. Washington, DC: American Psychological Association.

Harrell, J. P., Hall, S., & Tagliaferro, J. (2003). Physiological responses to racism and discrimination: An assessment of the evidence. *American Journal of Public Health, 93*, 243–247.

Helms, J., & Cook, D. (1999). *Using race and culture in counseling and psychotherapy: Theory and process*. Needham Heights, MA: Allyn & Bacon.

Henderson, K., & Sloan, L. (2003). Helping psychologists help victims of racist hate crime. *Clinical Psychology: Science and Practice, 10*(4), 481–490.

Jackson, J. S., Brown, K. T., & Kirby, D. C. (1998). International perspectives on prejudice and racism. In J. L. Eberhardt & S. T. Fiske (Eds.), *Confronting racism: The problem & the response*. Thousand Oaks, CA: Abbreviated.

Jones, J. M. (1997). *Prejudice and racism* (2nd ed.) New York: McGraw-Hill.

Kessler, R. C., Michelson, K. D., & Williams, D. R. (1999). The prevalence, distribution, and mental health correlates of perceived discrimination in the United States. *Journal of Health and Social Behavior, 40*, 208–230.

Klonoff, E. A., & Landrine, H. (1999). Cross-validation of the schedule of racist events. *Journal of Black Psychology, 25*, 231–255.

Krieger, N., & Sidney, S. (1996). Racial discrimination and blood pressure: The CARDIA study of young black and white adults. *American Journal of Public Health, 86*, 1370–1378.

Ladrine, H., & Klonoff, E. (1996). The schedule of racist events: A measure of racial discrimination and a study of its negative physical and mental health consequences. *Journal of Black Psychology, 22*, 144–168.

LaFromboise, T., Choney, S. B., James, A., & Running Wolf, P. R. (1995). American Indian women and psychology. In H. Ladrine (Ed.), *Bringing cultural diversity to feminist psychology*. Washington, DC: American Psychological Association.

Lawrence, K. (2001). Racism, oppression, and childhood trauma. In B. Everett & R. Gallop, (Eds.), *The link between childhood trauma and mental illness: Effective interventions for mental health professionals* (pp. 271–291). Thousand Oaks, CA: Sage Publications.

Loo, C. M., Fairbank, J. A., Scurfield, R. M., Ruch, L. O., King, D. W., Adams, L. J., et al. (2001). Measuring exposure to racism: Development and validation of a race-related stressor scale (RRSS) for Asian American Vietnam veterans. *Psychological Assessment, 13*, 503–520.

McNeilly, M., Anderson, N., Robinson, E., McManus, C., Armstead, C., Clark, R., et al. (1996). The convergent, discriminant validity of the perceived racism scale: A multidimensional assessment of white racism among African Americans. In R. Jones (Ed.), *Handbook on tests and measurements for black populations.* Richmond, CA: Cobb and Henry Publishers.

Murray, B. (2002). Psychology bolsters the world's fight against racism. *Monitor on Psychology, 33*(1).

Nagata, D., & Cheng, W. (2003). Intergenerational communication of race-related trauma by Japanese American former internees. *American Journal of Orthopsychiatry, 73*, 266–278.

Root, M. P. P. (1995). The psychology of Asian American women. In H. Ladrine (Ed.), *Bringing cultural diversity to feminist psychology.* Washington, DC: American Psychological Association.

Sanchez-Hucles, J. (1998). Racism: emotional abusiveness and psychological trauma for ethnic minorities. *Journal of Emotional Abuse, 1*, 69–87.

Scurfield, R., & Mackey, D. (2001). Racism, trauma, and positive aspects of exposure to race-related experiences: Assessment and treatment implications. *Journal of Ethnic and Cultural Diversity in Social Work, 10*, 23–47.

Sellers, R. M., & Shelton, J. M. (2003). The role of racial identity in perceived racial discrimination. *Journal of Personality and Social Psychology, 84*, 1079–1092.

Sue, S. (1999). Science, ethnicity, and bias: Where have we gone wrong? *American Psychologist, 54*, 1070–1077.

Tatum, B. (1997). *"Why are all the Black kids sitting together in the cafeteria?" and other conversations about race.* New York: Basic Books.

Thompson, C., & Neville, H. (1999). Racism, mental health, and mental health practice. *Counseling Psychology, 27*, 155–223.

Thompson, V. (1996). Perceived racism as stressful life events. *Community Mental Health Journal, 32*, 223–233.

Utsey, S. O., & Ponterotto, J. G. (1996). Development and validation of the Index of Race-Related Stress (IRRS). *Journal of Counseling Psychology, 43*, 490–501.

Williams, D. (1999). Race, socioeconomic status, and health: The added effects of racism and discrimination. In N. Adler & M. Marmot (Eds.), Socioeconomic status and health in industrial nations: Social, psychological, and biological pathways. *Annals of the New York Academy of Sciences, 896*, 173–188.

Williams, D. & Rucker, T. (1996). Socioeconomic status and the health of racial minority populations. In P. Kato & T. Mann (Eds.), *Handbook of diversity issues in health psychology. The Plenum series in culture and health* (pp. 407–423). New York: Plenum.

Worchel, S. (1999). *Written in blood: Ethnic identity and the struggle for human harmony.* New York, NY: Worth Publishers.

Yee, A. H., Fairchild, H. H., Wizmann, E., & Wyatt, G. E. (1993). Addressing psychology's problem with race. *American Psychologist, 48*, 1132–1140.

Index

About the Series and the Series Editors

It is expected that nearly half of the entire U.S. population will be of nonwhite ethnic and racial minorities by the year 2050. With this growing diversity, clinicians, researchers, and, indeed, all Americans need to understand that the Eurocentric psychological views particular to Caucasians may or may not be relevant or adequate to address mental health issues in racial and ethnic minorities. This series addresses those issues, aiming to better understand how these factors affect mental health, and what needs to be done, or done differently, to heal disorders that may arise.

JEAN LAU CHIN is a licensed psychologist and systemwide dean of the California School of Professional Psychology at Alliant International University. She is also president of CEO Services, which offers clinical, educational, and organizational development services emphasizing cultural competence and integrated systems of care. She holds a doctorate from Teacher's College of Columbia University. Dr. Chin's past positions include associate professor of psychiatry at the Center for Minority Training Program, Boston University School of Medicine; regional director of the Massachusetts Behavioral Health Partnership; executive director of the South Cove Community Health Center; and codirector of the Thom Child Guidance Clinic. She has authored, coauthored, or edited books including *Relationships among Asian American Women* (2000), *Community Health Psychology*

(1998), and *Diversity in Psychotherapy: The Politics of Race, Ethnicity and Gender* (1993).

VICTOR DE LA CANCELA is associate clinical professor of medical psychology at the College of Physicians and Surgeons, Columbia University. He is also deputy executive director of Tremont-Crotona Child Development Center, and a clinical psychologist serving with the United States Army Reserve.

JOHN D. ROBINSON is a professor in the Departments of Psychiatry and Surgery at the College of Medicine and Hospital at Howard University. He is a fellow of Divisions 1, 12, 38, 44, 45, 49, 51, and 52 of the American Psychological Association. In 1998, he received a letter of commendation from the president of the United States for teaching excellence. Robinson is a distinguished visiting professor at the Walter Reed Army Medical Center and at the Tripler Army Medical Center. He earned his EdD in counseling psychology at the University of Massachusetts–Amherst, completed a clinical psychology residency at the University of Texas Health Sciences Center at San Antonio, and earned an MPH at Harvard School of Public Health. Robinson worked earlier as chief of interdepartmental programs in the Departments of Psychiatry and Surgery at Howard University, and has also served as dean of the Division of Graduate Studies and Research at the University of the District of Columbia, clinical professor in the Department of Psychiatry at Georgetown University School of Medicine, and clinical attending faculty in the Department of Psychiatry at Harvard University School of Medicine at the Cambridge Hospital.

About the Advisers

JESSICA HENDERSON DANIEL is an assistant professor of psychology in the Department of Psychiatry at Harvard Medical School, and both director of training in psychology and associate director of the LEAH (Leadership Education in Adolescent Health) Training Program in Adolescent Medicine at Children's Hospital of Boston. She is also an adjunct associate professor of psychology in the clinical psychology program at Boston University. Daniel is the past president of the Society for the Psychology of Women, Division 35, APA; and is coeditor of *The Complete Guide to Mental Health for Women* (2003). Her awards include the 1998 A. Clifford Barger Excellence in Mentoring Award from Harvard Medical School; the 2001 Education Distinguished Alumni Award from the University of Illinois; the 2002 Distinguished Contributions to Education and Training Award from APA; and the 2003 Professional Award from the Boston & Vicinity Club, Inc., National Association of Negro Business and Professional Women's Clubs, Inc.

JEFFERY SCOTT MIO is a professor in the Department of Behavioral Sciences at California State Polytechnic University–Pomona, where he also serves as the director of the master of science in psychology program. He received his PhD from the University of Illinois–Chicago in 1984. He taught at California State University–Fullerton in the counseling department from 1984–1986, then taught at Washington State University in the Department of Psychology from 1986 to 1994 before accepting his current position at CSPU–Pomona. His interests are in the teaching of multicultural issues, the development of allies, and how metaphors are used in political persuasion.

NATALIE PORTER is vice provost for academic affairs systemwide at Alliant International University. She is also an associate professor of psychology. She received her PhD from the University of Delaware. Porter's research interests include feminist and anti-racist models of clinical training and supervision, cognitive and emotional developmental changes in individuals abused or traumatized as children, and feminist therapy supervision and ethics.

JOHN D. ROBINSON is a coeditor of *Race and Ethnicity in Psychology*, a Praeger series.

JOSEPH EVERETT TRIMBLE is a professor of psychology at the Center for Cross-Cultural Research at Western Washington University. Trimble was a fellow in the Radcliffe Institute for Advanced Study at Harvard University in 2000 and 2001. He is a research associate for the University of Colorado Health Sciences Center, in the Department of Psychiatry, National Center for American Indian and Alaska Native Mental Health Research. He is also a scholar and adjunct professor of psychology for the Colorado State University Tri-Ethnic Center for Prevention Research. In 1994, he received the Lifetime Achievement Award from the Society for the Psychological Study of Ethnic Minority Issues, Division 45, American Psychological Association. In 2002, he was honored with the Distinguished Psychologist Award from the Washington State Psychological Association. He has authored eighty-two journal articles, chapters, and monographs, as well as authored or edited thirteen books, including the *Handbook of Racial and Ethnic Minority Psychology* (2002).

MELBA J. T. VASQUEZ is in full-time independent practice in Austin, Texas. A past president of APA Divisions 35 (Society for the Psychology of Women) and 17 (Society of Counseling Psychology), she has served in various other leadership positions. She is a fellow of the APA and a diplomate of the ABPP. She publishes in the areas of professional ethics, psychology of women, ethnic minority psychology, and training and supervision. She is coauthor, with Ken Pope, of *Ethics in Counseling and Psychotherapy: A Practical Guide* (1998, 2nd ed.). She is the recipient of several awards including Psychologist of the Year, Texas Psychological Association, 2003; Senior Career Award for Distinguished Contributions to Psychology in the Public Interest, APA, 2002; Janet E. Helms Award for Mentoring and Scholarship,

Columbia University, 2002; John Black Award for Outstanding Achievement in the Practice of Counseling Psychology, Division 17, APA, 2000; and the Distinguished Leader for Women in Psychology Award, Committee of Women Psychology, APA, 2000.

HERBERT Z. WONG has provided management consulting, diversity training, and organizational assessments to over 300 government agencies, businesses, and other organizations. He was the cofounder and president of the National Diversity Conference, Inc., which presented contemporary issues and future directions of workforce diversity. He was a consultant to the President's Commission on Mental Health (1977), the White House Conference for a Drug Free America (1989), and the President's Initiative on Race–White House Office of Science and Technology (2000). In the past twenty-five years, Wong has written extensively on multicultural leadership, cross-cultural communication, and diversity issues. Wong received his PhD in clinical and organizational psychology from the University of Michigan.

About the Contributors

AFUA ARHIN is a nursing instructor at Florida A&M University in Tallahassee and a PhD student in nursing at the University of Florida in Gainesville. Her research interests include race relations, adolescent pregnancy, and learning styles of black students. She is married with two children.

THEMA BRYANT-DAVIS is an American Psychological Association representative to the United Nations. At the UN, she is cochair of the NGO Human Rights Sub-Committee for the Elimination of Racism. Bryant-Davis is the global and international issues chair for Division 35 of the Society for the Psychology of Women. She is coordinator of the Princeton University SHARE Program, which focuses on issues of sexual violence, including sexual assault, sexual harassment, and harassment based on sexual orientation. She received her doctorate from Duke University and completed her postdoctoral training at the Harvard Medical Center's Victims of Violence Program.

CAROLE BAROODY CORCORAN earned her PhD and her MA in social psychology from Miami University, after having received her BA summa cum laude in psychology from Wittenberg University. In 1991 Dr. Corcoran was appointed to the Lt. Governor's Task Force on the Prevention and Early Intervention to Reduce the Incidence of Sexual Assault, and in 2002 she was named to the Virginia Attorney General's Advisory Council on Domestic Violence and Sexual Assault. She is a co-founder of the Rappahannock Council Against Sexual

Assault, as well as co-chair of a National Task Force on Feminist Psychology for Division 35 (Society for the Psychology of Women) of the American Psychological Association. Dr. Corcoran has researched how to integrate race and gender into the curriculum and has helped coordinate several grants from the State Council of Higher Education for Virginia for developing programs in that area. She also co-founded the Race, Class, Gender Awareness Project and won Mortar Board's Outstanding Faculty Member Award. Nominated by Mary Washington College for the State Council of Higher Education's Faculty Awards Program in 1995 and 1996, Carole Baroody Corcoran was promoted to full professor of the psychology faculty in 1998. Dr. Corcoran was co-investigator on a $1 million grant awarded by the National Institute of Mental Health to investigate the outcomes of different types of traumatic life experiences in college women. She serves as an organizational development, training, and assessment consultant for creativity, leadership, and diversity. Dr. Corcoran is also involved in coordinating a pilot project using theater, dance, and spoken word with at risk adolescents. Presently, she is a Visiting Scholar at the University of Virginia Women's Center.

KAREN B. McLEAN DONALDSON is a professor and researcher in cultural diversity and curriculum reform. She has taught over thirty years at all educational levels local and abroad and has received numerous awards and recognition for her teaching, research, and outreach excellence. She is currently the systemwide executive director for CARE (Consortia for Applied Research in Education) and founder/director of the Cross-Cultural Studies Institute in the Graduate School of Education at Alliant International University. Donaldson is the author of two books, *Through Students' Eyes: Combating Racism in United States Schools* (1996) and *Shattering the Denial: Protocols for Classroom and Beyond* (2001).

JOHN F. DOVIDIO is the Charles A. Dana Professor of Psychology, and an adjunct professor of graduate studies in psychology at Colgate University. He received the Gordon Allport Intergroup Relations Prize in 1999 and 2000, awarded by the Society for the Psychological Study of Social Issues, Division 9 of the American Psychological Association. In 2000–2001, he was a member of the National Academy of Sciences' Institute of Medicine Committee on Understanding and Eliminating Racial and Ethnic Disparities in Health Care. Dovidio has authored or coauthored three books and eighty-seven journal articles, and edited or coedited four contributed volumes. He is editor-elect of the *Journal of Personality and Social Psychology–Interpersonal Relations and Group Processes*, editor of the *Personality and Social Psychology Bulletin*, associate editor of *Group Processes and Intergroup Relations*, consulting editor for the *British Journal of Social Psychology*, and consulting editor for the *Journal of Experimental Social Psychology*. His research interests are in stereotyping, prejudice, discrimination, social power, nonverbal communication, altruism, and helping.

SAMUEL L. GAERTNER is a professor of psychology at the University of Delaware. An editorial board member for the *Journal of Personality and Social Psychology*, he has conducted research, funded by the National Institute of Mental Health, for *Reducing Intergroup Bias: The Common Ingroup Identity Model*. He shared the Gordon Allport Intergroup Relations Prize with John Dovidio in 1985 and again in 1998 with John Dovidio and other former PhD students. Gaertner has authored or coauthored eighty-six articles and book chapters. He is an editorial board member of the *Journal of Personality and Social Psychology, Personality and Social Psychology Bulletin and Group Processes*, and *Intergroup Relations*. His PhD is from the City University of New York Graduate Center. His research interests include intergroup relations, prejudice reduction, discrimination, and racism.

GORDON HODSON is an assistant professor of psychology at the University of Wales–Swansea, United Kingdom. He coauthored the paper "Why Can't We Just Get Along? Interpersonal Biases and Interracial Distrust," which was a finalist for the 2003 Otto Klineberg Award. He also coauthored chapters in *Social Psychology of Inclusion and Exclusion* (in press), *The Social Psychology of Prejudice: Historical Perspectives* (in press), and *The Social Psychology of Good and Evil* (in press). He has served as a reviewer for a number of journals, including the *British Journal of Social Psychology* and the *International Journal of Psychology*. He earned his PhD at the University of Western Ontario in Canada. His research interests include stereotyping, prejudice, discrimination, social identity, and perceived threat.

BERTHA GARRETT HOLLIDAY is the director of the American Psychological Association's Office of Ethnic Minority Affairs, where she supports APA's involvement in a variety of initiatives related to increasing the participation of ethnic minorities in psychology, and public policy issues affecting the well-being of communities of color throughout the world. Holliday is a community psychologist with expertise in black child and family socialization, program planning and evaluation, community mental health and public policy, and the history of ethnic minority psychology. She has authored and published more than sixty related technical reports, journal articles, and book chapters. She has held a variety of professional roles including researcher, professor, program evaluator, program administrator, and congressional fellow. She holds degrees from the University of Chicago, Harvard University, and the University of Texas–Austin, and did postdoctoral study at Cornell University.

CARLA D. HUNTER is a doctoral candidate at Teachers College of Columbia University's Department of Counseling and Clinical Psychology. She is also a research assistant at the Borough of Manhattan Community College. She earned her MA in human development at Columbia, and her BA in psychology at Hamilton College.

YVONNE M. JENKINS is a staff psychologist at Boston College University Counseling Services. She is also on the faculty of the Jean Baker Miller Training Institute at Wellesley College and is in private practice in Brookline, Massachusetts. For several years, she was on the staff of Harvard University Health Services. A prolific author, Dr. Jenkins coauthored *Diversity in Psychotherapy: The Politics of Race, Ethnicity, and Gender* (1993) and *Community Health Psychology: Empowerment for Diverse Communities* (1998), edited *Diversity in College Settings* (1999), and has written several book chapters. Dr. Jenkins is particularly interested in college mental health issues and in the impacts of race, culture, and other social factors on mental and social health.

YUEH-TING LEE is professor and chairperson in the Department of Ethnic Studies at Minnesota State University–Mankato. He holds a PhD in social psychology from the State University of New York at Stony Brook. A cross-cultural psychologist by training, Lee has authored or edited six books and has published over sixty refereed journal articles on racial stereotyping, intergroup conflict, immigration, and related topics.

SHERI R. LEVY is an assistant professor of psychology at the State University of New York at Stony Brook. She earned her BA in psychology from the University of Michigan and a PhD in psychology from Columbia University in 1998, for which she received the 1999 Society for the Psychological Study of Social Issues Dissertation Award and an American Psychological Association dissertation research grant. Her research interests include understanding processes that lead to reduced prejudice and the role of people's ideologies in prejudice and intergroup volunteerism. She has conducted research and has published numerous papers on children and prejudice. In 1999, with Dr. Frances Aboud, she coedited the issue "Reducing Racial Prejudice, Discrimination, and Stereotyping: Translating Research into Programs" for the *Journal of Social Issues*.

MA'AT E. LEWIS-COLES earned her PhD in counseling psychology at Teachers College, Columbia University. Lewis-Coles has held positions as psychology intern at the New York Veterans Administration Medical Center and as psychology extern at Barnard College Counseling Services, Columbia University; and Harlem Hospital Center Department of Psychiatry.

CORANN OKORODUDU is a full professor of psychology and coordinator for African/African-American studies at Rowan University, where she has served as associate vice president for academic affairs and coordinated programs on women's studies and multicultural curriculum transformation. Over the years, both in Liberia (her birth home) and the United States, she has focused her agenda within psychology, higher education, and various communities of practice on the national and global levels, and on promoting human rights and inclusive institutional policies and practices. Okorodudu is past president of the Society for the Study of Peace, Conflict, and Violence, APA's Division of Peace Psychology. She currently serves as main representative for the American Psychological Association (APA). It is in this capacity that she led APA's delegation to the 2001 United Nations World Conference against Racism, Racial Discrimination, Xenophobia, and Related Intolerance in Durban, South Africa.

JOHN E. PACHANKIS is a clinical psychology doctoral student in the Department of Psychology at the State University of New York at Stony Brook. He earned his BA from Loyola University. His research interests include identity development of stigmatized group members and the development of anxiety disorders as a result of stigmatization. He is currently involved in clinical and research issues associated with gay, lesbian, and bisexual individuals.

LUISA F. RAMIREZ is a doctoral student in the political science department at the State University of New York at Stony Brook and is the recipient of a Fulbright scholarship. She earned her BA in psychology from Universidad de Los Andes (University of Los Andes) in Colombia in 1994 and her MA in political science, majoring in political psychology, from the State University of New York at Stony Brook in 2003. She also received a master's degree in political science from the Universidad de Los Andes in 2001. Her research interests include understanding the processes of prejudice and the formation of collective identities in ethnic minority groups.

FREDERICK SLOCUM is associate professor of political science at Minnesota State University. He earned his BA in political science at the University of North Carolina–Chapel Hill, and his MA and PhD at the University of Iowa. His research interests include investigation of the sources, structure, and political consequences of white Americans' racial attitudes toward blacks, including "symbolic racism" and other explanations of whites' attitudes.

EDWARD STEPHENSON received his PhD in social/personality psychology from the University of California–Santa Cruz in 1987. He has since taught at a variety of institutions including Nova University, where he was assistant professor of psychology for two years. He then served as an adjunct professor at several colleges and universities in the South Florida area, including Barry University, Florida Atlantic University, St. Thomas University, and Carlos Albizu University. Stephenson is presently associate professor of psychology at Florida Memorial College. His special areas of interest include the psychology of culture, minority mental health and counseling, the psychology of the African Diaspora, and the psychology of prejudice and discrimination. In regard to the latter, Stephenson is specifically concerned with the manner in which Caribbean blacks who live in the United States are affected by and cope with various forms of discrimination.

AISHA RENÉE THOMPSON is a research assistant at the American Institutes for Research. A graduate of Mary Washington College with a BS in psychology, she studied and researched under the instruction of Carole Corcoran. Thompson now provides support to the National Center for Mental Health Promotion and Youth Violence Prevention.

BRUCE A. THYER is dean and professor at the School of Social Work at Florida State University–Tallahassee. He is also a visiting professor in the School of Human and Health Sciences at the University of Huddersfield, England, and visiting professor in the School of Social Work at the Queen's University of Belfast, Northern Ireland. He holds a PhD in social work and psychology from the University of Michigan, and an MSW in social work from the University of Georgia. His past roles include Distinguished Research Professor of Social Work at

University of Georgia, associate clinical professor of psychiatry at the Medical College of Georgia, senior clinical social worker in the Anxiety Disorders Program at the University of Michigan Hospitals, and neuro-psychiatric procedures specialist for the U.S. Army. In the latter role, he earned a National Defense Service Medal and Good Conduct Medal. He is the founding editor of *Research on Social Work Practice*, consulting editor for *Children in Schools*, international advisory editor for *British Journal of Social Work*, and a member of the editorial boards for *Scientific Review of Mental Health Practice, Behavior and Social Issues*, and *Journal of Human Behavior in the Social Environment*. He is author or coauthor of 214 journal articles; and author, coauthor, editor, or coeditor of twenty-two books, including *Cultural Diversity and Social Work Practice* (1996) and the *Handbook of Social Work Research Methods* (2001). He has also contributed to sixty-two other book chapters.

TARA L. WEST completed her doctoral degree in social and health psychology at the State University of New York at Stony Brook in 2003. She earned her BA in psychology at Indiana University–Bloomington. Her research interests include increasing pro-social attitudes and behaviors, and understanding and reducing prejudice.